HERMANN DETERING
THE FABRICATED PAUL

Even when all the experts agree, they may be well mistaken.

Bertrand Russell, 1872-1970

Hermann Detering

THE FABRICATED PAUL

EARLY CHRISTIANITY IN THE TWILIGHT

Translated by Darrell Doughty

Title of the German original:
Der gefälschte Paulus - das Urchristentum im Zwielicht
First published 1995 by Patmos Press, Düsseldorf.
English Translation by Prof. Darrell Daughty†, 2003.

For Mrs. W. Hofstra-van den Bergh van Eysinga
As well as
Mrs. Dr. R. M. Mispelblom Beyer-van den Bergh van Eysinga
Mrs. M. J. Beukema-Faber
Mr. E. Frater Smid
and Mr. J. H. Ritzema Bos

© 2018 Dr. Hermann Detering
www.radikalkritik.de
ISBN 9781981040810

Contents

Abbreviations ix
   New Testament ix
   Pseudepigraphical and Early Patristic Books x
Toward Understanding xiii
The Investigation of the Pauline Letters 1
   The Interest Awakes 1
   The Sources 6
   The Basic Elements of Our Picture of Paul 8
   Acts — An Eyewitness Report? 10
   Paul in Wonderland 12
   With Rabbi Gamaliel 13
   Paul the Persecutor 14
   Paul on the Way to Damascus 16
   The Conversion 17
   Missionary Journeys 19
   Imprisonment 20
   From Acts to the Pauline Writings 22
   Original and Forgery in Early Christianity 25
   The Inauthenticity of the Pastoral Epistles (1, 2 Timothy, Titus) 32
   Differences in Language and Theology 32
   Did Paul Have a Secretary? 33
   Paul's Mantel 34

A Double Standard 35
Ephesians, Colossians, and 2 Thessalonians:
   Inauthentic 38
Letters from No-man's land 40
Contradictions 41
Did Paul Copy from Himself? 42
Paul as a Schoolmaster? 43
Whoever says A must also say B 45
Edward Evanson: the Uncomfortable Englishman 48
From Baur to Bauer 50
The Radical Dutchmen 55
Seeking Traces 64
Two Pauls 69
What does Luke Remain Silent about the Letters of Paul? . 77
The Silence of the Apocalypse 79
Justin and Aristides 80
1 Clement and Ignatius: Two Will-o'-the-wisps of New
   Testament Criticism 86

The Historical Origins of the Pauline Letters 99
De omnibus dubitandum: One Must Doubt Everything ... 99
Antiqua Mater 104
The First Witness to Paul: Marcion the Heretic 106
Marcion's Two Gods 110
When did Marcion Become a Heretic? 112
Marcionism and Gnosis 115
Marcion's "Discovery" 118
Mouse from Pontus — or Catholic Redactor? 119
Paul as an Apostle of Circumcision 121

An Initial Visit with the Pope — An Interpolated Trip to Rome 122
The Pauline Christ as Son of David 126
Paul teaches a Christ with only an apparent body — Paul as Docetist 133
Paul and the teaching of two Gods 135
Paul — the Domesticated Marcion 139
Paul — the non-Jew 141
What use was made of the Pauline letters in the second century? 145
The opponents of Paul 149
Marcion as Author of the Letters? 154

A Legend and its Historical Kernel 156
A Final Open Question 156
Fabrication Impossible? 157
The Legendary Paul 161
Paul and Thecla 164
The Face of an Angel 167
Fight with Beasts in Ephesus 168
From Paul of the Legends to the Historical Paul 170
The Doppelgänger: Paul and Simon 173
The Sinful Woman 179
Who was Simon Magus? 181
The flatterer 190
The visionary, miracle worker, and Missionary 191
The Son of Lawlessness 194
The Match-Maker 196
From Paul to Saul 199

Simon the Leper and Paul's Sickness 202
Simon and Helena — Paul and Thecla — Jesus and Mary
Magdalene 204
What Remains? 210
Plato's Allegory of the Cave and the Investigation of
Earliest Christian History 210
The Church and her Heretics 212
Paul and Jesus 214
The Foundations of the Christian Faith 217
The Pope, the Christian and "Fortunate Hans" 221
The Letter Kills... 224
The Role of the Church 229
General Index 231
Bibliography 237
Notes 251

Abbreviations

New Testament

Scripture quotations are usually from the RSV, *Revised Standard Version of the Bible.* Copyright © 1952 [2nd edition, 1971] by the Division of Christian Education of the National Council of Churches of Christ in the United States of America. All rights reserved.

Mt	The gospel according to Matthew
Mk	The gospel according to Mark
Lk	The gospel according to Luke
Jn	The gospel according to John
Acts	The Acts of the Apostles
Rom	Epistle to the Romans
1-2 Cor	First and second epistles to the Corinthians
Gal	Epistle to the Galatians
Eph	Epistle to the Ephesians
Phil	Epistle to the Philippians
Col	Epistle to the Colossians
1-2 Thess	First and second epistles to the Thessalonians
1-2 Tim	First and second epistles to Timothy
Tit	Epistle to Titus
Phlm	Epistle to Philemon
Hebr	Epistle to the Hebrews
1-2 Pet	The two epistles ascribed in the canon to

	Peter
Rev	Revelation of John

Pseudepigraphical and Early Patristic Books

Acta Pt c Sim	Acta Petri cum Simone
ATh	Acta Pauli et Theclae
aethHen	Enoch, Ethiopic
ApkElj	Apocalypse of Elijah
Clem	Clement
1 Cl	First Epistle to the Corinthians
Hom	Pseudo-Clementine Homilies
Recog	Pseudo-Clementine Recognitiones
Cyprian	
Ep	Epistula
Epiphanius	
Pan	Panarion
EpPtr	Epistula Petri
Eus	Eusebius of Caesarea
HE	Historia Ecclesiastica
Hippolytus	
Haer	Adversus omnes haereses
Ign	
IgnEph	Letter to the Ephesians
IgnRom	Letter to the Romans
IgnPoly	Letter to Polycarp
IgnMagn	Letter to the Magnesians
Ir	Irenaeus of Lyons
AH	Adversus Haereses
Jus	Justin Martyr
1Apol	First Apology
Dial	Dialogus cum Tryphone
Jos	Josephus
Ant	Antiquitates
Bell	Bellum Judaicum

MPL	Migne, Patrologia Latina
NHC	Nag Hammadi Codices
Origen	
comm in Rom	Commentarii in epistulam ad Romanos
in Luc hom	Homilia in Lucam
Philo	
Post	De Posteritate Caini
Tert	Tertullian
AM	Adversus Marcionem
haer	De praescrioptione haereticorum

Toward Understanding

On the following pages I would like to take the reader once more over the stretch of road that I myself traveled in my engagement with Paul and early Christianity and that finally led me to the conviction that the Pauline letters in their entirety are inauthentic. Perhaps at the end of this stretch of road we have traveled together readers will be surprised at themselves with regard to how effortlessly and easily they have followed a road at whose end stands the total destruction of their own familiar and beloved conceptions. Perhaps at the end of this road they will even come to realize how little they have really lost and how much they have gained.

It is possible, however, that the case will be entirely different. For the sake of better understanding, therefore, for all those persons who for various reasons are unable to either acknowledge or agree with my constructions, I would like to offer the following for consideration: I am fully aware that in many respects the ideas developed on the following pages are very sketchy. What is presented is not an historical theory set forth and unfolded in every detail, but rather a sketch, or "rough draft."

There are two reasons why I must accept the risk of presenting certain pieces in a somewhat abbreviated way and totally ignoring others, for which reason I might be misunderstood or accused of lacking historical knowledge of certain circumstances (which I didn't want to present at all): first of all, because I want to address not only the experts but also a wider reading public, and secondly, because it seemed very important to me to present a complete theory of inauthenticity in its inner coherence.

All previous challenges to the authenticity of the Pauline letters, even those of the Dutch radical critics, suffered from the fact that they were unable to provide *a satisfactory overall conception*. In my opinion, the radical theory gains plausibility not on the basis of a host of arguments against the authenticity of the Pauline letters (As I showed in my dissertation on Dutch radical criticism, sufficient arguments of this kind have been advanced in the past without scholars finding it necessary to alter their position), but above all by answering the question that now arises concerning what "really" took place. If Paul was not the writer of the letters, then who was Paul, i.e., who was the person in whose name the letters were written? Was he a legend, a historical figure, or merely a phantom?

This question, which has as its goal not only criticism and analysis, but also synthesis, can only be answered if an internally coherent, plausible overall conception can be presented. In order to bring the entirety into view, however, I naturally could not and may not immerse myself too deeply in questions of historical detail (to which I will gladly return in another place), but must limit myself to presenting more essential points of reference. I would strongly emphasize, however, that to my knowledge the book contains no tenet for which I failed to provide (historical) grounds.

In scholarship, the person who proposes alternative conceptual possibilities is more vulnerable than one who simply criticizes. In that I attempt to set forth an alternative theory for the origin of the Pauline epistles, many parts of the book possibly offer the critic a welcome place to attack. Maybe it would have been better to have dispensed with some theses which might seem all too provoking or audacious. That would have certainly spared me much criticism and much vexation that I must now deal with. I suspect, for example, that among the theses propounded in this book those with which I attempt to resolve the problem of the historical Paul (= *Paulus historicus*) will encounter the greatest consternation. I would certainly recommend to future critics that in evaluating this theory they do not let themselves be guided only by the historical-theological knowledge they learned in school. From the perspective of the inauthenticity of the Pauline letters and on the basis of tradition-historical considerations, the entire theory seems to be completely consistent and illuminating. In any case, this hypothesis, while explaining one of the most difficult problems of a branch of early Christian literature, is like a boomerang for me: the more forcefully I cast it away, the more vehemently to comes back at me.

In order to prevent misunderstanding, I would like to point out that with the theses of this book, which, after all, deals with only one piece of early Christian history, no claim at all is made to have discovered the complete historical "truth" concerning early Christianity. It is not at all my view that the results I arrive at in this book place in question or render null and void everything that the representatives of the authenticity hypothesis have said and written until now. I myself have learned from most of them and have always felt the greatest admiration for the analytical acumen of New Testament exegetes (above all in the last century) and for their skill in sniffing out the problems of the text and solving them (in an entirely different way, to be sure, than takes place here).

I would regret it very much, therefore, if the present book were regarded by biblical scholars only as a provocation. I myself understand this book rather as an invitation, as an offer of conversation to experts as well as interested laity. Perhaps I will be able to call forth from one or the other a new consideration of the authenticity question. But maybe the opposite will be the case, and the representatives of the authenticity hypothesis will be able to convince me with sound arguments of the correctness of their position and thus, in a good Christian way, call back their errant brother to the ground of clear, sound teaching.

All in all, I hope that this book will not only have an exciting and stimulating effect, but will also be a contribution to greater freedom in the theological discussion. Perhaps in the future it will be possible to discuss more openly and more candidly problems which for various reasons — not only for pure scholarly reasons, I believe — have been rendered taboo by theologians and whose consideration was reserved only for non-theologians. In this regard, precisely the decisive, fundamental questions in New Testament scholarship are much too important to be relinquished to dilettantes or visionaries. Professional theologians as well, and especially they, cannot allow the freedom to be able to think in new ways to be taken away. If the present book can make a small contribution to this, its purpose would be entirely fulfilled.

I certainly do not expect that this book will produce a "revaluation of all values." Assuming that one day the inauthenticity hypothesis becomes accepted by the majority of scholars, a great deal of water must still flow down from under the scholarly mills; a great number of scholarly works must be written that, in more tenacious and more patient scholarly work, further develop and substantiate what is suggested here in only a rough outline, or perhaps show this to be an erroneous path.

Even after reading this book, for most readers the Christian world will remain as it was until now. In the pulpits, in Bible classes, or in religious instruction, people will continue to speak of the apostle Paul and his letters. His adventures on missionary journeys, his letters to Christian churches will continue to provide material for edifying preaching, fanciful romances, and boring hours of instruction.

There is nothing at all to object to here. For me it would be sufficient if those persons who continue to speak of "Paul" were more aware than before that we have to do here also with only a working hypothesis. I would be happy if from now on everyone who appeals to the letters of Paul would at the same time bear in mind that the authenticity of seven Pauline letters in no sense represents an absolutely established historical fact, but—just as the hypothesis of inauthenticity—is only a hypothesis, and indeed, as every scholar who has struggled with the unending difficulties and problems of Pauline studies will confirm, a very complicated hypothesis.

In the future, the value of both hypotheses, the authenticity hypothesis as well as that of inauthenticity, will have to be accessed in terms of which of the two is best able to resolve the manifold problems of the Pauline letters in the most illuminating and simple way. Such a competitive battle between entirely different orientations would nevertheless then be something new in the history of New Testament scholarship, in which until the present time the hypothesis of authenticity has occupied an absolute and unquestioned monopoly.

Basically, I can wish nothing more and nothing else than that in a hopefully not too distant future the recognition of the authenticity of seven Pauline letters will no longer represent—as until today—the unexamined presupposition for New Testament research, but rather the result of thorough reflection. That I personally entertain great doubt about this and in my opinion the future will belong to the simpler, clearer, and historically more probable hypothesis of inauthenticity is a quite different matter.

Chapter 1

THE INVESTIGATION OF THE PAULINE LETTERS
AS A HISTORY OF THE DISCOVERY
OF THEIR INAUTHENTICITY

The Interest Awakes

For a long time, my interest in the person and work of the man to whom the following pages are dedicated was not particularly great. Even during my theological studies it was difficult for me to feel comfortable with the man from Tarsus. For me, as for so many other theological students, he still stood entirely in the shadow of that other man from Galilee. My interest in him resembled one's interest in the friend of a good friend. Although one is not sure how to deal with him, as a matter of simple courtesy one can also not entirely ignore him.

That my interest in the apostle nevertheless awoke one day had less to do with the man himself than that even while I was still a student the luster that surrounded the radiant figure of Jesus began to diminish. It wasn't that the person of Jesus had lost its fascination and mystery. But it could not be denied that as my struggle with the historical sources increased, the picture of the man from Nazareth, that at the beginning of my theological studies had stood so graphically before my eyes, became increasingly pallid and unclear. Even in introductory seminars we learned that only very little of what was transmitted to us as relating to Jesus really reached back to the historical Jesus. We heard that the teachings and pronouncements of Jesus as well as some of the narrative material represented later church constructions. The Gospels as a whole, therefore, were not reliable eyewitness accounts, but *kerygma*, i.e., proclamation, affirmations of faith. Instead of this, one could also have said "pious fantasy." But no one dared to make such a statement. And it would surely not really have done justice to the matter. Be as it may, however, the picture of the real—historical—Jesus remained scarcely recognizable behind the later "church constructions."

What our theological teachers taught us about the impossibility of knowing the historical Jesus (concerning whom we know nothing more than the fact that there had been such a person) as well as about the creative imagination of the Christian communities after Jesus was shocking for many students. Although my own personal relationship with the "Lord Jesus" had always been characterized by friendly reservation and rather a bit of north-German coolness, I could also not deny being somewhat disconcerted. What was critical about the whole affair was that the historical arguments that our teachers brought forth against the authenticity of certain teachings and stories of Jesus were immediately illuminating for me and that, in contrast to other students, after a few days I was already overcome. There could be no doubt that the historical contours of the man from Nazareth had been wiped out by later tradition so as to be unknowable. Thus, anyone who expected from the historical man Jesus some kind of guidelines or directions for the here and now must always be resigned to the fact that what seems to be an authentic pronouncement of Jesus in truth does not derive from him at all.

At that time, in connection with this, I encountered for the first time a problem that even later would engage me again and again, namely, the relationship between history and faith. I had always held the view that my personal faith must be independent from what took place (or did not take place) 2000 years earlier in Palestine. A faith that is based on particular historical findings, which from one day to the other can be depicted in an entirely different way by historians, seemed to me to be a highly questionable affair and incompatible with the nature of faith, which had to be a deep certainty of existential (not historical) fundamental truths. At the university, however, I now became aware that at least the Christian faith possessed a pronounced historical inclination. That is already made clear in the apostles' creed, which in its so-called second article recites pure historical facts (or at least facts which are perceived by the church as historical): "I believe in Jesus Christ... born of the virgin Mary, suffered under Pontius Pilate, crucified, dead and buried..."

The adherence of the Christian church to particular historical facts, so-called *facts of salvation*, seems to me, until today, to be intellectual and human impudence, since, on the one hand, no person is really in a situation to totally investigate the historical truth-content in these statements and since, on the other hand, the nature of faith becomes completely falsified if it is degraded to maintaining the likelihood of historical data.

In any case, the loss of historical certainty with regard to the person of Jesus of Nazareth had as its consequence that I gradually turned away from Jesus and to the historical Paul. That reflected the need for a stronger historical confirmation for faith. I wanted to know what the beginnings of the Christian faith were like. In addition, I hoped that from the figure of Paul, whom I assumed stood in the full light of history, an illuminating beam of light would also fall on the person of the Nazarene, swinging to and fro between kerygmatic appearance and historical existence.

Unfortunately, I would realize very quickly that this hope would be difficult to fulfill. Strange to say, it soon became evident that, although Paul had been a contemporary of the historical Jesus, he had nothing at all to say about him. On closer examination, his letters contain practically no statements about the historical figure Jesus. In his well-known book on Paul, the theologian Günther Bornkamm speaks of the "amazing state of affairs" that Paul nowhere speaks "of the Rabbi from Nazareth, the prophet and miracle-worker who ate with tax-collectors and sinners, or of his Sermon on the Mount, his parables of the kingdom of God, and his encounters with Pharisees and Scribes."[1] Everything that we learn from Paul about Jesus remains peculiarly pallid and unsubstantial: Jesus is "born of a woman, born under the law" (Gal 4:4); as the seed of Abraham (Gal 3:16) and a descendent of David (Rom 1:4), he belongs to the people of Israel (Rom 9:4); he suffered (Rom 8:17), he died (Rom 5:6, 8, 15; 8:34; 14:9, 15; 1 Cor 8:11; 15:3; 2 Cor 5:14f; Gal 2:19, 21; 1 Thess 4:14, 16; 5:10;) on the cross (Rom 6:6; 1 Cor 1:17f, 23; 2:2, 8; 2 Kor 13:4; Gal 2:19; 3:1; 5:11; 6:12, 14; Phil 2:8), he was buried (Rom 6:4) and resurrected (Rom 4:24; 6:4; 1 Cor 15:4, 12ff, 16f, 20; 2 Cor 5:15; 1 Thess 4:14). When and where all this took place, we do not learn. As in the apostles' creed, there is a yawning gap between the birth and death of Jesus. In contrast to the creed, in which at least Mary and Pontius Pilate are mentioned, in the Pauline letters not only is the name of Jesus' mother missing, as well as that of the Roman governor, but also other names and concepts imparted to us by the Gospels (e.g., John the Baptizer, Joseph, Galilee, Gethsemane and Golgotha). Only the leaders of the earliest community — Cephas (or Peter), James, and John — are mentioned (Gal 1:19; 2:7-9; 12; 1 Cor 15:5-7).

On the whole, therefore, one can say, if we were dependent on Paul alone for knowledge of Jesus of Nazareth, we would know nothing at all about him — little more than that there was a man named Jesus, that he died and, according to the belief of the writer of these letters, rose from the dead. We would not know *when* and *where* he lived.

Basically, the fact that Paul says nothing at all about the historical Jesus was very curious—just as strange as the related fact that immediately after receiving the revelation calling him to be an apostle he went to Arabia for three years instead of visiting the Jerusalem community (Gal 1:17), as one might expect, whether to make contact with its leaders or to acquire more information about the life of the person who had appeared to him at Damascus. Can one imagine that someone who had just experienced the decisive turning-point of his life through a revelation took no notice and had no interest in the earthly past of the one who stood in the center of this revelation?

In any case, I myself was not able to replicate the tenacious ignorance with which Paul dealt with the history of Jesus. The main theological arguments set forth at this point by most scholars—e.g., Paul was exclusively interested in the exalted Christ, or perhaps more radical, Paul employed Jesus only as a pattern for his own theological conceptions—were rationally illuminating, but too theoretical. They may have been satisfactory for an academic theologian who perceived the apostle primarily as the bearer of an idea (often only his own idea). But this would not suffice for someone who perceived Paul as a man of flesh and blood, whose conduct must be humanly and psychologically replicable. — Or was the Paul of Galatians finally not a flesh and blood being, but only the product of an theologian? — To be sure, at that time I had not yet asked myself this question. But I was surprised at how easy it was for most theologians to pass over this peculiar state of affairs—i.e., the puzzling silence of Paul with regard to Jesus—and return again to the day's agenda. I didn't want that to be the case for me.

Although I still had no explanation for this peculiar behavior of Paul, my historical (or should I rather say criminal?) curiosity about the apostle Paul was awakened for the first time. From the beginning, my interest him had less to do with his theology, which seemed to me in part very cloudy and inconsistent, but with the puzzle and inconsistency of his biography. Only later did I realize that there was a direct connection between the biographical and theological inconsistencies and that the theology of the writer of the letters is much easier to understand if the historical problems associated with the person of Paul are first resolved.

The Sources

Whoever wants to be informed about a particular person from the past or present, and not be dependent only on reports, conjectures or opinions of others, needs reliable sources. For many people, the study of sources, which, at least for early Christian sources also presupposes knowledge of foreign languages (old Greek, Latin, and Hebrew), seems to be a laborious, boring and dry affair. They immediately reach rather for secondary literature in order to be informed secondhand about the person they are interested in. I have never felt that way. For me, reading sources always presents an absorbing, indeed, downright exciting affair. It is well known that every biography, every study of a particular historical person, is always colored by the view of the one who writes. Such presentations might suffice for a first orientation; over time, however, it could become somewhat boring. The source material is already ordered in a particular way; everything is dovetailed into an overall concept, and there is nothing further to discover. Secondary literature reminds me of a park that is certainly beautiful to look at and in which everything is well ordered and arranged, but which for this very reason nevertheless produces sterility and boredom. Reading sources, on the contrary, seems to me like a path through a wild, desolate countryside. It is dangerous and full of adventure. A discovery could be waiting behind every tree or bush; with every line, every subordinate clause, every word, a door could be opened to another world, hidden until now; the writer could give up his secret and divulge that he is really someone entirely different than the researcher assumed until now. The "danger" of one's own reading of sources should not be underestimated. It consists in the possibility that in the end the reader will arrive at conception of things all his own that brings him into sharp conflict with conventional views and conceptions.

With regard to the apostle Paul, the matter of sources is rather simple. In general, it can be said that our historical knowledge of the apostle rests primarily on two "pillars."

a) Even today, the best known and most popular source of information is still the book of Acts; although Acts has a decided drawback in that its historical value is questioned today by an increasing number of scholars.

b) Although more prosaic, the letters transmitted in the New Testament under the name of Paul are more solid with regard to their historical value. We have to do here with thirteen letters, or fourteen if the letter to the Hebrews if included, although it makes no explicit claim of Pauline authorship.

- the letter to the Romans (Rom)
- the first letter to the Corinthians (1 Cor)
- the second letter to the Corinthians (2 Cor)
- the letter to the Galatians (Gal)
- the letter to the Ephesians (Eph)
- the letter to the Philippians (Phil)
- the letter to the Colossians (Col)

- the first letter to the Thessalonians (1 Thess)
- the second letter to the Thessalonians (2 Thess)
- the first letter to Timothy (1 Tim)
- the second letter to Timothy (2 Tim)
- the letter to Titus (Tit)
- The letter to Philemon (Phlm)
- [The letter to the Hebrews]

According to the generally held view today, only seven of these definitely derive from Paul:

- the letter to the Romans
- the first letter to the Corinthians
- the second letter to the Corinthians
- the letter to the Galatians
- the letter to the Philippians
- the first letter to the Thessalonians
- the letter to Philemon

In the view of most scholars, these letters represent the earliest literary testimonies of Christianity, which are supposed to have been written in the time between 50 and 60 CE, prior to the Gospels (written after 70 CE).

Before we turn to the letters of Paul and the numerous problems connected with them, however, we will deal with that source which for most Christians even today represents the crucial basis for their picture of Paul.

The Basic Elements of Our Picture of Paul

What do we know about Paul, or what do we think we know about him? Perhaps in religious instruction or somewhere else we once heard,

- that we have to do here with a Jew named *Saul*,
- that to begin with this person was a *persecutor* of the early Christian community,
- that outside Damascus he was then suddenly *converted* ("Saul, Saul, why do you persecute me?") to Christianity
- and then became the most important Christian *missionary* and undertook several missionary journeys through the Mediterranean region
- so that finally, after being take *prisoner* in Jerusalem, he was brought to Rome.

If we ask where this historical data derives from, which we regard as absolutely certain and which determines our picture of Paul, we have to admit that it is not from contemporary testimonies regarding the apostle and also not from his letters (from which some things can be derived only indirectly), but from Luke's Acts. This must be a severe disappointment for someone who is highly interested in established historical facts. He will anxiously ask himself, can a work that begins with an extensive description of the ascension of Jesus that in no way sounds particularly symbolic (Acts 1:9) be regarded as a reliable historical source? As has long been known in theological circles, in many ways Acts is more like an imaginary, marvelous romance than an historical portrayal, even if in the preface the writer takes on the appearance of an historian and follows the customs of an ancient historian in his presentation. As we will see in more detail, in its portrayal of the person and work of the apostle, Acts interweaves the earthly and the heavenly, the historical and the legendary, in a wondrous and indistinguishable way.

Acts — An Eyewitness Report?

For evaluating the historical value of Acts it is also important to observe with regard to the author of the work (="Luke") that we do not have to do here with an eyewitness, as was earlier often assumed. Basically, this is self-evident from what has just been said. One should reckon that an eyewitness would hardly find it necessary to relate legends for the reader instead of historical events. In any case, it is widely recognized in present day New Testament research, even by conservative scholars that, contrary to what was earlier often assumed, the author was not a traveling companion of Paul.

If that were the case, one must ask why Luke presents a picture of Paul that is entirely different from the picture of the apostle in the letters. Vielhauer observes, "The writer makes historical mistakes regarding the life of Paul that no companion would make," and offers as evidence for this, "apart from all the rest," the following peculiar circumstance: "A man who reserves the title and honor of an apostle exclusively for the twelve and consistently denies this for Paul, even though Paul claimed the apostolate for himself and defended it, cannot be a companion of Paul."[2]

For the assumption that the author of Acts was an eyewitness, appeal is often made to the so-called "we-accounts." In these passages the writer suddenly continues his account in we-form, which gives the impression to the reader either that the writer himself was present at the reported events as an eyewitness or that he at least made use of a source written by an eyewitness. For example, Acts 16:9-13 reads:

And a vision appeared to Paul in the night: a man of Macedonia was standing beseeching him and saying, "Come over to Macedonia and help us." And when he had seen the vision, immediately we sought to go into Macedonia, concluding that God had called us to preach the gospel to them. Setting sail therefore from Troas, we made a direct voyage to Samothrace, and the following day to Neapolis, and from there to Philippi, which is the leading city of the district of Macedonia, and a Roman colony. We remained in this city some days; and on the Sabbath we went outside the gate to the riverside, where we supposed there was a place of prayer; and we sat down and spoke to the women who had come together.

It is clearly recognized today, however, that the "we-accounts" are a skilful literary fiction. According to Vielhauer, who can be cited here as a representing the opinion of many other scholars, the author of these passages "employed the literary means of the personal report in order to feign eyewitness character for some passages concerning Paul."[3]

With rejection of eyewitness character for the writer of Acts, also disposed of is the view deriving from early church tradition, according to which we have to do here with the *doctor* and *fellow worker* of Paul name Luke who is mentioned in Colossians (4:14) and Philemon (24).

Summary: The author of Acts is an otherwise unknown to us, Christian writer (from the second century), who himself did not know Paul personally. What he tells us about Paul and his activities are not first-hand reports. The heightened interest of the author in miraculous, wondrous stories, healing-, escape-, and punishment-miracles, and the "predominance of personal legends"[4] gives the impression rather that we have to do here not with a presentation of history, but with the transmission of legendary tradition.

Paul in Wonderland

The reader will perhaps take exception at the curious heading with which I now make a transition to a discussion of Paul in Acts. But at this point I could not forgo the allusion to the well-known children's book by the Englishman Lewis Carrol. I certainly do not want to claim thereby that the literary value of Acts resembles that of a children's book — whereby I also don't want to say anything against children's books (there is wonderful literature among them). But I would like to call attention to a situation that is important to consider again and again, namely, that the great majority of historical statements made in Acts about the life and person of the apostle Paul are legendary in character — Uta Ranke-Heinemann even speaks of "the fairy-tales of Acts"[5] — and thus are to be enjoyed only with great caution.

Although all this is known to most theologians and recognized by them, it must nevertheless be strongly emphasized again and again because the consequences that result from this are still too little considered. One admits may well admit that in Acts we in no way have an historical work in our present-day sense. But then, out of an understandable dilemma — apart from the letters, from where else should we get our information about the apostle Paul and early Christianity? — again and again, all the misgivings not withstanding, one still turns back to Acts to cannibalize it for early Christian history.

The basic methodological principle that one follows in doing this is sincerely simple: everything that somehow seems miraculous or imaginary is *unhistorical*; and everything, on the contrary, that proceeds in a rational and natural way and also agrees somehow with the letters is *historical*. This method, however, which in its most cultivated form is even employed by the critical New Testament scholar Günther

Bornkamm in his prudent and well-considered book on Paul, has fatal similarity with that of a man who, at any cost, wanted to hold on to a historical kernel in the story about little red riding hood and, to this end, removed all the mythic components (the wolf who speaks, red riding hood and grandmother in the stomach of the wolf) in order to hold fast to the historical existence of a little girl named red ridinghood who visited her grandmother in the forest sometime long ago and met a wolf on her way.

Now — in spite of Ranke-Heinemann — Acts is not a fairy tale of the brothers Grimm. But the example should nevertheless remind us to exercise caution in determining the historical kernel for many of its stories. We must obviously reckon with the possibility that our attempt to determine the kernel will be like peeling an onion: we think we have reached the kernel but always hit only another peel. — With regard to the entire subject, Richard Pervo correctly remarked: "[Luke] was bumbling and incompetent as a historian yet brilliant and creative as an author"[6]

With Rabbi Gamaliel

For the author of Acts, although Paul is a Jew, his family home was not in Palestine, but in the Jewish diaspora; he is said to have been born in Tarsus (Acts 9:11, 30; 11:25; 21:39; 22:3), in those days a Hellenistic city (today in Turkey) with a mixed, Greek and oriental population. Paul is supposed to have received his religious training from Rabbi Gamaliel (Acts 22:3). The Jewish-rabbinic tinge that one notices in many passages in the Pauline letters is usually explained from this background. The name of Rabbi Gamaliel (Gamaliel the Elder or Rabbi Gamaliel I, †50 CE) is also well-known in Jewish tradition. This certainly does not prove, however, that the information in Acts is also historical. In any case, in Jewish writings of the first two centuries CE there is no mention of a rebellious student of Gamaliel named Paul or Saul. It is also very remarkable that the supposed student of Gamaliel, who certainly would have received instruction from him in the original Hebrew text of the Old Testament, cites passages from the Old Testament exclusively from the Greek version—as if in his life he had never learned Hebrew! (see below ⇒ Paul—the Non-Jew).

Paul the Persecutor

Paul first appears on the scene in Acts as a persecutor of Christians. He is present when Stephen, the archetypal Christian martyr, is stoned, and as we are told at the very end of the story, he "took pleasure in his death" (Acts 8:1). The story of the death of Stephen the martyr is portrayed by Luke in very dramatic colors. The theatrical and histrionic character of the presentation is only exceeded by modern biographers of Paul, for whom the stoning scene offers a welcome opportunity to teach the reader (who is presumably comfortably stretched out on his couch at home) the meaning of fear, through a very thorough and detailed portrayal of the strange and archaic death penalty with which those of the Jewish religion punished the blasphemer. Dieter Hildebrandt speaks of the "critical choreography of the concentric stoning: One is surrounded on every side. The faster ones have caught up with the sacrifice. A very loose corral is built, just narrow enough to prevent an escape but still at a favorable distance from the throwing and thrashing of the others; for after the first stoning of the witness, dozens of arms are raised all at once, a whole whirl or projectiles is released, flying rubble, a chaotic bombardment. Even the torturers do not go entirely without bruises, or a minor injury, or a bloody nose."[7]

In Hildebrandt's literary fantasy Paul is "only a sneering observer of the gruesome scene. But that allows him to appear all the more loathsome. The others at least have fury in their stomachs, the scalp is deluged by an orgasm of rage, they are beside themselves over Stephen the blasphemer. But Saul knows how to control himself and does not dirty his hands. He simply watches with satisfaction."

If unlike Hildebrandt one does not read fantastic things into the text which are not there (Paul as a "sneering" observer), one will perhaps come to the conclusion (if one sets aside the literary effect it makes) that the entire stoning scene produces very little for a biography of Paul. As Hildebrandt, indeed, rightly observes, Paul is mentioned only on the margin, as though it were a footnote and as evidence for which side the pre-Christian Saul-Paul was on, namely, on the side of fanatical, anti-Christian Pharisaism.

One could certainly still go a step further. According to the Jewish historian of religion H.J. Schoeps, it is a fully open question whether the entire stoning story relates an historical event. Schoeps points out the remarkable circumstance that, in spite of great significance as an archetypal martyr, Stephen plays no great role in early Christian literature and that his martyrdom falls entirely into the background next to that of James the brother of the Lord in 66 CE. For these reasons and others, Schoeps can doubt "the historicity of the supposed Hellenistic Deacon Stephen."[8] He observes that we very probably do not have to do here with a "historical figure, but with a substitute figure introduced by Luke for tendentious reasons, on whom teachings troublesome to the author are unloaded."[9] For the most part, the material Luke uses for developing his destined death—Stephen is stoned after his speech against the Temple—contains the same motifs as the account of the stoning of *James* the brother of the Lord[10]. In Schoeps' opinion, the same destiny is imposed on the "substitute man" Stephen as on James the brother of the Lord. "The retouching of the facts allowed Luke... to unload the anti-cultic disposition, which was entirely foreign to him," and which finds expression in the speech of Stephen, the enemy of the Temple, "on the spokesperson for the Greek contingent within the early community and to place this in the mouth of a peripheral figure in the events."

Paul on the Way to Damascus

As a zealot for the law, Paul supposedly also distinguished himself later in the persecution of Christians. He obtained "letters" from the Sanhedrin in Jerusalem that legitimated even his persecution of Christian communities in distant Damascus.

But Saul, still breathing threats and murder against the disciples of the Lord, went to the high priest and asked him for letters to the synagogues at Damascus, so that if he found any belonging to the Way, men or women, he might bring them bound to Jerusalem (Acts :9:1f).

It has been noted again that Paul did not have the slightest authority to undertake a persecution of Christians in Damascus, which was an independent city and not subject to the jurisdiction of the Jewish central authority (Sanhedrin). Hyam Maccoby: "Outside Judaea ... the High Priest had no such police authority, and it is therefore difficult to understand how any 'letters' he might give to Saul 'authorizing him to arrest' followers of Jesus would have any validity. The difficulty is all the greater in that Damascus at this time was not even under Roman rule, having been ceded by Caligula (ad 37). It belonged to the independent Arab kingdom of Nabataea, under the rule of King Aretas iv (9 BC-AD 40). This King, who was jealous of his independence, would hardly take kindly to the entry into his territory of an emissary of the Roman-ruled area of Judaea for the purpose of arresting and dragging away citizens or even aliens who were under his protection."[11]

An interesting explanation of this historical riddle, which was discussed at the very beginning of the discovery of the Qumran scrolls, but then dropped and forgotten, has been tossed into the discussion again by R. Eisenman. He presumes that the term "Damascus" is a *code name* for the group of Jewish sectarians who had gathered together in the Qumran settlement. Accordingly, Paul's expedition supposedly led him not to the Damascus in Syria, but to that Damascus which is spoken of in the so-called *Damascus Document*.[12] This explanation would naturally only be plausible under the given presumption and would make sense only if Christians dwelled in Damascus (= Qumran) at the time of Paul, which for Eisenman, who identifies the residents of the Qumran settlement with the early Christians, was in fact the case. To be sure, until today this thesis has been energetically disputed by the majority of scholars — without being in a position, however, to offer a different, better explanation.

The Conversion

Just outside Damascus a sudden reversal then took place through the best known episode from the life of Paul: his conversion. It is often said that the conversion made a Paul out of the earlier Saul. But this now proverbial turn of speech does not fully correspond with the circumstances reported by Luke. For Luke, the Jew Saul who was converted to Christianity continues to be called Saul for quite a long time. The reader first learns that Saul also had a second name (namely, the Roman name Paul) very incidentally in Acts 13:9, when Saul-Paul has succeeded in converting

Sergius Paulus, the Roman proconsul in Cyprus, to Christianity.

Paul's sudden conversion experience outside Damascus, from which authors and artists in every age have found inspiration again and again—one thinks, for example, of the well-known picture *The Conversion of Paul* (1600) by *Caravaggio*—is described three times by Luke.

Now as he journeyed he approached Damascus, and suddenly a light from heaven flashed about him. And he fell to the ground and heard a voice saying to him, "Saul, Saul, why do you persecute me?" And he said, "Who are you, Lord?" And he said, "I am Jesus, whom you are persecuting; but rise and enter the city, and you will be told what you are to do." The men who were traveling with him stood speechless, hearing the voice but seeing no one. Saul arose from the ground; and when his eyes were opened, he could see nothing; so they led him by the hand and brought him into Damascus. And for three days he was without sight, and neither ate nor drank (Acts 9:3-9).

In spite of the fact that the account of Paul's conversion is repeated three times, which emphasizes the significance Luke obviously attributes to this event, the individual items reported therein are not very productive for the biography of the apostle. We will see below in more detail that Luke's presentation is clearly not to be understood as a rendering of historical events, but as a tendentious rejection of the claim put forwards by the writer of the letters to be an eyewitness and thereby a legitimate apostle of Jesus Christ. In addition, some of the material from which the author constructed his conversion story shows remarkable similarity with another well-known conversion stories from ancient literature. This too does not exactly speak for the historicity of the Lukan presentation.

Following other scholars, Ranke-Heinemann calls attention to a parallel between Acts 26:14 and a segment from a drama by the Greek poet Euripides. In Acts the voice speaks to Paul-Saul: "Saul, Saul, why do you persecute me? It hurts you to kick against the goads."

What we have in this saying is a citation from the *Bacchae* of Euripides, in which the persecuted God (In this case, Dionysius) speaks to his persecutor (In this case Pentheus, the king of Thebes) as in Acts: "You turn a deaf ear to my words... Instead of kicking against God's goads as a mortal, you should rather offer sacrifices" (787ff.).

Ranke-Heinemann concludes: "This Dionysius episode has obviously been taken over into the Damascus scenery. An ancient persecution-saying is taken up in a Christian persecution-saying. Even the detail that because of his meter Euripides uses not the singular, but the plural 'goads' is taken over by Luke". Of course, Ranke-Heinemann characterizes the "fairy story about the process of Paul's conversion" as a "harmless fairy story."[13]

Missionary Journeys

In contrast to the presentation of Galatians, where the writer explicitly says that he did not immediately confer with "flesh and blood," but first went to Arabia (Gal 1:17), in Acts we are told that following his conversion Paul to the Christian church in Damascus, where he is healed of his blindness by Ananias. After an unsuccessful attack on the life of the new convert to Christianity, Paul goes to Jerusalem to the apostles there (2 Cor 11:32).[14]

Soon afterward comes the first missionary journey (Acts 13:2ff.), which Paul undertakes along with his companion Barnabas, and which leads the two missionaries to the island of Cyprus, where Paul is even able to convert the Roman proconsul there, named Sergius Paulus, to Christianity (Acts 13:7-12).

After the apostolic council in Jerusalem Paul, to whose work of all the rest of Acts is dedicated (Acts 15:36ff.), travels over almost the entire Mediterranean region. The apostle is portrayed by the writer of Acts primarily as a miracle worker and missionary (not as an independent theological thinker), who successfully continues further on the way that —according to Acts— Peter first trod.

On his second missionary journey, which takes the apostle to Macedonia and Achaia, Paul travels for the first time on European soil. Because of the hatred and jealously of the Jews, Paul is imprisoned, but set free again through miraculous circumstances (an earthquake! Acts 16:26) and through God's ever-present assistance. At the Areopagus in Athens the apostle preaches the message of the resurrection (Acts 17:19), which stands at the center of his preaching (The Paul of Acts has never heard anything about justification by faith alone).

Imprisonment

After the return to Antioch by way of Ephesus and Caesarea, an additional missionary journey is attached, which, after a long stay in Ephesus, where he becomes involved in the rebellion of the silversmiths, takes the apostle again to Macedonia and Greece. This is followed by the last trip to Jerusalem. Evil premonitions torment the apostle, who soon after his arrival in Jerusalem is arrested, at the instigation of fanatical Jews from the diaspora, who hinder his work here as they do every-where else.

After the proceedings before the governor's council in Caesarea and the hearing before the Roman governor, Felix, and his follower, Festus, Paul appeals as a Roman citizen to Caesar, and after a speech before king Agrippa, is brought to Rome. In connection with this journey to Rome, the writer of Acts also tells us many more wonderful things about a shipwreck and escape, poison snake bites that have no effect, sick people being healed, etc.

Luke leaves us in the dark only about the end of Paul's life, although there would certainly have been many wonderful stories to tell here. We do learn, however, that immediately after his arrival in Rome, in spite of his chains, Paul has the opportunity to converse with Jews who were there and to testify "from morning to evening... about Jesus from the law of Moses and the prophets."

Uncertainty exists, however, regarding the further fate of Paul. Was he condemned to martyrdom, as reported in the apocryphal Acts of Paul? Or did the apostle travel from Rome even further to the West, to evangelize there also? The account in Acts breaks off abruptly.

And he lived there two whole years at his own expense, and welcomed all who came to him. preaching the kingdom of God and teaching them about the Lord Jesus Christ quite openly and unhindered (28:30-31).

The peculiar end of Acts has given rise to many questions for exegetes (similar to the equally peculiar ending of Mark). It is often assumed that the writer of Acts had an apologetic reason for concluding his work in this way. News of the martyrdom of Paul would eventually have exposed the apostle to suspicion of scheming against Rome. Since this could not be Luke's view, for whom it was most important to demonstrate for his contemporaries how loyal and absolutely harmless Christianity was from a political perspective, he concluded his presentation of the apostle's activity in the way he did.

From Acts to the Pauline Writings

After working intensively on Acts, I realized that the attempt with its help to get closer to the person of Paul had failed miserably. The biographical information it contained about the apostle seemed to be mostly legendary in character. That was true not only for the activity of Paul as a miracle worker or, for example, his marvelous escape from prison in Philippi, but also for information that at first sight appeared to be reliable and which in fact is perceived as historical by many biographies of Paul, e.g., the apostle's instruction by Rabbi Gamaliel, his activity as a persecutor of Christians, and his conversion.

Against this background, the closer I came, the contours of the figure of the apostle, which to begin with had been sharply profiled and stood before my eyes almost as if they were carved in stone (like the well-known picture of the four apostles by Dürer), began to drift apart like a smokescreen. Whoever immersed themselves in the world of Acts and took pleasure in its wonderful stories, the great deeds and adventures of the apostle, his heroism and courage in the face of martyrdom, in order to directly pose the question regarding the historical value of all this — for such a person it would be like someone who received a gift of gold in a beautiful dream and now upon awakening had nothing. It became more and more clear to me that anyone who would base their historical knowledge of the apostle on Acts must tumble into the deep, golden abyss of fairy tales and legends. Historical certainty could never be found here. The question whether anything at all in the presentation Acts could have historical value could basically not be answered by a historian who was aware of his responsibility. If one did not want to simply dismiss everything as unhistorical (one really could not blame someone who reached such a radical conclusion), all that remains is the simple statement that we have to do here with an apostle, who presumably worked around the middle of the first century, who was an important missionary, and who may have died in Rome.

Besides Acts, of course, there are still more literary witnesses to Paul in the New Testament, which have remained out of view until now: the letters. Since, in contrast to Acts, we have to do here not with testimonies about the apostle, but with testimonies of his own, the situation would seem to be entirely different. The figure of the apostle as well as the history of the early Christian community, that had just dissolved before my eyes into a fog of fanciful and phantom-like figures, must necessarily take on clearer, firmer contours. For the first time in the literature of the New Testament, we had writings which seemed to be a true historical foundation stone and whose historicity and authenticity could not be doubted. For the first time, we had here written documents which reflected the life of the early Christian church first hand, so to speak, not in legendary, transfigured retrospect, and in which one could sense the living breath of a real personality in every line.

It became clear to me what enormous significance the Pauline letters had for the historian of early Christianity. If we had to do here (at least in some cases) with the earliest Christian documents and with authentic letters from the hand of the apostle Paul — and at that time, like other theologians, I took this for granted —

Then they obviously must reflect the situation in which they were written, which would mean that, from a historical perspective, we find ourselves in the middle of the first century

CE, i.e., in that very time that one later characterized as "earliest Christianity."

Then what the letters impart concerning the earliest community in the first half of the second century must also be more or less valid, and Acts, which contains many points of contact with the letters, could also be drawn upon as an additional historical source.

Then what Paul says about Jesus must have been said around the middle of the first century, so that one can with certainty begin with the historical existence of the man from Nazareth before the conversion of Paul. What the apostle communicated about him, to be sure, was little enough, but even here, once one had obtained the necessary certainty, one could fill out Paul's somewhat pallid picture of Jesus with additional interesting details from the Gospels.

In these ways the rest of the New Testament writings could be more and more firmly connected with the letters. And finally one could arrive at the comforting result that the entire ship of the early Christian church with the all its known apostolic crew laid at anchor in the safe harbor of the first century.

I understood not only what it means for theologians to possess the Pauline letters, I also understood what it would mean if—for one reason or another— they were lost, or if their authenticity were called into question, like the rest of the New Testament writings—an idea, to be sure, which still seemed completely impossible to me. Since New Testament scholarship has obviously fastened the entire weight and load of their theories to this single hook, namely, the Pauline writings regarded by them as authentic, all those things whose fate, just a moment ago, they still believed could be connected with the authenticity of the letters would also be dragged into the abyss. The figure of the apostle Paul and our knowledge about him would become questionable. The historical value of the four Gospels and Acts, which derives from one of the Gospel writers, would again become questionable. The history of the man from Nazareth would also become questionable. In short, all our trusted and beloved conceptions of early Christianity would become dubious.

Such a prospect, however, seemed purely hypothetical for me, since I regarded the authenticity of the Pauline letters, or at least a core of these letters, as having been demonstrated. The thought that even with the testimony of the Pauline letters we have to do not with a direct reflection of events around 50 CE, but with much later documents was impossible possibility.

Nevertheless, in the course of time this impossible possibility would gradually become a certainty for me. With closer examination, one after the other of the thirteen letters in the New Testament canon under the name of Paul turned out to be "inauthentic," i.e., not proceeding from the pen of the apostle who lived in the first century. At the end, the number of those letters from the Pauline corpus which withstood critical examination shrunk to a small, hard core, with Galatians and the Corinthian letters at the center — until these also finally had to be given up.

Before I come to the Pastoral Epistles, as well as Colossians, Ephesians, and 2 Thessalonians, with which criticism of the Pauline writings begins, a few general comments regarding literary forgery in early Christianity are necessary.

Original and Forgery in Early Christianity

Whoever deals with the writings of New Testament very soon encounters — also and especially outside the Pauline epistolary literature — the phenomenon of forgery, or as one says in a somewhat more refined way, pseudepigraphy.

The history of investigation of the New Testament has led to the conclusion, generally accepted today, that of the twenty-seven writings of the New Testament—apart from those that supposedly derive from Paul—not a single one can be traced back to an apostle or a student of an apostle. Although the titles of the four Gospels— *The Gospel According to Matthew; The Gospel According to Mark;* etc.—seem to indicate with regard to the four authors that we have to do with apostles, or students of apostles, and are thus direct or indirect reports by eye witnesses, the majority of exegetes today would reject the possibility, for example, that Matthew the tax-collector wrote the Gospel of Matthew or that the interpreter of Peter named Mark wrote the Gospel named after him.

The view has generally prevailed that the Gospels were first transmitted anonymously until they were attributed to Matthew, Mark, Luke, and John (presumably shortly before the formation of a "canon" of New Testament around the end of the second century).[15] The fact that the Gospels all have false attributions is related to the fact that the decisive condition for including a Christian writing in the New Testament canon, which henceforth would serve the church as a plumb line (= canon) for her preaching, was the principle of apostolicity. To be recognized by the Church, a writing must be of apostolic origin, i.e., traceable back to an apostle or to a student of an apostle.

Today hardly any scholar would think of identifying the author of the Gospel of Matthew with Matthew the apostle, who appears in all four apostolic lists in the New Testament and according to early church tradition was regarded as its author. The same is true for Mark and Luke. The Gospel of John as well would not be regarded today by hardly any scholar as the work of John the apostle, although even in the past century "on every page" one heard "the heart beat of the disciple whom Jesus loved."[16]

The situation is not much different for the other writings of the New Testament, i.e., above all, the letters. Even Catholic theologians do not regard the epistle of James as the work of "James the brother of the Lord" (Gal 1:19), as the letter's introduction obviously suggests when the author refers to himself as "James, a servant of God and Lord Jesus Christ," but, as is nicely said in the Catholic *Einleitung* to the New Testament by Wikenhauser-Schmidt, is regarded rather as a "pseudonymous writing," whereby "the author... [has] made the most sparing use... of the principle of pseudonymity, in that he only [!] claims for himself the name of James the brother of the Lord."[17] For a long time the epistle of Jude has been seen not as the work of "Judas the brother of the Lord," but as the work of an "author from the post-apostolic time."[18] According to the today's view, the first epistle of Peter can in no way derive from the apostle Peter[19], nor can the second... and so one could continue.

The production of pseudepigraphic writings is in no way met with only in early Christian literature; it was also common elsewhere in antiquity. It was especially common in Jewish apocalyptic literature to disclose revelations and visions under the name of a patriarch or some other authority from the ancient past. Also popular was literature that placed "final words" in the mouth of a famous person, whereby it took on for the reader the status and dignity of a last testament. In Jewish literature, for example, there is a writing named *Testament of the Twelve Patriarchs*. As the forefather Jacob addressed his twelve sons shortly before his death, so also here, before their own death, Jacob's twelve sons address their descendents, to communicate to them their final wishes and to illuminate them concerning future events that they have already foreseen. Even in the Greek-

Hellenistic world, however, pseudepigraphy was certainly an everyday practice. Among others, for example, some letters are known to have been forged in the name of Plato.[20]

The most important reason why ancient writers provided their productions with false authorial attributions was probably that in this way they could invest them with greater authority. In a very conservative society, like that in antiquity, which had especially high esteem for traditions and values from ancient times, a writing stemming from ancient times and that moreover one that had been written by a legendary, mythically-elevated figure, would naturally have great importance.

With regard to Christian literature, the previously mentioned perspective of apostolicity played a great role. It was, above all, the Catholic church that quickly recognized that it was important to possess a solid and reliable foundation in its struggle against other churches (e.g., the Gnostics, Marcionites, and Ebionites). To justify themselves and in order to controvert the legitimacy of the other churches, they developed not only the principle of right belief (confession) and the apostolic succession of bishops, but for this purpose also created their canon of writings, in which only writings that were apostolic (or at least made this claim) found entry. Because the Catholic church could now claim to be the rightful heir of Jesus and the apostles, it was able to drive its opponents from the field, who, even though they made the same claim, were less successful. These then became "heretics." The Catholic church, on the other hand, being the most powerful "sect," held the upper hand and henceforth defined what Christian "orthodoxy" had to mean for all the faithful.

If one recognizes that the idea that something must be truly apostolic in order to be divinely inspired and canonically legitimate is historically conditioned and arose from a struggle for power in the church, it is much easier to comprehend the concept and phenomenon of literary forgery in early Christianity. Historical understanding makes it possible for us to evaluate a writing independent of its apostolicity or non-apostolicity. We recognize that the value of a New Testament writing's contents does not depend on whether it is authentic or not. A forgery could contain more "original" ideas that a supposed original. The person who has learned to pay attention to content and who regards content, not authorship, as the final and decisive authority to which one feels obligated will be less disturbed by the problem of forgery.

Nevertheless, I am naturally aware that it is not easy for many Christians to live with the fact that we find "forged" writings in the New Testament canon. One is taken aback and asks, How is it possible that a religion with a high moral claim like Christianity can be based on writings that do not derive from those persons in whose name they were written?

According to their individual temperament, origin, and religious background, each person/Christian reacts very differently to the knowledge that most writings in the New Testament are falsifications. Basically, two different reactions are possible. The first could be called churchly-apologetic. Its representative are all too inclined to play down or make light of the matter of forgery. One should "not really" speak of forgery, since the intention of the pseudepigraphical author (e.g., in the case of the Pastoral Epistles) was "to allow the voice of the apostle be heard even after his death, to insure his continuing 'presence' (cf. Col 2:5 with 1 Cor 5:3)" — so the theologian Andreas Lindemann, with regard to the author of the so-called deutero-Pauline writings.[21] Moreover, the concept of "authenticity" is said to be vague. Since for the Catholic New Testament scholar Norbert Brox "the 'authenticity' of a writing is shown by its Christian content, not by historical traces of the actual author,"[22] even an "inauthentic" writing—depending on the amount of Christian content—can prove to be authentic. Against such attempts to soften or obscure the fact of literary forgery, it continues to be important to always call things by their right names. Thus, Ranke-Heinemann states: "It should not be denied that... forgeries were a wide-spread practice in the early church. This does not make them legitimate. It is and remains religious counterfeiting."[23]

Nevertheless, one does not need to go as far as that furious critic (Karlheinz Deschner) who would like to deal with the entire history of literary falsification in early Christianity under the theme *Criminal History of the Church*[24]. This throws out the baby with the bath water. Criminalization of early Christian pseudepigraphy is misguided and inappropriate for the actual circumstances, which have nothing to do with the circulation of counterfeit coins or bills. We observed above that the origin of forgeries must be looked at from the historical circumstances of its own time. They were supposed to satisfy the need of many Christians who require binding rules and the authority of an apostolic age. One should also not find objectionable the fact that in addition the attempt was made to pursue church politics in this way, since extensive use was made of these instruments in all Christian camps. Finally, one will have to say that most of the writings included in the New Testament under false names are of such high theological and literary quality that the world of religious literature would be far poorer if the authors of the pseudepigraphic works had abided by our modern rules of play and produced the writings under their own names. For then, we have to fear, if they had not been linked with the lustrous name of an apostle, they would not have been regarded as worth transmitting; they would have remained literary ephemera and would not have survived over the centuries.

From what we have said here about the problem of literary forgery with reference to the Christian faith, one could (correctly) conclude that the question is often given far too much importance. In fact, in general, it is less the simple, faithful Christians, who quickly recognize that the Pauline letters in no way become less valuable by the discovery of their inauthenticity, than the representatives of the church and scholarship, who have a difficult struggle with this problem.

For many scholars it is a question of their own reputation. One can understand that a biblical researcher who throughout his life-long, scholarly occupation with the Pauline letters has proceeded as a matter of course from the integrity of letters generally recognized today as authentic, and on this basis has written many brilliant books, would find it difficult to bear if someone could prove to him that all his work until now rested on a fiction. For him what may not be, cannot be.

For the church there is also very much at stake — at least according to its own self-understanding. Because it regards itself, now as before (the reference here is primarily to the Roman Catholic church), as the legitimate heir of Christ and his apostles and until today bases its authority on this claim, the discovery that all the New Testament writings are forgeries and in no way stem from the time of the apostles makes many things uncertain. If the Church acknowledges that the historian who advocates this view is correct, it must give up its own claim of authority — or (which would certainly be more beneficial) perceive this as a questioning of its own self-understanding and base its authority in the future on spiritual empowerment, not historical.

The Inauthenticity of the Pastoral Epistles (1, 2 Timothy, Titus)

By and large, in Protestant as well as Catholic circles today, there is agreement that the so-called Pastoral epistles — i.e., the two letters to Timothy as well as the letter to Titus, called Pastoral epistles because they are directed to the shepherds (pastors) of communities, not the communities themselves — cannot stem from the writer of the other letters, or, as the case may be, from Paul. Hans von Campenhausen, the Protestant theologian, speaks in this regard of "a typical forgery, although of unusual spiritual distinction."[25] The authenticity of 1 Timothy was doubted already in the nineteenth century. It was first contested by J.E.C. Schmidt (1804)[26] and Friedrich Schleiermacher (1807)[27]; and their judgment was then taken over by J. G. Eichhorn (1812)[28] and extended to the other Pastoral Epistles.

Differences in Language and Theology

In general, in evaluating the Pastoral Epistles, one employed and still employs criteria relating to language and style as well as criteria relating to content. The results of word statistics already show that there are great differences between the Pastoral epistles and the other Pauline letters regarded as authentic. The number of words which appear neither in other Pauline writings nor anywhere else in the writings of the New Testament (so-called hapaxlegomena) is very high (26% = 175 words), while, on the contrary, of the 884 words in the Pastoral letters (personal names not included) 306 (36%) are not found in the other Pauline letters.[29]

The appearance of a number of concepts that derive in part from the vocabulary of the Hellenistic world (e.g. "piety," "prudence"/"discretion," "good conscience," "epiphany", instead of "parousia" for Paul, "ruler" = "despotēs, "saviour," "trustworthy word"), stands in contrast to the absence of a number of central Pauline concepts (e.g. "covenant," "body of Christ," "righteousness of God," "revelation," "freedom," "cross" among others), all of which one should not expect in every letter, but whose total absence is remarkable... This language reflects a different kind of theological thinking and a different church situation."30 But the stylistic differences are also striking and can be noticed even through the English translation of the Greek original. Brox observes: "In contrast to the passionate, sometimes explosive style of Paul, we find no trace of similar energy in the Pastorals. In contrast to the apostle's numerous insertions, incomplete sentences, and hardly understandable phrases, stands the calm flow of speech in the Pastoral Epistles."31

Did Paul Have a Secretary?

The attempt has been made to explain the linguistic-stylistic differences by the hypothesis of a secretary. It is said that Paul did not write the letters himself, but only sketched out a rough draft and gave this to a secretary, who then filled in the details and formulated the wording. For various reasons, this hypothesis is very improbable. Among others, it collapses because of the many differences in theology and content that distinguish the Pastoral Epistles from the presumably authentic Pauline letters, and which Paul would hardly have allowed his secretary to get away with. I give only three examples. While for the writer of the presumably authentic letters faith is understood primarily as an act, in the Pastoral epistles the focus is primarily on content (1 Tim 3:9; 4:1), i.e., "orthodoxy with regard to fundamental, uncompromising apostolic teaching that must be accepted and held fast."32 While the opposition between sarx and pneuma (flesh and spirit) is fundamental for the "authentic" Paul, these are nowhere referred to in the Pastoral epistles. Finally, the theology of the law and works occupies a far more important place in the Pastoral Epistles than in other Pauline letters, which (in their original stratum) are clearly antinomian and in which all legalistic elements were introduced later.

Paul's Mantel

Finally, another important argument against the Pauline authorship of the Pastoral Epistles is the impossibility of accommodating them in the framework of Paul's biography. In Wikenhauser-Schmidt's Einleitung, the investigation of the "presumed historical situation of the Pastoral Epistles" reaches the conclusion: "All three Past(oral Epistles) thus presuppose that at the end Paul was resident in Asia, or perhaps in the East (so Titus). Of all the situations referred to in the three letters. however, none fits in the life of Paul up to his conveyance to Rome as a prisoner in the fall of 60... If the three letters really derive from Paul, therefore, they must have been written in the time after his two-year imprisonment in Rome (61-63), and it must thereby be presupposed... that he had then been exonerated and set free."[33]

Precisely this assumption, however, is highly improbable and is rightly rejected today by almost all exegetes. The situation of the Pastoral Epistles is thus shown to be an "ostensibly historical" fiction by an author writing in the name of Paul.

In investigating the situation of 2 Timothy, a small detail often plays a very large role, namely, the mantel of Paul, which he supposedly left behind when he departed from Troas. Writing in the name of Paul, the author of 2 Timothy asks his protégé Timothy:

When you come, bring the mantel that I left with Carpus at Troas, also the books, and above all the parchments. (4:13)

In view of the supposed "obscurity" of these details, many exegetes have spoken of the "simple realism," the "uniqueness of the situation and of the relationship between writer and recipient." J. Jeremias, the great New Testament scholar, even saw this as the "main argument for the authenticity of the Pastoral Epistles."34 However, one can certainly only speak in such a way if one thinks very little about the writer's pseudepigraphic inventiveness and imagination — which many scholars are certainly inclined to do.

A Double Standard

It is now certainly interesting that many indications that in the opinion of New Testament scholars speak for the inauthenticity of the Pastoral Epistles are also to be found in the presumably authentic Pauline letters — without the same consequences being drawn from this as in the case of the Pastorals! We obviously have to do here with a double standard.

Thus, Walter Schmithals, the Berlin New Testament scholar, for example, represents the view that "the setting forth of identical, enduring ordinances of a legal kind for the most diverse missionary regions" does not correspond "with the diversity of communities in the time of Paul" and thus could not be intended "for fellow workers whom Paul has just seen or will see very soon."35

In this connection, however, it must be remembered that on this point the situation of the supposed authentic letters of Paul does not differ from that presupposed by the Pastorals: here also the apostle produces precisely his most encompassing writings, richly garnished with all kinds of exhortations and universal teachings, just on the eve of his upcoming visit in the churches. Romans is supposed to have arisen in this situation, i.e., shortly before the apostle's arrival in Rome; and 2 Corinthians likewise, shortly before the apostle's arrival in Corinth. Here also one might ask whether it would not have been better for the apostle to reserve his shrewd recommendations until he had become familiar with the problems of the community "face to face."

The expressed self-stylization of the apostle is also often used as an argument against the authenticity of the Pastoral Epistles. In 1 Tim 1:16 the writer speaks of the "mercy" that he (Paul) received, "that in me first Jesus Christ might display all patience for an example to those who were to believe in him for eternal life." About this,. Brox writes: "Such absolutizing of one's own person...is not Pauline.... Nowhere in his authentic letters does Paul ascribe to himself such a key position in the process of salvation. We have before us not statements by the apostle, but statements about the apostle."[36] — But, is such an "absolutizing of one's own person" really not Pauline?

Even the Paul of the supposedly authentic letters, who was set apart while still in his mother's womb and called to his office by the grace of God (Gal 1:16), does not exactly distinguish himself by excessive humility. In 1 Cor 11:1, for example, he can present himself as an example and proudly appeal to his readers: "Be imitators of me, as I am of Christ" (cf. also 3:10; 4:11-13, 16; 9:19-27; Phil 3:17; 1 Thess 1:6 – Eph 5:6). The writer of Philippians can imagine no greater gift for his readers than to suffer what he himself has already suffered: "For it has been granted to you that for the sake of Christ you should not only believe in him but also suffer for his sake, engaged in the same conflict which you saw and now hear to be mine" (1:29). Indeed, in the mind of the writer of Philippians, the suffering of the apostle not only possesses normative character, but obviously already has a redemptive significance—like that of Christ: "Even if I am to be poured as a libation upon the sacrificial offering of your faith, I am glad and rejoice with you all" (2:17). It is no wonder that even the writer of Philippians can appeal to his readers: "Brethren, become fellow imitators of me, and mark those who so live as you have an example in us" (3:17).

Here also, the self-assurance of the apostle at times reaches such a degree that one must either diagnose all the symptoms of pronounced megalomania — or in considering such statements, to be consistent, we must arrive at the same conclusion as for the Pastoral Epistles, which are generally regarded as inauthentic, namely, that we have to do here not with "statements by the apostle, but (with) statements about the apostle." The hardly tolerable self-stylization thus betrays the later, pseudepigraphic author of the letter, who, filled with admiration, looks back on the transfigured picture of the hero faith from the past.

In addition, it should also pointed out that the situation in the supposedly authentic Pauline letters is often just as contradictory and confusing as in the Pastoral Epistles. According to Walter Schmithals, "the writer of the P(astorals) is not interested in sketching an authentic historical situation for the letter, or not in a position to do so."[37] What should we say then about the writer of Philippians, who one time portrays the apostle as a prisoner (1:7, 13, 14) and then again as a free man (2:25)? Or about the writer of 2 Corinthians, regarding whose situation exegetes can obtain any clarity at all only if they occupy themselves with complicated hypotheses of segmentation; i.e., they believe they can reduce the difficulty of conceiving a unified situation by declaring the letter to be composition from several small letters, or "postcards," written at entirely different times in entirely different situations, which were then supposedly joined together by a redactor? Peculiar here is only that the redactor obviously did not regard it necessary to inform the reader in a redactional note about this procedure, by which he arbitrarily atomized (why actually?) the precious memory of the apostle.

Finally, it must still be said that the reference to a later development in teaching found in the Pastoral Epistles as an argument against the authenticity of the letter is also a double-edged sword, since one can advance this argument with equal justification against the supposedly authentic letters of Paul. Here also we encounter a series of conceptions which cannot be otherwise documented anywhere in the presupposed time of origin. The Christ-hymn in Philippians (Phil 2:6-11), for example, contains strong echoes of the conception of the descent of the heavenly Sophia, which is first evident only in the second century and fully developed first by the Gnostic Valentinus (for Valentinus, see below ⇒ *Marcionism and Gnosis*) [38].

Also the other echoes of Gnostic conceptions, and indeed not only those that can be presupposed already in the first century, but those that derive from the more developed Gnosis of the second century — for example, the cursing of the earthly Jesus, 1 Cor 12:3, first documented at this time, belongs here — show that not only the Pastorals but also the other Pauline letters share the religious atmosphere of the second century, not the first.

Ephesians, Colossians, and 2 Thessalonians: Inauthentic

On the basis of contradictions in content and theology, the letter to the Ephesians, the letter to the Colossians, and the second letter to the Thessalonians are also regarded as inauthentic by most scholars today.

In the same way as the Pastoral Epistles, in reading Ephesians and Colossians linguistic and stylistic differences first catch the eye. While Colossians contains 34 words that appear nowhere else in the New Testament, and 15 that appear elsewhere only in Ephesians, the letter to the Ephesians itself contains some 39 hapaxlegomena and 90 words that do not appear in the Pauline letters designated as authentic[39].

Many sentences in Ephesians and Colossians strike one as excessively verbose. "One misses the liveliness characteristic of Paul."[40] In its place, we encounter long complicated sentences, in which the writer prefers to connect "abstract ideas to one another with genitive constructions"[41] and string these together until it is entirely incomprehensible (e.g., Col 1:9-12):

Therefore, we too, from the day we heard of it, asking that you be filled with the knowledge of his will in all spiritual wisdom and understanding, to lead a life worthy of the Lord, fully pleasing to him, bearing fruit in every good work, and increasing in the knowledge of God, being empowered with all power, according to the might of his glory, for all endurance and patience with joy, giving thanks to the Father, who has qualified us to share in the inheritance of the saints in light.

Although, from a literary perspective, the results of the whole stylistic process might provide little edification, for many readers it produces the impression of great theological significance: what is obscure must also be profound. Whether this is true cannot be investigated here. The stylistic peculiarities of Colossians and Ephesians, which some would also explain by appeal to liturgical influences, decisively diverge from the presumably authentic letters of

Paul, and indeed to such an extent that even the Einleitung by Wikenhauser-Schmidt calls it an "evasion" if one speaks here of Paul's "late style" or appeals once more to the secretary-hypothesis in order to save their Pauline origin.[42]

Letters from No-man's land

Apart from linguistic-stylistic peculiarities, a large number of inner contradictions and factual problems can also be cited against the authenticity of the letters. Especially characteristic of Ephesians is the letter's "lack of situation."[43] The superscription "To the Ephesians" was not part of the original document. "It is most likely that the words 'in Ephesus' were originally missing"[44]. The occasion of Ephesians is nowhere clearly visible. It seems to have been "written in a historical no-man's land." This certainly does not indicate the presence of an actual letter, which generally is written in a definite historical situation for a definite historical reason. We have the impression here that we have to do rather with an edifying tract in the form of a letter,[45] i.e., a theological writing that only later was given a historical cloak and that only later was placed under the great name of the apostle. The "letter" may also be a reworked sermon, or baptismal liturgy; Margaret Y. MacDonald: „Like the question of the identity of the Colossian false teachers, the nature and purpose of Ephesians have been the subject of extensive debate. The lack of reference to specific church matters, coupled with a liturgical-catechetical style, has led to the suggestion that it is perhaps best to view the work mainly as a liturgical tract or a sermon rather than as a letter in the usual sense — that is, as a theological work merely cast in the form of a letter ... Ephesians presents its readers with many interpretative puzzles. The very intention of the author of Ephesians to write to a community in Ephesus cannot be taken for granted."[46]

In addition, the writer of the letter hardly seems to have a *personal relationship* with the Christians addressed here, which is strange, since Paul is supposed to have resided in Ephesus for a long time. According to Eph 6:21, the readers should know everything about Paul; but according to 1:15; 3:2, they know about each other only through hearsay. The readers are addressed once as Gentile Christians (1:13; 2:1f., 11f., 13, 19; 3:1), then as former Jews (1:11f.)[47], and then again very generally as Christians (1:15-23; 3:12; 4:17). Here also one wonders whether the writer had any knowledge at all of the concrete circumstances in the local community, or whether from the very beginning he did not imagine the recipients of the letter to be the *entire* church.

Ephesians contains signs of familiarity with other Pauline letters, e.g., Romans, 1 and 2 Corinthians, Galatians. Here also one can distinguish teaching material (chs. 1-3) from exhortatory material (chs. 4-6). Eph 3:3 is related to Gal 1:12-16 and is something like the earliest commentary on Galatians. The writing originally may have been intended to be attached to the earliest collection of Pauline writings. As in the other Pauline writings, the picture of Paul is *idealized*: Paul suffers and is imprisoned "on your behalf, the Gentiles" (3:1); his theological and christological concepts show that a long development has taken place. The community was not founded only a short time ago, but has obviously existed for a very long time.

Contradictions

Just as in Ephesians, so also in Colossians one can observe a series of small contradictions. The author writes one time in the singular (1:23b-4:18) and then again in the plural (1:1-1?, 23a), as if he himself were not really certain which possibility he should choose. The case is similar for the question concerning his imprisonment. One time he finds himself in prison (4:10, 18); but then it is said that he toils and strives for the community (1:29; 2:1). It is entirely unclear how both should be reconciled with one another. The writer himself probably did take the situation in which he placed his hero not very seriously.

Also when reading, the writer seems one time to portray Gentile Christians (1:21, 27; 2:11), and another time Jews (2:13)[48]. With regard to content, the writing contains allusions to the Old Testament (Ps 110:1) as do the other Pauline letters. In particular, Ephesians seems to have been known to the writer of Colossians — probably, as for Marcion, with a different name, namely, the letter to the Laodiceans (2:1; 4:13-16) — and heavily used by him (see p. 122).

If one adds some further observations, e.g., the fact that Paul already appears as a "dogmatic authority," who is known by all Christians, and that he has already completed what Christ suffered for the community, and if one adds as well that the Christian community seems to have already existed for some time and that the gospel has already been preached in all the world (1:6, 23), then the tradition, according to which Paul wrote this letter around the year 63 in Rome, can hardly be correct. With Colossians, we have to do rather, as with Ephesians, with an edifying-dogmatic tract in the form of a letter, intended to be read (4:16) at the gathering of the community (for worship).

Did Paul Copy from Himself?

Just as Ephesians seems to connect with a series of passages in Colossians, so also 2 Thessalonians agrees in many places with some passages from 1 Thessalonians, partly in verbatim echoes.[49] Apart from 2:2-9, 11-12, there are only nine verses in 2 Thessalonians without parallels in 1

Thessalonians![50] From the indisputable existing literary dependence of the second letter on 1 Thessalonians, it has been concluded that the second letter originated with use of the first. Because one could not assume that in the writing of 2 Thessalonians Paul had copied himself, there must have been a later hand at work in the origin of the second letter. The letter is thus pseudonymous.

In view of these very reasonable considerations, all attempts to nevertheless save the authenticity of 2 Thessalonians — 1 Thess is directed to the leader of the community, 2 Thess to the entire community[51]; 2 Thess was originally addressed to the community in *Philippi*[52]; 2 Thess is a literary composite[53] — are not very convincing.

The occasion for 2 Thessalonians cannot be easily deduced from the tendency of the letter, which in terms of content clearly presents a correction of what is said in 1 Thessalonians. The writer of the letter obviously fears that the remarks in 1 Thessalonians about the immediacy of the impending parousia of the Lord could have negative consequences for the ethical conduct of the community. He attempts to prevent this, among other ways, by reference to the good old apostolic tradition (2:15) and stimulation of orderly conduct (3:6-12) — and by delaying for a while the "coming of the Lord" (which obviously made readers of the first letter very uncomfortable), and embelishing it with a rich replenishment of apocalyptic events.

Paul as a Schoolmaster?

The view held by the majority of theologians today that not all of the thirteen letters ascribed to Paul in the New Testament actually derive from the apostle naturally raises the question concerning the real author, or authors, of these writings. Who in early Christian times would have had an interest in writing and distributing letters in the name of the apostle? One most often assumes here that the deutero-Pauline writings and the Pastoral Epistles were the product of a Pauline school. In the course of his activity as a teacher (possibly during his time in Ephesus), Paul is supposed to have gathered students and fellow workers around himself, who constituted a "school," after the model of ancient schools of philosophy. After the death of the apostle, the pseudepigraphical writings were produced in the circle of students and fellow workers, who intended to give new voice to the theological inheritance of their master in different times and different circumstances.

Of course, in the same way as the assumption of a Johannine school, the darling, pampered child of present day theologians, the entire theory has a decisive catch to it. In the same way as the assumption of a Johannine school, it represents a *fiction, a pure hypothesis,* for which not the slightest basis can be found in the New Testament.

As a rule, arguments in favor of this assumption offer only vague references to the contemporary teaching activity and schools of wandering pagan teachers, who suggest this hypothesis, as well as the fact that Paul often mentions fellow workers in his letters. That is obviously too little to prove beyond all question the existence of a Pauline school, especially because, as we will see later, from the perspective of church history, the fellow workers of Paul mentioned in his letters are just as intangible as their master himself, or, as the case may be, his churches. In any case, the early church historians, Hegesippus and Eusebius, know nothing at all about a "Pauline school" or about any students of Paul who would have played a special role therein — and they would have really had to have known!

If all that still remains then is only the reference to the existence of forged letters, which is employed to demonstrate what in reality must be independently demonstrated, we find ourselves in a circular argument. First, the existence of a school is hypothesized in order to explain the pseudepigraphic writings as the product of a Pauline school; then on the basis of the pseudepigraphic writings as the product of a Pauline school, one concludes, razor sharp, that a Pauline school existed. That is not very convincing! Basically, what applies to the Johannine school also applies here. Already in the last century, Franz Overbeck, a critical theologian and friend of Nietzsche, remarked that we have to do here with a "scholarly invention" that is "groundless," the "splendid example of a fantasy," since one "not only knows nothing about its founding but also nothing about who belonged to it."[54]

The question about the real origin and the real writer of the Pauline pseudepigrapha is thus not satisfactorily resolved with the hypothesis of a Pauline school. We will have to return to this question later.

Whoever says A must also say B

For every reader who has followed me thus far a question must intrude that also arose for me very early, as I occupied myself with the Pauline letters and the problem of their authenticity: How far can criticism of the Pauline writings go? Is their a definite point, a border, at which it is said, Thus far and no farther! Or on the contrary, if it has been shown that a portion of the letters are inauthentic, must not the rest be investigated, even if to begin with they inspire in us the appearance of authenticity and genuineness?

Many people perhaps believe that the existence of inauthentic letters necessarily has the simultaneous presence of authentic letters as a presupposition, that the former belongs to the latter almost like a shadow and thus necessarily presupposes it. They think that if there had not been an apostle Paul who left behind authentic letters, no later person would have come up with the idea of writing letters under the name of Paul. This assumption, however, is not persuasive. One can easily imagine that not only the writer(s) of the Pastoral Epistles, the deutero-Pauline letters, and 2 Thessalonians, but also the writer(s) of the rest of the Pauline letters, possessed from tradition only the report of the life and work of the apostle, and that the whole fiction of an apostle who wrote letters (who, as we will see, the writer of Acts knew nothing about at all, of even wanted to know about) was their own invention. To illustrate this with an example from our own time (to be sure, regarded as inappropriate by some people): even the forged diaries of Hitler "discovered" by Heidemann/Kujau (1983) had no connection with a really existing, authentic diary of Hitler; rather the fiction of a Hitler who wrote diaries entered the world at the same time as the forgeries.

Against an investigation of the authenticity of all the letters, the objection could be made that there are hardly any witnesses from early Christian times that seem to exhibit such a personal, individual character as, for example, the Pauline letters to the communities in Corinth or Galatia. One would have to concede that precisely these letters at least have the immediate appearance in their favor. The sharply imprinted profile of a living, historical personality seems to be disclosed in them. In view of their passionate, combative character, with their multiplicity of personal allusions, they awake in the reader, at first glance, the character of something impossible to be mistaken about, something that cannot be invented, something "authentic," which makes it seem impossible to raise at all the question of genuineness. Nevertheless, apart from the fact that from time immemorial it has been part of the task of scholarship to place in doubt and critically interrogate even what appears to be obvious, the observation that letters transmitted in the New Testament under the name of the apostle are distinguished by the ""living stamp" of his spirit will not be really satisfactory as long one is not able to establish where and how he became acquainted with this spirit. The fact that the writer of Galatians was obviously a person with a passionate temperament and a sharply defined personality cannot be proof that we actually have to do here with Paul. Otherwise, for example, one would also have to regard the scribblings in the letters of the young Werther as authentic documents. It all comes down to the question whether the writer who transmitted letters under the name of Paul can be shown, by means of the historical circumstances in which he appeared and which are reflected in his letters, to be that person whom he claims to be. The letters transmitted under the name of Paul, therefore, can only be regarded as really authentic if it has been shown that they fit seamlessly and unbroken into the time and historical circumstances presupposed by their writer.

For other reasons as well, an examination of the question of the authenticity of the Pauline letters is certainly not superfluous. As we observed above, the history of the investigation of the New Testament writings has led to the generally recognized conclusion that of the all-together twenty-seven writings in the New Testament — apart from those that supposedly derive from Paul — not a single one can be traced back to an apostle, or a student of an apostle — and this is the case even though all the writings of the New Testament claim direct or indirect apostolic authorship, which then constitutes the presupposition for their inclusion in the canon! One probably does not at all need an especially critical mind to permit the question with what grounds present day scholarship still justifies the very self-confidently expounded judgment that the Pauline letters, or as least some of them, which critics today still regard as "genuine," are authentic writings of the apostle from the middle of the first century. To put this question another way, with what justification do the modern critics decree the apostle Paul to be the exception — indeed the only exception! — to the principle they themselves established, namely, that the writings contained in our canon, without exception, do not stem from the writers named in them, but rather from pseudonymous authors?

In any case, these few preliminary considerations already make clear that the question concerning the authenticity of those letters which scholars until now, for whatever reasons, have excluded from the discussion of authenticity could prove to be thoroughly rewarding. This is obvious from our previous observations. Whoever says A must also say B. If in the opinion of scholars some of the Pauline writings are clearly inauthentic, what is the situation then with the rest?

Edward Evanson: the Uncomfortable Englishman

Everyone who occupies himself with the history of research in a particular area of interest soon ascertains that most of the questions which stirred him and which at first seemed new and exciting had at sometime already been asked. This is also true for the question about the authenticity of all the Pauline letters. This question was also once asked and investigated, and indeed at the very beginning of historical-critical occupation with the Pauline letters.

The first person who dared to challenge the authenticity of one of the letters held to be sacrosanct by today's research was the Englishman, Edward Evanson (1731-1805). Evanson, who had served as pastor in Longdon (Gloucestershire) since 1770, was in every way an independently minded theologian. As a convinced Unitarian, he rejected the Christian doctrine of the Trinity as well as the idea of incarnation. Like all Unitarians, in the confession of a trinitarian God Evanson saw an infringement of the fundamental idea of monotheism. Because as an ordained pastor, however, he was obligated to read the Apostle's Creed every Sunday, or the (especially trinitarian oriented) Nicene Creed, he either made arbitrary modifications or read so fast that no one could understand him. This was the reason then that the congregation complained about him to his superiors and criticized, above all, the "underplaying" of the Nicene creed. Evanson replied that he read the Nicene creed, which "exceeded the limits of his conceptual power," only as an obedient servant of the law.[55] At the same time, he declared himself prepared to read it more slowly in the future. With regard to his abbreviation of the liturgy, this was a serious matter of conscience. And in any case, within a few months Parliament would make a statement concerning reform of the liturgy. Until then, his accusers should be patient, "certainly not a long time to bear with a weaker brother's qualms of conscience for men who are so strong in their own true faith."[56]

Evanson nevertheless remained stubborn and made further changes in the worship service immediately on the following Sunday, in which he left out what were for him offensive liturgical phrases ("both God and man," as well as "Father, Son and Holy Ghost"). Afterward he explained in writing that he was not appointed by the Lord-Chancellor to preach "incoherent nonsense of dumb superstition," but "the true and proper word of God."[57] So on 4 November, 1773, a complaint against him was presented. On account of an error in process, however, this was rejected, and Evanson was exonerated by a higher authority. Evanson died on 25 September, 1805, in Colford, after working for still some years on reform and renewal of the worship service.

Evanson contested the authenticity of Romans, above all because of contradictions with Acts, whose witness he regarded as historically correct. While Romans presupposes the existence of a Christian church whose faith is known in all the world, Acts has nothing to report about a Christian community in Rome when Paul arrived. Moreover, Evanson asked, how a congregation could already exist in Rome if at the time the vision called Paul to Macedonia the gospel had not yet been preached in Europe. While it is presupposed in Romans that the Jews in Rome are already familiar with the gospel, in Acts Paul would like to make the gospel known to Jews in Rome (Acts 28:17-29). Above all, for Evanson Romans 11 shows very clearly that the writer of the letter cannot be Paul, but someone writes *after the destruction of Jerusalem* presupposed by the parable of the olive tree.

From Baur to Bauer

The Tübingen theologian Ferdinand Christian Baur (1792-1860) was one of the most important New Testament scholars of the past century and the first in Germany to submit the New Testament to a comprehensive historical critique.

Not only the Pastoral Epistles, regarding whose authenticity Friedrich Schleiermacher had already before him allowed doubts to be expressed,[58] but also both Thessalonian epistles, Colossians, Ephesians, Philemon, and even Philippians—i.e., letters "whose authenticity," according to an early New Testament scholar, "could have never been contested with any appearance of justification"[59]—fell victim to the unmerciful criticism of the man from Tübingen. Baur left only four pillars standing: *Romans, the two Corinthian epistles, and Galatians.* Obviously troubled by the fact that he had already stuck his neck out, Baur now made every effort to insure that "not even the smallest suspicion of inauthenticity" could ever be raised against these letters, because they "bear the character of Pauline originality so indisputably that one cannot even imagine with what justification any critical doubt could ever be maintained."[60]

Nevertheless, Baur's view that there was only a basic collection of four authentic "major epistles" was revised by most of his friends and critics. For them, the reduction to only four letters seemed all too arbitrary. For most German critics, Baur had gone *too far*, and they strived in the time that followed to show that, alongside the "major epistles," at least three additional epistles, which had been rejected by Baur as inauthentic, should be regarded as authentically Pauline: 1 Thessalonians, Philippians, and Philemon.[61]

Of course, there was still another radical critic in Germany, for whom Baur *had not gone far enough*. Instead of stopping when he was only half-way home, Baur should have done what seemed only consistent to do, namely, recognize the inauthenticity of *all* the epistles. Such was the criticism advanced by Bruno Bauer (1809-1882).

While Ferdinand Baur should be numbered among the most important New Testament critics of the nineteenth century, Bruno Bauer certainly belongs among the most original. Bauer was the *Enfant terrible* among theologians of that time. Like Baur, Bauer was a student of the philosopher G.W.F. Hegel. As a youth he had been a personal friend of Karl Marx and Friedrich Engels. Later, having identified in the meantime with the political right wing, he turned against them.

As a teacher of theology, Bauer presented a severe provocation for his contemporaries. In view of the theses that the theology professor from Berlin presented in his books and at the rostrum, that should hardly be surprising. The normally upright and decent man, whom contemporaries portray as a likable and unassuming person, seems to have evolved here from a Dr. Jekyll to a Mr. Hyde. In a letter from 6 December 1841, he writes to his friend Arnold Ruge about his occupation as teacher and theologian: "At the university I lecture before a large audience. I do not recognize myself when I declare my blasphemies at the rostrum — they are so enormous that the students' hair stands on end, these children, whom no one should provoke — and think about how piously I work at home on the defense of holy scripture and revelation. In any case, it is a very evil demon who lays hold of me every time that I ascend the rostrum, and I am so weak that I submit to him unconditionally."[62]

The "demon" to whom Bauer submitted had whispered to him that all the Pauline letters were inauthentic and that an historical person named Jesus very probably never existed. If he had existed, Bauer argued, this Christ would then be conceived "as a real historical appearance .... before which human beings must shudder, a figure who can only impart fear and horror."[63] Bauer's reference here was primarily to the Christ portrayed in the Gospel of John, which he perceived as an unhistorical construction.

The provocation that Bauer represented for his scholarly colleagues was so great that in 1842 he was removed from office. However, Bauer was not thereby released from his demon — he continued to write as a vegetable merchant and anchorite of Rixdorf (Berlin-Neukölln) Bücher, in which he developed his view of early Christianity without Jesus and Paul — but at least Bauer's theses could no longer damage the minds of his students.

Bauer was convinced not only that the Paul in Acts represents an imaginary historical figure, but also that the representation of the apostle in the letters "sprung from the same ground of deliberate reflection."[64] Although Bauer impressively displayed the inconsistency and half-heartedness of other theologians, who, like Baur, had more or less retreated to four major epistles, he was not able to plausibly carry out his own initiative.

Bauer offered no reasonable and systematic analysis of the literary character of the Pauline letters, but saw his task rather to "scold" the author like a schoolmaster, often in petty ways, and to finally convict him again and again of self-contradiction.[65] Even the forward with which Bauer introduces the investigation of the origin of Galatians, which has as its goal the "exposure of the compiler,"[66] does not suggest anything good. From the very beginning, Bauer takes for granted the fictional character of Galatians. He is filled with unfathomable mistrust, which leads him to raise suspicion with every word and again and again to triumphantly tear the mask from the face of the "compiler," with whom, in addition, he seems to stand in a tense human relationship. As criteria for evaluation, Bauer usually calls attention to presumed or actual stylistic deficiencies, which he unmercifully exposes and rectifies.

Even though the entire process is often more arbitrary than systematic, here and there insights and perceptions appear that witness again and again to the brilliant, critical mind of the writer, and which constitute the real significance of this work. In a certain sense, the reader is drawn into a dramatic "unveiling struggle" in which one finally does not know what he should admire more: the cleverness of the "insidious hierarch,"[67] or the acuteness of the critic who exposes him step by step.

Bauer finally comes to the following conclusion: none of the letters circulated under the name of Paul, including the so-called major letters, stem from the pen of the apostle; on the contrary, they are written by various authors, and all are the product of Christian self consciousness in the second century.

The primary arguments for the inauthenticity of the Pauline epistles are the influence of Gnosticism,[68] most evident in the Corinthian letters, which for Bauer belonged to the second century, as well as the dependence of the writer of the letters on the Gospel of Luke (which was traditionally regarded as supposedly later) and Acts, which Bauer attempted to demonstrate for individual letters.

According to Bauer, 1 Thessalonians presupposes Acts, 1 and 2 Corinthians, Romans, and Galatians; Philippians presupposes 2 Corinthians, the first and second sections of Romans, as well as 1 Thessalonians; and the writers of Ephesians and Colossians are supposed to have made use of 1 Corinthians and Galatians. The four major letters originated in the following order: Romans; 1 Corinthians; 2 Corinthians, Galatians.[69] Their writers were strongly opposed to the views of Acts, which they presuppose and to some extent deal with polemically.

In his book *Christus und die Caesaren* (*Christ and the Caesars*[70]), Bauer explains that "progress in the redaction of Acts as well as the production of the Pauline epistolary literature was carried out in the decades from the final years of Hadrian's reign to the first half of Marcus Aurelius's, and each circle had the other in view in its work. At the highpoint of this conflict, *Galatians* sketched a portrait of the apostle that was directed point for point against an edition of Acts very much like the one we have today."[71]

According to Bauer, the name of Paul could be connected with such epistolary literature because "the figure of this champion of a universal community and of freedom from the law through faith already existed."[72] For Bauer, this figure was obviously not historical, but legendary — as the name already indicates, and whose symbolism (Paul = the small one) Bauer dealt with at length (see below ⇒ *The Doppelgänger: Paul and Simon*).

Bauer, who as we already noted also rejected the historical existence of Jesus, was dismissed by other scholars as a "fantasizer." Until today, no real debate with him has taken place.

The Radical Dutchmen

Dutch radical criticism refers a movement arising in the nineteenth century within New Testament scholarship in the Netherlands, some of whose representatives rejected the historical existence of Jesus and who were usually conceived of as a group: the Dutch Radical School. The representatives of this school include, among others, Allard Pierson (1831-1896), the well-known theologian and historian of art and literature, after whom the Allard Pierson Museum on Oude Turfmarkt 127 in Amsterdam is named; his friend Samuel Adrianus Naber (1828-1913), a philologist; Abraham Dirk Loman (1823-1897), professor of theology in Amsterdam; Willem Christiaan van Manen (1842-1905), a scholar from Leiden; and the philosopher G.J.P.J. Bolland (1854-1922), also from Leiden. The last offshoot and representative of radical criticism in this century was the theologian, Gustaaf Adolf van den Bergh van Eysinga (1874-1957).

The designation "radical" was obviously ascribed to this movement with a certain amount of sarcasm, since in the eyes of many people they intended to destroy not only the wild branches of the Christian tradition but also its roots (*radix*, from which the word *radical* is derived, means "root"). The Dutch critics referred to in such a way, however, gladly used this concept for themselves and gave it a positive meaning.

With regard to time, the history of Dutch radical criticism can be very precisely defined. The beginning of Dutch radical criticism is usually perceived in the publication of

Pierson's *Sermon on the Mount* in 1878, a work in which doubt was already expressed with regard to the authenticity of the so-called major letters as well as the historical existence of Jesus. The history of Dutch radical criticism closed with the death of Van den Bergh van Eysinga; or at least since then is no longer represented in universities. Only a small academic circle of "Van-der-Berghians" survives today, but this plays hardly any role in present day Dutch theology.

Loman was certainly one of the most outstanding personalities among the Dutch radical critics. His lecture *Über das älteste Christentum (On Earliest Christianity)*, given on December 13, 1881, in the house of the Free Church of Amsterdam (today an avant-garde center in Weteringschans 6-8 in Amsterdam), ignited a storm of indignation in the audience. In his lecture, Loman claimed that Christianity in its origin was nothing else than a Jewish-Messianic movement and that the figure of Jesus had never existed, but represented a symbolization and personification of thoughts that could only make full headway in the second century. A gnostic messianic community later appeared alongside the Jewish-Christian messianic community. In the period between 70 and 135 CE the two groups opposed one another with bitter animosity. Only in the middle of the second century did they achieve a reconciliation, in which the gnostic community had Paul as its representative and the Jewish-Christian community had Peter. The result of this process of reconciliation was the formation of the Roman Catholic Church. According to Loman, the letters of Paul are all inauthentic and represent the product of the newly-believing, gnostic-messianic community.

Later radical critics regarded Loman's lecture as a kind of manifesto, in which the rough elements of the new paradigm—the radical-critical theory regarding early Christian history, Loman's hypothesis—were set forth. The significance still attributed to Loman's lecture in radical-critical circles at a later time is shown by the fact that in the house of the *Vrije Gemeente* Van den Bergh van Eysinga and his students celebrated December 13th as a special memorial.[73]

In general, the agreement of representatives of the radical school was confined to the two basic theses: the denial of authenticity for all the Pauline letters and/or the historical existence of Jesus. So both theses were not always held simultaneously. Van den Bergh van Eysinga remarks: "There are radicals who accept the historicity of Jesus while rejecting the epistles," although, to be sure, "the opposite case, that one rejects the historicity of Jesus but nevertheless maintains the authenticity of the Pauline letters... cannot be documented."[74] The historical existence of Jesus was questioned by only a few radical critics, and even Loman, who originally questioned it, later withdrew this thesis. On the other hand, the thesis that all the Pauline letters are inauthentic was held by all radical Dutch critics.

My first "encounter" with so-called Dutch radical criticism took place when, as a theological student, I was curiously browsing the pages of a newly acquired *Introduction to the New Testament* and in a section dealing with the Pauline epistles stumbled upon the existence of something called "radical criticism," whose representatives had the audacity to deny the Pauline authenticity of the four major epistles and to explain them as "the fallout of anti-nomistic currents from the period around 140 CE."[75]

I was skeptical, since the designation "radical criticism" itself could not portend anything good. In the same way as the English Bishop J.A.T. Robinson obviously did ("radical critics ... oscillating wildly")[76], at that time I imagined a radical to be like a wild thrashing critic, half man and half wild animal. Moreover, I already knew about Bruno Bauer, who likewise had contested the authenticity of all the Pauline letters, and indeed with what I then regarded as very questionable methods and results. In the same way as the denial of authenticity for the Pauline letters, which seemed to be related with this, such attempts seemed to me to be determined by very transparent prejudices, lacking any scholarly seriousness. In any case, I could agree in the depths of my heart with the author of my *Introduction to the New Testament*, the famous New Testament scholar W.G. Kümmel, when he pays no further attention to such fantastic theories in what follows and only remarks in half a sentence that their representatives began with "untenable literary presuppositions and an atrocious historical construction."[77]

At that time, what I had read about these foolhardy scholars (all of them held teaching positions) was still sufficient to convince me that additional information would hardly be required for my further theological education and would probably also be unrewarding. Even though a knowledge of Dutch radical criticism in fact turned out to be unnecessary for completing my theological exam, however, it was certainly evident that such knowledge was absolutely indispensable for a more intense, scholarly engagement with the Pauline letters.

In reading the Pauline letters I later encountered more and more questions that, when I was a student, I had either never thought about at all or had regarded as having been already answered long ago. A series of these questions was already discussed above. Since the common answers did not satisfy me, even when they were advanced with reference the often-entreated "critical consensus," and since the remarkable certainty suddenly radiated by theology teachers when one asks them about the historical bases of the Christian faith deeply disturbed me, I began more and more to seek refuge with persons who with regard to the church and theological history were outsiders and "skewed-thinkers," whom during the course of my studies I had heard something about in standard textbooks and introductions only in footnotes, parenthetical comments, and marginal remarks.

With regard to the radical theologians, I nevertheless knew at least that they obviously had undertaken a general assault on the traditional picture of early Christian history as it has been taught in universities, largely without change, from Baur until today. I did not know in detail for what reason and with what arguments this had been carried out and with what arguments it had been repelled by traditional theology.

The question about what kind of arguments these were — on the basis of my previous engagement with the Pauline letters, I thought I could surmise some — had to be put off for a long time because of my lack of knowledge of the Dutch language. In time, of course, this problem began to engage me in such a way, the curiosity became so unbearable, that I could no longer resist the temptation. I went to the library and procured for myself all the literature available in Germany about and by the Dutch critics, purchased a Dutch-German dictionary, and began to read.

With the first, still somewhat stumbling reading of some classic radical-critical writings in the original Dutch, I already suspected that the key might lay here for the many questions and problems which had caused me so much trouble in my occupation with the history of early Christianity and especially with the Pauline letters.

I was more interested in the arguments with which Dutch theologians and philologists had contested the authenticity of all the letters than with the answers they had given for many difficult questions in Pauline research. Even if a single argument, considered for itself, would not always have decisive significance, in connection with many other arguments it nevertheless builds what one characterizes as "cumulative evidence." This is what one calls a scientific theory that is constructed from many different individual arguments, where each, considered for itself, need not be completely convincing.

In what follows, I obviously cannot repeat all the arguments with which the authenticity of all the Pauline writings has been contested. In a series of brief points, however, I can note some questions and problems which could give a moment's pause even for those who until now have never doubted the authenticity of all the Pauline writings.

- "Paul, slave of Jesus Christ, called to be an apostle, set apart for the gospel of God..." "Paul, called to be an apostle of Jesus Christ by the will of God..." "Paul, an apostle, not from men nor through a man, but through Jesus Christ and God..." "Paul, a prisoner for the sake of Christ Jesus..." – Does someone write here about himself or about *someone else*? Do we have to do here with a statement about one's self or with a statement *about* the (revered) apostle (of a legendary past)? – Consider this: The greetings employed by Greeks and Romans were *very unpretentious*. Even the great Cicero could simply write: "Cicero greets Atticus" (*Cicero Attico salutum dicit*)[78].

- Gal 1:1: "Paul... to *the churches* in Galatia." 1 Cor 1:1: "Paul, to the church of God which is in Corinth, to those sanctified in Christ Jesus, called to be saints, *together with all those who in every place call on the name of the Lord Jesus Christ, their Lord and ours*. The poor letter carrier!

- Gal 1:11: "*I want you to know*, brethren, that the gospel preached by me was not of men." Had Paul left the Galatians ignorant of this central point of his teaching until now?

- Gal 2:6: "And from those who were reputed to be something — what they once *were* (ēsan) makes no difference to me." Why *were*? "*Are*" the apostles then no longer present when the author of Galatians writes his letter? Have they already died? Does the author of Galatians by this time look back on the apostolic age as closed?

- In Galatians 6:11 Paul calls attention to the large letters of his handwriting: "See with what large letters I am writings with my [own] hand." Why? Obviously because he wants to provide his readers with an indication of the authenticity of the letter. Question: Why must the apostle already protect his letters from falsification? Were forged letters already in circulation *in his lifetime*? Hardly. – If already in his own lifetime Paul represented such an authority that is was worthwhile to produce false letters in his name, why then do we hear nothing about the great apostle and his letters for another 100 years? – The writer's reference to his handwriting in 2 Thessalonians 3:17 — "I, Paul, write this greeting with my own hand. This is the mark in every letter of mine; it is the way I write" — is regarded by most exegetes as a sign of the letters inauthenticity. Why is the corresponding reference in Galatians not so regarded?

- 1 Cor 3:1f: "But I, brethren, could not address you as spiritual persons, but *as fleshly persons, as babes in Christ*. I gave you milk to drink, not solid food; for you were not ready for it; and even now you are not ready for it, for you are still fleshly." 1 Cor 2:6: "Yet among the *perfect ones* we impart wisdom." Is the writer of 1 Corinthians himself really clear about *to whom* he is speaking?

- Rom 1:1f: "Paul... set apart for the gospel of God... namely, the gospel concerning his Son, who was descended from David according to the flesh..." 2 Cor 5:16: "Even though we once regarded Christ according to the flesh, we regard him thus no longer."
Can the writer of Rom 1:1-2, who places so much value on the family tree of Jesus and his *descent from David*, be the same person who write 2 Cor 5:16?

- Is it conceivable that on the eve of his sojourn in Rome he wrote one of the longest letters in ancient literature to the church there? Why does he write a letter at all that goes beyond a brief announcement of his coming? Would he not be able in a short time to provide a much better and more lively testimony through his personal presence with the Roman community?

- After Paul received his revelation, he goes *into the desert* (to Arabia, Gal 1:17) — and not to the Jerusalem church! Does that make psychological sense? Transfer that for a moment to a follower of Socrates in southern Italy, who has come upon one or another of Plato's dialogues and now feels called to become a disciple of Socrates: "He took pleasure in the fateful death of the philosopher, for he was a sophist with body and soul. But he became aware of something different. To think like Socrates, to feel, to teach, to live like Socrates, to fully identify with him, that — so he had understood, grasped by intuition — is the one thing necessary. Would he now hurry to Athens? Plato was still alive. Alkibiades was still alive. From them and from so many others he will attempt to learn what Socrates thought, felt, taught — what spirit spoke from his environs. No. He goes to Egypt, remains there for three years, and then writes and speaks about Socrates during his entire life and comes to be regarded by a credulous world as the most credible witness to the Greek philosopher, as the most reliable interpreter of his life and work."[79]

- Why does *the Jew* Paul speak of Greeks and *Barbarians* (Rom 1:14) if according to Greek understanding of the concept the latter term can only refer to himself? Why must the Jew Paul first *become* a Jew (1 Cor 9:11)? Why does *the Jew* Paul forbid men to cover their heads during the worship service (1 Cor 11:4)?[80]

- Why does Paul undergo a battle with beasts in Ephesus (1 Cor 15:32) even though as supposedly a Roman citizen he could not be sentenced *ad bestias* at all? Even if he was not a citizen of Rome, how could he have survived such a thing?

- Why does the author who presumably wrote 1 Thessalonians between 50 and 60 look back upon the destruction of Jerusalem in 70 CE? 1 Thess 2:16: "God's judgment has come upon them [the Jews] at last!" (cf. also Israel's "rejection", 11:15ff. and the "severity of God" in 11:22).

- For the persecutions of Christians, of which mention is made again and again in the Pauline Epistles (Rom 8:35; 12:14; 1 Cor 4:12; 2 Cor 4:9; 12:10; Gal 6:12; 1 Thess 2:14 etc.) there is no evidence *before Nero*. The putative persecution of Christians in 64 after the fire of Rome is, moreover, historically disputed.[81]

- Speaking of persecutions is — apart from those under Domitian (c. 81–96 CE; Justin, 1Apol 31, Eusebius, *EH* 3.17ff.), Trajan (c. 98–117 CE) and the ones the Jewish Christians were exposed to under Bar Kochba 132-135 (Justin, *Apol.* 1,31; Eusebius, *EH* 4. 8,4) — only possible in connection with the so-called *Aposynagogos*, i.e., the exclusion of Christians from synagogue life. And indeed, the *Aposynagogos* itself is unattested before Justin in the middle of the second century (Justin, *Dial.* 16:4; 47:5; 93:4; 95:4; 96:2; 108:2f; 133:6 , cf. 17:1).[82]

In the next section, I would like to deal with one of the most important questions: Why are the letters of the great Christian apostle, who claims godly authority for his office, and whose literary and theological level was hardly reached again in early Christian literature, first attested only in the first half of the second century? Why is the Catholic Justin in the middle of the second century silent with regard to the Pauline writings? Why do we first encounter a canon of letters with Marcion the heretic?

Seeking Traces

The Pauline letters are regarded as the most important documents of early Christian history in the first century, and Paul is its most important witness. It is expected of a reliable historical witness that his own historical identity can be credibly demonstrated. Tertullian, the church father, was not at all satisfied with the fact that the author of the Pauline letters represents himself in his letters as an apostle from early times (In this Tertullian was more critical than many New Testament critics today).[83] Such a claim is not sufficient by itself to produce certainty on this point. What is the situation then with the other witnesses for the apostle and his letters?

With regard to the person of the apostle, in the search for non-Christian sources for Paul one finds oneself in a similar dilemma as in the attempt to document the historicity of Jesus with non-Christian source material: the ancient sources are silent.

The dilemma is even greater since the silence stands in flagrant contrast to the overwhelming significance that the apostle is supposed to have had according to the writer of Acts and the early Christian tradition. Should we not expect that the sensational, public appearance of the apostle, his preaching and his missionary work, must also have had at least a distant reflection outside the churches founded by him?

Even if we do not regard by far everything that Acts tells us about the work of Paul as historical — even if one ignores his appearance before king Agrippa (Acts 15:13f) or the high council in Jerusalem (Acts 22:30), his marvelous release from imprisonment in Philippi (Acts 16:24ff), the uprising he caused in Ephesus (Acts 19:23ff), and the excitement he stirred up in Athens (Acts 17:18ff) — when all these elements, largely banished to the realm of legendary stories by present day scholars, are set aside, there nevertheless remains, the bright reflection of an extraordinary personality who could hardly have remained unknown to a Greek or Roman writer or historian of that time. Even if we limit ourselves to only the major letters of Paul, a person and events remain which the ancient world could not have ignored and which must also have attracted attention beyond the narrow circle of Christian churches. Where indeed do we encounter such a man, who like Paul in Ephesus was thrown to the wild beasts in the arena (1 Cor 15:32), who received "five times the forty stripes minus one" (2 Cor 11:24), who was ship-wrecked three times, adrift in the sea for a night and a day (2 Cor 11:25) — and survived all this! — who traveled from Jerusalem as far round as Illyricum in order to preach the gospel and evangelize (Rom 15:18f), who was able to escape from Damascus in a dramatic way (2 Cor 11:32)...? The puzzling answer is "Nowhere"! Neither in Graeco-Roman nor in Jewish literature do we find a trace of all this.

The figure of the apostle of the people, who is elevated in Acts to transcendent, almost divine status (Acts 14:11), obviously attracted so little notice among the Greeks and Romans that they do not mention him with one word. In this regard, there was a number of ancient writers who could have and must have been interested in the figure of the apostle: for example, Josephus, the Jewish-Roman historian, who is already met in connection with the question concerning the historical Jesus, who in his work *The Jewish War* relates the history and pre-history of the Jewish wars up to the fall of Masada in 73 CE and in his *Jewish Antiquities*, which appeared around 94 CE, described the history of Jews from the creation of the world until 66 CE. As already in the case of Jesus, so also with regard to Paul, Josephus, who otherwise displays the history of the Jewish people in great detail, and even somewhat garrulously, remains remarkably silent. Josephus, the friend of Romans, knows nothing about Paul, the Roman citizen, and also nothing about Saul, the zealot for "the traditions of the fathers" (Gal 1:14). The Saul known to Josephus is a relative of king Agrippa[84] and shares only the name in common with the Saul of the New Testament.

Josephus' silence might seem strange, but it is nevertheless honest. The regretful lack of historical reports about the apostle Paul would have been easy to remedy through some insertions and interpolations. That Christians, for their part, did not succumb to this temptation might have something to do with the fact that it was easier to tolerate the absence of any kind of historical reports about the apostle than the disturbing silence that surrounded the person of Jesus by Josephus.

In addition to Josephus, one could think of a number of other ancient writers who could have referred to the apostle in one way or another: Plutarch (c. 45-120 CE), who was open to all religious movements of his time, Epictetus (c. 55-135 CE), Seneca (c. 3 BC – 65 AD), Pausanias (c. 115-180 CE), Aulus Gellius (c. 130-180 CE), Lucian (120-180 CE), to only name a few. They were all familiar with the theaters of the apostle's activity and one or the other must have heard something about it — but they are all silent.

If what follows from all this is that the figure of the apostle to the nations, who was portrayed in such radiant and gleaming colors by Christians, was fully unknown to the "nations" of the first and second centuries, a look at the Jewish sources from the first and second centuries shows that here as well nothing seems to have been known either in a positive sense about the Jew who surpassed all his contemporaries in his zeal for the religion of the fathers or in a negative sense about the despiser of the law and apostate.

However, not only the person, but also his work, namely, the letters written under the name of the apostle, are all obviously entirely unknown into the middle of the second century. As the majority of present day scholars recognize, the historical course of the Pauline letters in the first and second centuries is one of the most obscure and puzzling chapters of New Testament research.

The elevated claim with which Paul appears in his letters in his capacity as an apostle called by God (Gal 1:1f) stands in curious contrast with the fact that the apostle seems to have completely forgotten in the theological discussion from directly following his death until the time of Marcion. Not only were the churches supposedly founded by Paul further developed on a different, Catholic foundation, particularly strange is that the letters, to which the apostle is indebted until today for the largest part of his fame, seem to have been forgotten for almost an entire century, until we encounter them in the middle of the second century in the hands of a heretic, of all places, the heresiarch Marcion, who was excommunicated by the Catholic church in 144 CE.

This view of the historical course of the Pauline letters in the first and second centuries is by no means an individual opinion, but is a largely accepted understanding in recent research today.[85] I would call attention, for example, to the New Testament scholar Ernst Käsemann, who in his essay "Paul and Early Catholicism" provides a brief sketch of the effects and after-effects the apostle had on the Christian church of his time. Even for Käsemann, the finding is by and large negative: in the churches founded by Paul the memory of the apostle disappeared in a very short time. For Käsemann, the Pauline churches are "after a single generation already entangled in Hellenistic enthusiasm" without being able to preserve the inheritance of the apostle. Even the Apocalypse of John "gives no indication that Asia Minor was indebted to the apostle." To be sure, apart from the insignificant witness of Ignatius, Käsemann knows a "great exception" — i.e., Marcion — which also makes clear "in what circles the theologian Paul continued to be esteemed." In view of these very meager results, Käsemann's formulation at the beginning of his article is entirely confirmed: "Historical research has perhaps its final and deepest value in the fact that it disillusions. How true this is even and especially of Paul has scarcely received sufficient recognition until now."[86]

To be sure!

Two Pauls

A problem that has occupied Pauline research for a long time is the fact that the picture of Paul in Acts differs essentially from that which we meet in the letters presumed to be authentic. In comparing Gal 1:11-2:10 with the relevant passage in Acts, for example, we observe a significant divergence. While according to the presentation in Gal 1:17, after his conversion Paul spent three years in Arabia, Acts knows nothing to report about this. In the presentation of Acts it is as if after his conversion Paul remained in Damascus for some time and preached Christ in the synagogues there (Acts 9:20), until he was finally driven out by Jews there and came to Jerusalem.

While in Galatians Paul's second visit in Jerusalem is occasioned by a "revelation" (1:16), in Acts he is commissioned to go to Jerusalem by the churches in Antioch (11:22).

While the fifteenth chapter of Acts (vv. 23-29) contains the so-called "apostolic decree," that prescribes that Gentiles abstain from "blood and what is strangled and unchastity" —a requirement that was continuously followed by Catholic Christians of the second and third centuries and which had no efficacy only in Gnostic and Marcionite communities[87], the writer of Galatians knows nothing about this decree in the passage where he relates the meeting in Jerusalem.

The differences between the letters regarded as authentic and Acts, however, do not relate only to individual historical data, but are fundamental in character. Acts gives us an entirely different picture of Paul than the letters.

The following two characteristics are commonly raised up as the essential features of the Lukan picture of Paul.[88]

1. Luke sketches the picture of the apostle in such a way that he appears as a *typical representative of Judaism*, as a Jew who is faithful to the law.

In Acts, for example, Paul *not only approves of circumcision, but even practices it himself!* (Acts 16:3: the circumcision of Timothy).

This passage can be compared with Acts 21:21, where Luke mentions the concern of some Jewish-Christian zealots for the law who have heard a rumor about Paul that he teaches Jews to forsake Moses by telling them that they should not circumcise their children or observe Jewish customs. To provide the Jewish-Christian zealots for the law with a public demonstration of his faithfulness to the law, Paul is supposed to become a Nazarite for a while and pay the expenses of four men who would become Nazarites — which he promptly does (Acts 21:18ff; In ancient Israel a Nazarite – from the Hebrew *nazir* = to separate oneself, consecrate oneself – was a man who was set apart by a vow for special service to God and who distinguished himself from his religious brethren by an ascetic way of life. For example, a Nazarite had to abstain from wine for a specified time; for reasons of purity he could not touch a dead body; and he could not "let a razor travel over his head," that is, he must let his hair grow long like the Old Testament hero Samson. One could regard him as a Jewish "monk for a time"- often for a lifetime.)

In contrast to this, Paul of the letters (in the non-interpolated passages of the corpus paulinum) explicitly and vehemently rejects the law and circumcision. Paul's criticism of the law reaches its peak in Philippians where, in the course of a furious polemic, circumcision is characterized as nothing less than castration (Phil 3:2).

2. A further characteristic of the Lukan picture of Paul is the subordination of the apostle to the Jerusalem representatives of the church.

a) Luke emphasizes that, in contrast to the other apostles, Paul had not been an eyewitness to Christ. In all three presentations of Paul's conversion, it is important for Luke that Paul fell down on his face. This and the blinding of Paul have the same significance every time: afterward, Paul can no longer see! Consequently, he did not experience an appearance of the exalted Christ like the rest of the apostles, since all he saw was the great heavenly light.

According to the presentation of Luke, therefore, "Paul is dependent on hearing... That Paul first identifies the exalted Christ in dialogue emphasizes that he had not seen him. And that he converses with the Lord in heaven shows that Jesus did not come to earth."[89]

The tendency that Luke pursues with this presentation of the conversion of Paul can be understood against the background of his picture of Paul and his concept of an apostle. According to Luke's understanding, only one who has seen Jesus Christ is an apostle. Against this background, the writer of Acts endeavors to fundamentally distinguish Paul's conversion and calling from the calling of the twelve.

In this regard, the fact that Luke reports the calling of Paul three times shows how important this distinction between Paul and the twelve apostles was for him. In contrast to the twelve, Paul had never seen Jesus! The resurrected Christ had never left heaven at all, but had merely called to him from heaven and, in other respects, referred him to the church, which had long been built on the foundation of the twelve.

The New Testament scholar Walter Schmithals can say: "The greatness of Paul for Luke consists precisely in his devoted dependence on the twelve apostles."[90]

In contrast to this, the writer of the letters presents the matter in an entirely different way. In Gal 1:1f and 1 Cor 9:1ff Paul explicitly emphasizes that he is entirely equal to those who were apostles before him. He has "seen Jesus our Lord" (1 Cor 9:1). He claims for himself and his gospel the same direct relationship with the resurrected Jesus as the apostles.

b) The words that Jesus directs to the apostle in Acts 9:6, that he should go into the city in order to hear there what more he should do, make it entirely clear that the conversion of Paul is exclusively centered on establishing contact with the Jerusalem church and its representatives. Günter Klein observes: "The direct contact with the heavenly world exhausts itself therefore in the goal of bringing Paul to the threshold of the meeting with Ananias and remains this side of any material instruction. This—and so also the conveyance of the disoriented Paul into the orientation of faith—remains the exclusive prerogative of the representative of the church."[91]

In contrast to the presentation of Galatians, conversion and calling are therefore not identical with one another for Paul. In Acts, conversion only plays the role of a road sign by which Paul is directed to the representatives of the Jerusalem community: it is here that he first receives the decisive instruction and authorization for his further work.

c) Closely related with this is the further circumstance noted by Klein, namely, that the difference between the presentation of Acts and that of Galatians "that first meets the eye" concerns "the absence of the figure of Ananias."[92]

While Acts reports that directly following his conversion Paul turned to Ananias, the representative of the church, in Galatians Paul denies "as sharply as possible that there was any kind of incident that might suggest the possibility to conceive his apostleship as being 'from men,' indeed, even as only 'through men.' Thereby it is expressed with complete clarity that not only a direct but also any kind of mediated human role in his conversion is excluded. The contrast with the Lukan scheme, for which the idea of mediation is constitutive, is total."[93]

Klein remarks that the "highly polemical inclination" of the prescript of Galatians, which is primarily concerned with the rejection of opposing constructions, wants to address this issue in every conceivable expression, and in the formulation of positive circumstances is entirely dependent on the preceding negation."[94]

d) The subordinate position attributed to Paul in relation to the other apostles is exemplified above all by the conduct of the apostles during the so-called apostolic council.

While the Paul of Galatians, for example, "in order to completely maintain his independence, so that the fact that he sets his gospel before the leaders in Jerusalem would not make him appear to be subordinate and dependent, declares that he went to Jerusalem as the consequence of a revelation (Gal 2:1),"[95] according to the Lukan presentation he follows a resolution of the church in Antioch (Acts 15:2). While according to the statements in Galatians the Jerusalem pillars imposed nothing on Paul, according to the presentation of Acts the apostolic decrees are imposed on Paul and his churches.

All this (b-d) contradicts the picture mediated to us by Galatians. Here the apostle is represented as fully *sovereign*. He is an apostle "not from men nor through a man, but through Jesus Christ." It was a *revelation* that caused him to go to

Jerusalem to confer with the apostles there. He comes without having been sent by his own church or summoned by those in Jerusalem.

Since, as we have seen, the differences between Acts and the presumably authentic letters of Paul are in many cases irreconcilably great and fundamental in character, they require a decision by the historian: one must give preference to either the presentation of Acts or that of Paul as more historically adequate.

It is very obvious that for the great majority of scholars the decision would be in favor of the Paul of the letters, and the presentation of Luke in Acts, as a rule, is characterized, more or less emphatically (sometimes even polemically), as a tendentious falsification. A.J. Matill, who can be named here as representative of many others, declares that "in Acts and in the letters there are *two Pauls*, the historical Paul of the authentic letters and the legendary Paul of Acts."[96]

One must ask whether the decision by Matill and the majority of present day scholars in favor of the Pauline letters, which seems so obvious and beyond question, is not somewhat rash. There is indeed a *third* possibility, usually left out of consideration, that can lead us beyond the narrow alternative that either the Pauline letters or Acts must be correct. How would it be if from a historical perspective *neither* Luke *nor* the author of the Pauline letters was "correct"? If the Paul of Acts as well as the Paul of the letters, as Bruno Bauer expressed it, "sprung up from the same ground of deliberate reflection"?

As we have seen, by closer observation it becomes clear that Acts and Galatians are "in conversation" with one another, that "in their work" the authors of both writings have each other "clearly in view."[97] It follows from this, whatever one may think in particular about the relationship of mutual dependence, that both writings, whose respective statements, in spite of, or perhaps precisely because of their differences, fit together like two pieces of a puzzle, must have originated at approximately *the same time*. It is unthinkable that one piece of the puzzle (Galatians) is many decades older than the other and that the (implicit) polemic of Acts was conserved over many decades in order to appear again in a time in which the debate about the apostleship of Paul (after his death) had long since become insignificant. On the other hand, it is difficult to imagine that the writer of Galatians did not know Acts, or one of its predecessors, which, last but not least, is indicated by the "highly polemical tendency" that present day scholars called attention to.

Even apart from this, the likewise fictional character of the picture of Paul we encounter in the letters is clear. The many improbabilities and inanities with which Acts burdens us from a historical perspective, and which cause many scholars to consider Acts as a historical source regarding the apostle Paul either not at all or only to a very limited extent, are also met in the Pauline letters! We would see this even more clearly, or course, if we first freed ourselves from the prejudice that in the letters we have to do with first-hand sources, and if we had the same critical distance with regard to the letters as we do with regard to Acts. Instead of this, the automatically presupposed and, in general, hardly further considered axiom of authenticity leads us either to not even notice the many discrepancies and problems in the letters regarded as authentic or to plaster over *those we do notice* with all kinds of possible and impossible explanations. Our *prior decision* that in the letters we have to do in every case with documents having great historical authenticity is so unshakable that, as improbable as they might be individually, all these explanations are legitimate. If we once began to doubt the possibility of such explanations (As a rule, hardly anyone believes the explanations as such except for the one from whom they originated), in the same breath we would have to ask the decisive, fundamental question about the authenticity of all the letters—and no one wants to do that.

Our prior-decision has the effect that we have forgotten how be amazed at things that we should really wonder about: for example, that the writer of the letters claims he went to Jerusalem *because of a revelation*, as Allard Pierson already noticed, smells suspiciously of apologetic (the writer obviously counters the accusation that his apostle, if anything, is no sovereign apostle, but as Acts claims, had been *sent*) and gives rise to the suspicion that for the writer of this passage the historical possibility (or impossibility) of a "revelation" that would cause him to go to Jerusalem at the appropriate time for the apostolic council had escaped his sight[98]. Or for example the writer's incidental remarks that he had fought with wild animals in Ephesus (1 Cor 15:32), that after many other hardships ("five times I received from the Jews forty [lashes] minus one; three times I was beaten with rods; once I was stoned") he was "adrift on the deep sea for a day and a night" (2 Cor 11:24f.: literally *on the bottom of the sea*!); that he was received by the churches in Galatia "as an angel of God... as Christ Jesus" (Gal 4:14: Why? And how did the Galatians know Christ Jesus, whom the apostle had yet to preach to them for the first time?); and so forth. If we would read these passages and others in a different context, we would recognize without a moment's hesitation that we have before us either overblown exaggerations of someone's runaway imagination or—what is more probable—literary fiction. In addition to what has been said, we now come to a further important point, which we have not considered at all until now.

What does Luke Remain Silent about the Letters of Paul?

The list of Christian writers who must have known the Pauline writings but whose work nevertheless betrays nothing of the sort is considerable. Surprisingly, the writer of Acts also belongs to this group. Even Luke knows nothing about the literary activity of the apostle! For Luke the activity of Paul (and Peter) is limited to that of a missionary and worker of miracles. He seems to know nothing about any correspondence of Paul with his churches; in any case, he says nothing about this.

How should one explain this peculiar situation that the first and only New Testament author who concerns himself with the life history of Paul does not waste one word regarding the apostle's letters to his churches, which seemed so important to Christians a few decades later that they found them worthy of inclusion in the New Testament canon? Can one imagine that a present day writer would write a biography of J.S. Bach without mentioning his musical works? What is hidden behind Luke's remarkable silence?

According to the generally accepted conception, Luke writes after the death of Paul, and thus looks back on the life and work of the apostle. If he does not mention the letters of the apostle, the reason for this must be sought in following three explanations:[99]

1. Luke *knew* the Pauline writings, but for certain reasons would not, or could not mention them;[100]
2. Luke *did not know* the Pauline writings, even though they already existed;[101]
3. Luke did not know the Pauline writings because in his time no literature at all in the name of Paul yet existed.

It is self-evident that today Luke's remarkable silence with regard to the letters of Paul must be explained either with 1) alone, or perhaps with 2), since 3) would presuppose the *inauthenticity* of all the Pauline letters, which is an impossible possibility for research that continues to hold fast to the axiom of authenticity for all the Pauline writings, and that until now has not once considered this as even a temporary working hypothesis.

To be sure, the reasons given for the fact that Luke did not know the Pauline writings, although they already existed, strike one as entirely artificial. The assumption that in the course of his search for details about the life of the apostle Luke heard nothing about the letters that were supposedly so highly revered and highly valued in the churches is extremely improbable.

More probable, on the other hand, is the Klein's assumption that by "suppressing the Pauline writings" Luke wanted to "neutralize the theology of Paul that was regarded as sinister by orthodox thinking."[102] In other words, Klein's thesis means that Luke knowingly ignored the Pauline letters because in many ways these were disturbing for the church of his time.

This thesis, that proceeds from the correct observation that in their language and theology the Pauline letters come remarkably close to the Gnosticism perceived as heretical and for this reason must have seemed "sinister" to the orthodox church of the second century (I return to this below ⇒ *Marcionism and Gnosis*), must nevertheless collapse in the form represented by Klein because in the Pauline writings — in their present canonical form — alongside much that is Gnostic there are also some anti-Gnostic ideas, which are not only well in accord with the thinking of the orthodox church but also could be made excellent use of against the Gnostics.

The Silence of the Apocalypse

What is true for Acts also holds for the last book in the New Testament canon, The Revelation to John, which according to prevailing opinion was perhaps written in the time between 90 and 95 CE[103]. One should also be able to presuppose a knowledge of Paul and the Pauline letters for the author of the Apocalypse, since the seven letters contained in the writing are addressed to churches that belong in the region of Paul's missionary work: Ephesus, Smyrna, Pergamum, Thyatira, Sardes, Philadelphia, and Laodicea.

Here also we are disappointed. The author of the Apocalypse, who according traditional opinion writes only a few decades after Paul,[104] seems to have heard nothing about Paul or his letters. At the same time, he had all kinds of reasons to talk about him. Above all, the apocalyptic writer, who was filled with passion for Christian martyrdom, could not have ignored Paul's own martyrdom in Rome.

Moreover, how should the serious differences be understood between the Christianity presupposed by the Pauline letters and that which the apocalyptic writer addressed? In comparison with the former, must not the latter seem to come from another world? While the writer of the Apocalypse still conceives Christianity as entirely a national-Jewish affair, the writer of the Pauline letters presupposes a Christianity that has emancipated itself from Judaism and the law long ago.

In addition, as Käsemann observes, the writer of the Apocalypse of John gives no indication "that Asia Minor is indebted to the apostle."[105] In light of the astonishingly negative historical findings, that is even saying a bit too much. The radical critic Loman did not leave it be with simple astonishment, but bravely drew the consequences: it seemed to him that defending the authenticity of the major epistles was something more difficult that opening all the seals and locks of the Apocalypse.[106]

Not only important New Testament writings wrap themselves in silence with regard to the apostle Paul and his letters (Paul is mentioned for the first time in the New Testament in 2 Peter 3:15, which according to the prevailing view today is supposed to have originated in the middle of the second century),[107] outside the New Testament as well in the period between 50 and 150 CE we encounter hardly any church writer who can definitively witness to the existence of letters stemming from the apostle Paul.

Justin and Aristides

Justin, the "philosopher and martyr," who lived in Rome (ca. 165 CE) and descended from Flavia Neapolis (today Nablus) in Palestine, is one of the most important church writers of the second century. According to his own statement, he had first been a teacher of Platonic philosophy before he was converted to Christianity (Dial 2.6).

Justin also seems to not yet have heard of Paul. In any case, his writings do not indicate that he knew an additional apostle alongside the twelve. Likewise, Justin seems not to have known letters that had been written under the name of Paul.

Of course, there is something that makes the whole affair somewhat more complicated, but also more puzzling, than the New Testament witnesses considered until now. It is the often noted fact that, in spite of his obvious ignorance of Paul, Justin's writings occasionally, in some places, sound "Pauline," i.e., their language and theology has a certain Pauline coloring. For example, in his *First Apology* Justin attempts to derive the possibility of resurrection from the image of a man and human seed: just as in a wondrous way the man comes forth from human seed, so also the human body will be resurrected and take on immortality (1Apol 19).

> But as at first you would not have believed it possible that such persons could be produced from the small drop, and yet now you see them thus produced, so also judge ye that it is not impossible that the bodies of men, after they have been dissolved, and like seeds resolved into earth, should in God's appointed time rise again and put on incorruption.

That could directly connect with 1 Cor 15:38, where the author of the Pauline letters employs a corresponding image: "But God gives it a body as he has chosen, and to each seed its own body."[108] This echo of Pauline theology and language, that can also be observed elsewhere and can hardly be accidental, is strange. If Justin knew the Pauline letters, why does he fail to mention him as a missionary and founder of churches, as a great Christian theologian, or as a martyr and hero of the faith? How can we explain the strange fact that Justin speaks in Pauline phrases without mentioning Paul or his letters?

Since we often encounter this phenomenon in our search for traces of the apostle in second century writings, the question will be pursued in somewhat more detail in what follows. It can finally be explained, however, only when we interrogate our last and decisive witness, Marcion, the "rediscoverer" of the Pauline letters who was excommunicated from the Catholic church.

If we hold fast to the traditional understanding, namely, the view that all the (major) Pauline letters are authentic, the following possible explanations emerge[109]:

1. One can deny that the passages that sound like Paul should be traced back to the Pauline writings and or that Justin knew of any Pauline tradition;

2. One can assume that Justin did indeed know Paul, but deliberately *ignored* him because he was the primary witness for Marcion, the heretic whom Justin fought;

3. One can presume that Justin refrained from mentioning Paul out of respect for his Jewish dialogue partner, because "there may have been no reason for Justin to draw on the Pauline writings";

4. One can disregard what is found in the text and make Justin an ardent follower of Paul.

The first possibility, for example, is taken up by. Schmithals. He declares: "That the Oriental Justin must have devoted himself in Rome to the Pauline tradition is an unreasonable demand. Did Rudolf Bultmann in Marburg devote himself to the literature of Hans Bruns, or Billy Graham in Berlin to the writings of Ernst Fuchs? Hardly!"[110]

The anachronistic comparison Schmithals makes between Justin, Bultmann and Billy Graham is hardly sufficient to provide a satisfactory explanation for those passages that contain echoes of Pauline writings. Apart from the fact that one cannot compare the situation on the theological "book market" in those days with that of today, one should also consider that writings that are about to be elevated to the rank of canonical dignity are not easily ignored.

That Justin does not mention Paul because he deliberately ignores him is forcefully maintained in our time by Günter Klein[111]. He rightly refers to it as a "very strange affair": An orthodox writer, who is nevertheless a witness for how things were in Rome around 150, leaves behind in his work not one trace of that apostle to the Gentiles who decades earlier had enjoyed the highest respect in this very same church, as 1 Clement indicates, and Ignatius as well indirectly. Did he know nothing about him, and none of his writings? That would have been fully impossible at this time and in this place. The only possible conclusion is that he wanted to ignore him." [112]

Klein provides the same kind of explanation here as in the case of Luke, who in his view was "embarrassed" by Paul and in this way attempted to limit the popularity of his writings. With regard to this explanation, therefore, the same thing must be said as there.

That the third possible explanation is correct is highly questionable, [113] since one can find many starting points in the Pauline letters for conversation with a Jewish dialogue partner. And the fourth explanation is even less probable, since the fact that Justin nowhere mentions Paul by name seems to be completely ignored.[114]

Two possibile explanations for solving Justin's enigma still remain. But both of these explanations, of course, would presuppose what is obviously unthinkable for most theologians, namely, that the (major) Pauline letters do not derive from the apostle and are therefore inauthentic.[115]

Explanation 5: In view of the fact that Justin does not explicitly mention the Pauline letters, one could surmise that they *did not yet exist*, or

Explanation 6: that they were not yet circulating as letters of Paul.

To begin with, there could have been only general theological tracts, which—having originated in heretical (Marcionite) circles—were already by and large identical with the later Pauline letters, but did not yet sail under the flag of the apostle. This would explain the fact that Justin's language now and then exhibits Pauline echoes, but that at the same time he nowhere speaks of the apostle. He does not do this because he obviously did not know him, either as an apostle or as the writer of the literature he sometimes used and in which various questions about Christian life were addressed. This literature could later have been brought into the form of letters and attributed to the apostle. This presumption offers a possible explanation for why Justin nowhere mentions Paul, even though he makes use of Pauline phrases. That theological writings that had originally not at all been conceived as letters could circulate as theological treatises for a long time before they were reworked into "apostolic letters" is indeed a phenomenon known elsewhere. In the view of many scholars, for example, the letter of James could have been such a treatise, which through the introductory address and greeting with the name of James, the "brother of the Lord" and apostle, became a letter from early, apostolic times. And Hebrews as well, as one can see at a glance, has hardly anything to do with a real "letter," but is basically nothing else than a theological "essay," which was first transformed into our "letter" to the Hebrews through the addition of some epistolary formalities. The name alone divulges that it can hardly be a real letter: for example, who would perceive a letter *to the Germans* as an authentic letter — with postmark and stamp? In any case, the possibility can not be excluded that the Pauline letters also originally circulated in the Christian bookstores of the ancient world only as "interesting literary publications," as the Swiss radical critic Rudolf Steck expressed it. The Pauline letters as well contain many passages that give a strong impression of theological-dogmatic or ethical treatises. It would be entirely possible that individual "building blocks" of this kind were later furnished with an epistolary frame and published as testimony from apostolic times.

But even if Justin already possessed the Pauline writings as letters — not in their present canonical form, but in an earlier version, there could have been a serious reason why he would have remained silent about it. Justin could have been aware that the Pauline letters represented forgeries (by Christian heretics). Because of their theological content, he did not want to deny them respect; but he obviously also could not recognize them as documents from apostolic times, just as little as could recognize Paul as an apostle, whom he either did not know at all, or knew only as the patron saint of the heretics.

This conjecture, which leads us into the middle of the entire question concerning the authenticity of the Pauline writings and which will engage us later in connection with the interrogation of our chief witness, Marcion, cannot be pursued further here. At this point, it is sufficient to observe that Justin knows nothing about the existence of an apostle Paul nor anything about letters written under his name, which in the middle of the second century for a representative of the Roman church, to which Paul had once written the letter to the Romans, must seem very strange.

It is also strange then that the Christian philosopher Aristides, who at about the same time was writing in Athens, in his writing addressed to the Caesar Hadrian, in which he defends Christianity against accusations by the pagan world, speaks not a single word about the supposed founder of the first Christian churches in Greece, even though—here we encounter a phenomenon similar to Justin—he sometimes uses Pauline formulations[116]. As with Justin, the Christianity of Aristides had already largely separated from Judaism—but any reference to the person who with his theology supposedly created the presupposition for this is missing. As with Justin, the preaching of the gospel is exclusively the work of the Twelve (whether he silently includes Paul among them or does not know him at all is unclear).

1 Clement and Ignatius: Two Will-o'-the-wisps of New Testament Criticism

In our investigation of witnesses to the Pauline letters in the literature of the first and second centuries we have until now (along with some writings less important for our work) left two writers out of consideration: the writer of 1 Clement and the martyr-bishop Ignatius of Antioch. Both writers are perceived by most scholars today as the earliest witnesses to the (major) Pauline letters.

According to widespread opinion today, in *1 Clement* we have a writing from the church in Rome to the church in Corinth, that supposedly originated in 81-96 or 93-97 and whose author was a certain Clement of Rome, who presumably was "a leading person in the Roman church, one of their bishops or Presbyters."[117]

In this writing, whose purpose is seen to be the restoration of peace and order in the quarreling Corinthian community, Paul is spoken of several times — 5:5-7, where the persecution and suffering of the apostle is alluded to; Paul is characterized as a "herald in the East and the West," who "received the true fame for his faith," (5:6) and is portrayed to the Corinthians as "the greatest example of patience" (5:7); then 47:1, where the community is reminded of the "letter of the blessed Paul," in which the quarrelsome Corinthians were once already admonished to unity, and indeed by highest apostolic authority. If it is already clear from the second passage that the writer of *1 Clement* knew 1 Corinthians, on the basis of other passages it also cannot be denied that he knew some of the other Pauline letters.

The martyr-bishop *Ignatius of Antioch,* who around 110[118] was supposedly brought from his home in Antioch to Rome in order to suffer martyrdom there, is a remarkable figure. In his seven letters that he writes on the way to different churches in Asia Minor and to the church in Rome, he also shows that he knows the apostle Paul and his letters. In his letter to the Ephesians he refers to the Ephesians as "common-initiates with Paul" (12:2), who mentions the church in Ephesus "in all of his letters." Peculiar here is only that the "common initiation" of the supposed founder of their community has been so quickly forgotten that later they could make the disciple John, who had supposedly already been executed in Jerusalem in 44 CE, the founder of the church.[119]

In his letter to the Romans (4:3), Ignatius mentions "Peter and Paul" in one breath, and in other passages also it is clear that the author of the Ignatian letters knew not only Paul but also his letters, which he sometimes cites or alludes to.

Even if knowledge of the apostle Paul and some of the letters written in his name can not be disputed in for either the writer of *1 Clement* or Ignatius, it is nevertheless very doubtful that the two apostolic fathers fulfill another essential presupposition for their reputation as witnesses for the authenticity of the Pauline epistles. What is the situation with regard to the authenticity of *their* "letters" and the question of their dating? — If one can believe the majority of today's theologians, the authenticity of the letters and their origin around the turn of the first to the second century is beyond doubt[120].

To be sure, thoroughgoing skepticism is appropriate when scholars appeal to the "critical consensus" or "generally recognized results." Apart from the fact that until now in this scholarly field the majority decision has seldom led to reliable results, it has also often been seen in the past that opinions having been supported for a long while by a broad "critical consensus" at some point end up in the scholarly waste basket as entirely out of date.

The case with regard to *1 Clement* and the Ignatian letters is somewhat different because the authenticity of these "letters' was very contested for a long time in the past! Johannes Haller rightly calls attention to the fact that for a long time these letters were "regarded as unauthentic... Today one regards them as authentic, but how long can one do that? The price of such documents tends to rise and fall with the scholarly market..."[121]

In fact, to confirm this one must only glance briefly at the fluctuating *history of research* for these letters. Surprisingly, the theologians of our grandfathers' and great-grandfathers' generations often show themselves to be far more critical than their descendents today. Not only *1 Clement*, which because of its enormous length, that for a real letter was highly unusual, stirred up doubt among old-time scholars, the Ignatian letters also took on the smell of forgery very early. Until the seventeenth century, the Ignatian letters were known only in the so-called "longer recension," which contained not only seven letters like the collection today, but six additional letters. The Catholic character of these letters (among which was a letter from Ignatius to Mary!) was so obvious that it required no great scholarly effort to recognize that they represented a pseudepigraphic products from a later time. The Protestants of the Reformation were among the first to suspect that the letters of the martyr-bishop, who carried out energetic propaganda for the office of the monarchial bishop on his way from Syria to Rome, were forgeries. They were joined later by most of the theologians of the Tübingen School — although in the meantime the situation had changed somewhat (in favor of the authenticity of the letters) and since the seventeenth century there had existed not only the thirteen letters of the longer recension but also the seven letters of the "middle recension," whose Catholic elements were not so striking to the eye.

In any case, towards the end of the last century there was a "conservative" turn, introduced by the investigations of the German scholar Theodor ahn[122] and J.B. Lightfoot,[123] both of whom, with a great display of erudition, attempted to demonstrate the authenticity of the seven letters of the middle recension, without providing satisfactory answers, to be sure, for the decisive questions raised previously by those who contested their authenticity. After their judgment received in 1878 the blessing of Adolf von Harnack, who at that time was the greatest German authority in the area of early Christian history, the authenticity of the seven Ignatian letters was established in Germany as a generally recognized scholarly result. After Harnack's harsh dictum, "Whoever regards the Ignatian letters as inauthentic has not studied them intensely enough,"[124] only a few still had the courage to again place the question of authenticity on the day's agenda.

As in the case of the Ignatian letters, so also for *1 Clement* a quick look at the history of research suffices to relativize the opinion expressed with great self-confidence by many theologians today that we have to do here with an authentic writing from the close of the first century. The leading scholars of the Tübingen School did not perceive this writing as an authentic letter. Here also it was again the German scholar Harnack who authoritatively supported the authenticity of the writings still disputed at that time and thereby determined the course of future research until today. After Harnack, at least in Germany there were few researchers who dared contest *1 Clement*. In view of the numerous questions and problems that *1 Clement* and the Ignatian letters had earlier posed for scholars — and which were not really solved by Zahn, Lightfoot, or Harnack — this is more than curious and perhaps only understandable against the background of these scholars' great authority. What may also have played a role for some theologians was the view that the letters were quite important not only for dating the Pauline letters but also for dating some other New Testament writings (e.g., the Gospel of Matthew) and that calling their authenticity into question could produce further consequences, which made it seem advisable not to ask this question to begin with.

Whatever the case may be, whoever picks up *1 Clement*, for example, and reads it without prejudice will encounter so much nonsense and so many contradictions that they will not be able to suppress the question. In spite of the introductory address to "the church of God that sojourns in Corinth," and in spite of the obligatory mentioning of some names as well as other epistolary formalities, do we have to do here with a *real letter*?

Can a document consisting of about 9400 words be accepted without further ado as a writing that was sent from Rome to Corinth with the intention of actual correspondence? Apart from the fact that the size of an average letter in antiquity, as one can determine from collections of ancient papyrus letters we possess,[125] was not substantially different from our letters today and consisted of one to two pages (rather less than more, since writing was such an arduous affair in antiquity), the situation in which the author intervenes with the pen, the party conflict in Corinth, required great haste! If he wanted to accomplish something with his writing, he could hardly sit there and spend weeks or months drafting a writing whose size surpasses that of many ancient books, especially since in view of conditions of conveyance in the ancient world he would have had to reckon with considerable delay in delivery. With the passing of one or two months, the situation which the writer presupposes in his writing could be entirely different, and his writing hopelessly out of date.

If the party conflict in Corinth and the replacement of the presbyters with younger members of the church was in fact the real incentive for the letter from the church in Rome to the church in Corinth, it is furthermore completely impossible to understand why the writer only comes to speak of this in chapter 44 (!) and in the first two-thirds of the writing exhausts the patience of the Corinthians with discussions of the resurrection, the omniscience and omnipresence of God, and such things, which although edifying, have no importance for the matter at hand.

In addition, there is the consideration that the entire controversy addressed by the writer of *1 Clement* remains strangely unclear and vague and that the information about it is very contradictory, as even supporters of its authenticity today must concede:

> "He [Clement] emphasizes that the uproar can be traced to 'a few rash and self-willed persons' (1.1; in 47.6 it is only 'one or two persons'), but then accuses the entire congregation (46.9 = 'your uproar'). As motives he identifies jealousy; envy and contentiousness; lack of love, humility and discernment. But he does not identify the actual background of the Corinthian conflict (!), just as little as he identifies the actual motives for the—certainly uninvited—intervention by Rome in the inner affairs of the Corinthian church (!). Without doubt, these are closely related, but there is nothing else to learn about either. The opponents in 1 Clement left behind no witnesses; nor can their views be reconstructed from the writing, since it does not debate their arguments, but simply condemns them morally. With regard to the circumstances in Corinth as well as Rome's motives, if one is not willing to give up, one is dependent on hypotheses."[126]

If one begins with the presumption that we have to do here with a real letter, all the peculiarities cited here should give one cause for thought!

Finally, the conflict as such lacks any inner probability: how can the Corinthian church, founded so long ago, rise up against their presbyters on account of only a few ringleaders? The "attempt at mediation" that the writer undertakes (from Rome!), in which he one-sidedly condemns the "troublemakers" in Corinth, as if they acted from base motives, is also entirely unrealistic and shows the fictional character of the whole thing. Already in the last century, Gustav Volkmar raised the consideration that the letter could hardly be intended for the entire community in Corinth, as the address would have us believe, but only for that part of the community to which the displaced presbyters and their followers belonged.[127]

The tensions and obscurities revealed here are due to the contradiction between the situation presupposed in the writing and the author's real intention. The real intention of the author, of course, is not the resolution of an actual conflict in a diplomatic way, but something quite different: his writing, that is directed not to *one* church, and also not to the church in Corinth, but to *all* the churches in the Catholic universe, is intended not to mediate, but to instruct and — here a typical Catholic tendency of the letter becomes visible — to warn against uprisings and disorder in the churches! The writings leads us into a time, most probably the middle of the second century, in which the distinction between priests and laity (40:5: there are much different rules for laity than for ecclesiastical officer-holders) already announces the Roman clericalism. Over against all inclinations to opposition, the authority of the church is enjoined in an impressive example.

For this purpose the writer employs the motif of party conflict already known to him from 1 Corinthians and uses this as a pretence, cloaked in the form of a letter, for an edifying, exhortative discourse on the theme "Peace and Harmony in the Church." For the writer of *1 Clement*, the church in Corinth is an exemplary church, in which he would like to see his ideal church realized, in essential agreement with that of the self-aggrandizing official Roman church: consider the harmonious picture of the church he sketches, in which the young submit in humble subordination to the old, the laity to the priests, the wife to the husband (chs. 1-2) — the Roman Catholic ideal of the church in its purist form!

Once one has recognized the writer's real intention, it will no longer seem strange if there are other peculiarities as well that would look odd in a real letter. Who would expect, for example, in real letter, which moreover is written by the church in Rome to the church in Corinth, to find the exhortation (34:7), "Let us therefore come together *in the same place* (*epi to auto*) with harmony of conscience and earnestly call upon the Lord as from one mouth, that we may share in his great and glorious promises"? In view of the geographical distance between Rome and Corinth, one can only wonder how the writer imagined the *common* visit of a holy place. In this passage it becomes clear: for a moment the writer has forgotten the situation presupposed by the letter and falls from the role of writer of letters into the role of a preacher, which he also gladly takes over in other passages as well: see the passages with strong liturgical characteristics (20.1-12; 38.1-4 and the concluding prayer, 64), which make one think of a sermon rather than a letter.

In other places, the author succeeds very well in imagining himself in the role of a letter writer: for example, in the introduction to the letter, where it reads:

> On account of the sudden and repeated misfortunes and calamities that have befallen us, we have been somewhat delayed in turning to the questions disputed among you, beloved, and especially the abominable and unholy sedition, so inappropriate for the elect of God (1:1).

In these lines, many people have wanted to see a reference to an actual situation of persecution (under Nero or Domitian). As Van den Bergh van Eysinga already recognized, however, what we have here is only a conventional apology, which the author of 1 Clement readily employs to give his writing the appearance of an authentic letter.[128] According to the operative Roman law, persecutions did not usually arrive overnight.

In the same way as *1 Clement*, the seven so-called letters of Ignatius also are all pseudonymous works.

The situation presupposed in the letters must already raise suspicion. The bishop of Antioch has become a victim of persecution of Christians in his own city, and the punishment is not to be carried *here*, as would usually be the case, but, accompanied by a small body of Roman soldiers, he has been sent on a journey through half of the Mediterranean world, from Syria to Rome, to be thrown to wild animals in the arena there!

Although Ignatius is a prisoner, he nevertheless has the remarkable opportunity during his trip through the city of Smyrna in Asia Minor to make contact with the local bishops of the churches in Ephesus, Magnesia, and Tralles, and to hand over to them a letter to each of their churches. In a similar way, the churches in Philadelphia and Smyrna, as well as Polycarp, the bishop of Smyrna, receive letters from Troas. Since in spite of his sentence Ignatius is obviously still uncertain whether he will be put to death in Rome, he also writes a letter to the church in Rome, in which, delirious in the face death and craving martyrdom, the bishop entreats them not to prevent his martyrdom by intervening with the authorities.

> I beseech you, do not be an untimely kindness to me. Let me be food for the beasts, through which I can attain to God! I am God's wheat, and I am ground by the teeth of wild beasts that

I may be found pure bread of Christ. Rather entice the wild beasts, that they may become my tomb and leave no trace of my body, so that when I fall asleep I will not be burdensome to anyone... I long for the beasts that are prepared for me, and I pray that will be quick with me. I will even entice them to devour me quickly... Fire and cross and struggles with wild beasts, cutting and tearing asunder, rackings of bones, mangling of limbs, crushing my whole body, cruel tortures of the devil, let these come over me that I may attain to Jesus Christ! (IgnRom, 4-5)

This has been perceived as the product of a pathological longing for martyrdom.[129] But the matter is likely to be much simpler. In the case of this citation as for the Ignatian writings in their entirety, we have to do not with real letters, but with something entirely composed at a writing table. Their author is not the martyr-bishop Ignatius, but someone later, perhaps a pseudonymous writer around the middle of the second century, who puts himself in the role of the legendary martyr-bishop and was able thereby to give free flight to his fantasy since at that time he hardly needed to fear that the hysterical, overblown death in the arena he conjured up would ever become a reality. The empty and hollow pathos of the declamation, the entire surrealistic scenario that we meet in the Ignatian letters, including the artificial background situation, obviously modeled on the journey of Paul as a prisoner, all this shows that we have to with the product of a typical "writing table author."

Given the artificiality of the basic situation, a series of remarkable contradictions and improbabilities we observe becomes understandable. Ignatius writes that he has been condemned (*IgnEph* 12:1f; *IgnRom* 3:1), but in another passage is nevertheless still uncertain whether (and how) he will die. He is in chains, but nevertheless able to visit the churches of Asia Minor and write letters! A passage in the letter to the Romans throws light on how grandly the author handles the geographical and historical details. In *IgnRom* 5:1 Ignatius writes to the Romans from Smyrna that "from Syria to Rome, by land and by sea" he has been fighting wild beasts (meaning his Roman guards), which is a peculiar remark if one considers that the bishop's journey by sea is still before him.

Like the writer of *1 Clement*, the author of the seven Ignatian letters also drops out of his role as bishop and martyr again and again. In *IgnEph* 5:3, for example, the seems to have entirely forgotten that he writes as a bishop, and exhorts the church like someone who has never been invested with the office of bishop: "Let *us* then be careful not to oppose the bishop" (cf. IgnEph 11:1; 15:2; 17:2; IgnMagn 10:1). It is also strange that Ignatius, who is still uncertain whether he will experience the martyr's death in Rome, can self-consciously anticipate the result of martyrdom and characterize himself as *Theophoros* ("God-bearer") and *Christophoros* ("Bearer of Christ"), which according to practice at that time characterized the martyr only *after the death*.[130] Here also it is evident that the letters stem from a later writer, who already looks back on the martyrdom of the legendary bishop.

The historical existence of a bishop in Antioch named Ignatius need not necessarily be doubted. As the theologian Daniel Völter showed, there existed a tradition according to which Ignatius was martyred in winter 115-116 *in Antioch* by order of the Caesar Trajan.[131] Presumably, this tradition was known to the author of the letters. He enlarged on this in his own way by adding the journey to Rome, and then used it as background for his literary production, in which he let the last weeks and days of the heroic, death-disdaining martyr come alive once again.

That the seven Ignatian letters are not authentic letters is shown by the fact that in general they are stylistically very carefully constructed, which one would hardly expect for letters having originated under the arduous conditions of an imprisonment journey. In addition to this, in the only letter addressed not to a church, but to a person, bishop Polycarp, the absence of any personal relationship with the addressee is particularly remarkable:

> Ignatius, who is also called Theophorus, to Polycarp, who is bishop of the church of the Smyrnaeans, or rather has God the Father and the Lord Jesus Christ as bishop over him, abundant greeting. Welcoming your godly mind, which is grounded as if on an unmovable rock, I glory exceedingly that it was granted to me to see your blameless face, for which I remain glad in God. I exhort you in the grace with which you are endued to quicken your course and to exhort all men so that they might be saved. Live up to your office with all diligence, both fleshly and spiritual... (IgnPoly 1).

Nothing could be more general and non-committal! It must be clear to every reader that in the letter to Polycarp we have to do not with an actual correspondence, but with literature, an artificial letter. Whoever regards the letter to Polycarp as inauthentic, cannot maintain the authenticity of the rest of the Ignatian letters.

Finally, it should be noted that the number *seven* is also remarkable for an assembled collection of letters. In view of the importance that the number seven had in antiquity (as the symbol of fulfillment), it seems to have symbolic significance. If one assumes that we have to do here with authentic letters, it must be asked how and by whom their collection was brought about. The real situation is much more simple: the letters were conceived as a collection from the very beginning, as parts of a whole, in which one "letter" presupposes the other. Thus, in IgnEph 20:1, for example, Ignatius declares that plans to write "a second small book"[132] (Significantly, the writer does not speak of a "letter"), in which he will discuss "the plan of salvation with reference to the new man Jesus Christ, his faith, his love, his suffering and resurrection." This second book is then the letter to the Magnesians. That the letter to the Magnesians presupposes the letter to the Ephesians is shown by IgnMagn 1:2, where the desire is expressed that the churches might experience a three-fold unity, "a union of the flesh with the spirit of Jesus Christ... a union of faith and love... a union of Jesus with the Father"; for what we have here is a recapitulation of the most important ideas from the letter to the Ephesians!

In view of the almost total absence of a substantial debate about reservations regarding the authenticity or the seven Ignatian letters and *1 Clement* that have been put forward in the past, it can hardly be maintained that the self-assuredly expressed judgment by modern research that we have to do here with authentic letters inspires much confidence. In my opinion, it is time for present-day theologians to free themselves from the spell of Harnack and other authorities of the past in order to submit the "letters" to a renewed critical examination — even with the risk that the two old lighthouses, which illuminated New Testament criticism for many years, so as to shelter a large part of New Testament literature in the safe harbor of the first century, will turn out to be will-o'-the-wisps.

Chapter 2

THE HISTORICAL ORIGINS OF THE PAULINE LETTERS

De omnibus dubitandum:
One Must Doubt Everything

My own observations as well as my occupation with Dutch Radical Criticism had brought me in the meantime to a place where the inauthenticity of all the Pauline letters was established for me. In spite of this, however, this negative result was not sufficient for me. In my mind, the primary task for all historical problems was not to determine what had not been the case, but what in fact had been. As I understood it, the historian must always finally be in the situation not only to submit the presumably historical course of history to criticism, but also to reconstruct what actually unfolded. In my opinion, the decisive and finally convincing argument against the authenticity of the letters that the Hollanders still owed us could only be the reconstruction of the real course of history. In my investigation until now two questions had still not been answered:

1. If Paul did not write the letters, who did write them?
2. If someone else wrote them in the name of Paul, who then was the historical Paul?

Since in the mean time I had reached a dead point in my research, I thought that a study trip in the homeland of Dutch Radical Criticism could be useful for me. I hoped that a trip to Amsterdam and Leiden could help me discover additional radical-critical literature, that was not available in German libraries. Above all, I was interested in a book whose existence I had heard about [only in the Hollanders' writings, who mentioned it often. The mysterious book came from an Englishman named Edwin Johnson, and had a similarly mysterious title, *Antiqua Mater*.

If one left the highway, the city of Leiden was at first not much different from any average city in northern Germany. But I was nevertheless not disappointed: the city that had existed in my imagination existed in fact. I found it a bit later, when I came to the heart of the old town: a piece of old Holland, like a picturesque Grachten idyll, the gabled houses, the court yards, the cool, clear Vermeer-atmosphere.

I went from the Nieuwe Beestenmarkt on the Princess canal and then along the marvelous Rapenburg Canal in the direction of the university, and passed by the house of the famous philosopher René Descartes (1596-1650), who had lived and studied here while he was in Holland. *De omnibus dubitandum*—this dictum of the philosopher, often cited by Loman, automatically occurred to me as I passed by the somewhat small and inconspicuous, gabled Dutch house. "Everything should be doubted": beginning from this starting point, Descartes had found his certainty, the certainty of thinking[1]. The reverse side of the maxim, the dark side of the picture, that everything is uncertain, everything should be doubted, he found in the dictum *Cogito ergo sum*: "I think, therefore I am." Here the philosopher of the Enlightenment obtained firm ground under his feet. The doubt had led him not into despair, but into the certainty of rational thinking. For a person in the twentieth century, of course, this exercise could no longer be carried out again in the same way. In the wake of the Enlightenment, rational thinking had been too strongly disavowed for that. If something fascinated me about Descartes' doubting everything and questioning everything, it was not what he discovered at the end of his long and certainly wearisome road; it was rather starting point, the doubt. "Without doubt," doubt represented the most powerful driving force in human intellectual life. Doubt is chaotic, unencumbered; it can lead to the highest heights and the lowest lows at the same time — thus obviously a vexation and a devilish temptation for an orthodox person. And nevertheless, this temptation represents nothing else than life's temptation of the intellect itself, which again and again impels our doubting eyes to be opened to disclose another side of itself.[2]

Meanwhile, I arrived at the old university building in Leiden, which reminded me of a Gothic church. In fact, there was a nunnery on this spot before a university existed. I went purposefully to the modern library, which I suspected would contain a number of treasures for me, whose recovery would occupy me in the days to come. In the library I acquired a list of books from the estate of *G.J.P.J. Bolland*, the philosopher and radical critic of Leiden, that had been left to the university library after his death. The list was exceptionally comprehensive and, as I suspected, contained a number of books on radical criticism. Surveying the list, after a short time my eyes fell on the title of a book I had sought above all others and which had attracted my interest for weeks: the *Antiqua mater*. Bolland had actually had this book in his possession. I quickly filled out a few loan-cards, so I could attend to the rest of the list. And indeed, in a few minutes a friendly library attendant brought me a stack of books among which was the *Antiqua mater*. The work of 308 pages, published in 1887 by Trübner & Company, was not as voluminous as I had expected.

On the first page of the book, beneath the title of the book, printed in beautiful old-English script, and the subtitle, there was a citation relating to its title. It came from a biography of the poet Abraham *Cowley* (1618 –1667): "He had an earnest intention of taking a review of the original principles of the primitive Church: believing that every true Christian had no better means to settle his spirit, than that which was proposed to Aeneas and his followers to be the end of their wanderings, *Antiquam exquirite Matrem.*" *Antiquam exquirite Matrem*!

The peculiar title of the book was thus derived from a citation from Vergil's *Aeneid (3.96)*. The author had appropriated it for his own theme, the history of the investigation of early Christianity. For him, the search for the "ancient mother" was the search for the origins of Christianity. The mother whom we revere without knowing her face to face. To take up the search for her means to devote oneself to the search for the spiritual origins of the Western world. This search was like a long, difficult journey, where we could not know how it would turn out and what would await us at the end, if we finally met her face to face — whether we would even recognize her, or whether we would delighted, or disappointed, or perhaps even terrified.

In accordance with the theme of his book, the learned Bolland, who clearly loved to provide all his books with a personally written remark, attached a quotation from the poem *The Lost Church* by Ludwig Uhland:

> Oft, yonder forest's depths within,
> Is faintly heard a chiming peal;
> None know from whence the sounds begin',
> E'en legends scarce the spot reveal.
> The church hath passed away, but still
> The chimes come softly on the wind;
> Once pilgrims would the pathway fill
> Which now none knoweth where to find.[3]

I did not know exactly what Bolland wanted to express with this quotation. Disappointment, because, in his eyes, the author of the book had not found the way to the *Antiqua mater*? Doubt as to whether the way to her could be found at all by means of historical criticism? Then Bolland certainly would have misunderstood the title *Antiqua mater*, which for Johnson obviously referred only to the historical origin of the Christian church.

Be as it may, the citation from Uhland's poem, which I had not previously known, was nevertheless splendid. In a very poetic way, it characterizes the spiritual-historical situation not only for someone in the nineteenth century, but also for our own situation in the twentieth century. If people take notice at all of their roots, and do not live rootlessly oriented on consumption and success in the present, they must be filled with deep sorrow precisely with regard to their religion, Christianity.

With the dawning of historical doubt, *de omnibus dubitandum*, and with the rise of historical consciousness, Western people lost the security their religion had mediated to them until now. The path to the ancient church was no longer possible, in any case no longer in the way generations before them had gone.

> Once pilgrims would the pathway fill
> Which now none knoweth where to find.

Apart from such general considerations, however, I was more interested at the moment in the content of the Antiqua mater, concerning which I had previously read only a few allusions. What might be special about the book? Might there be pointers in it that went beyond the simple negation of the "It was not so"? For me, the question concerning the origin of the Pauline letters had still not been satisfactorily explained. Van Manen's assumption of a Pauline school, that even today still enjoys great popularity in a modified form, was completely unacceptable, even if one must recognize that the radical Dutch critics had already made many correct observations. A question remained open here, and I hoped to find information about it in the Antiqua mater. I was certainly not disappointed.

Antiqua Mater

Edwin Johnson began his investigation with the question concerning extra-Christian witnesses for early Christianity and the historical Jesus. According to Johnson, apart from the New Testament, we learn very little about the history and origin of Christianity. Most pagan writers show no acquaintance with Christianity, although the Jews are often mentioned. For Johnson, therefore, the silence of classical writers is finally more significant than the few places in ancient literature (in Pliny the Younger[4], Suetonius[5]) where we have to do either with later interpolations or, as for Tacitus[6], with a confusion of Christians at the time of Trajan with Jewish messianic figures from the time of Nero. On the whole, as a witness for the reality of everything that, according to what is mediated in the New Testament, supposedly took place with regard to Jesus and the apostles, the testimony of classical literature from the first two centuries is not very auspicious.

Johnson goes further. Among the extra-canonical Christian sources, the apostolic fathers are worthless for historical investigation, since we have to do here with anonymous writings, which are also difficult to locate with regard to time. Only with Justin (whom we mentioned above) in the middle of the second century do we stand on somewhat reliable historical ground. Of course, what Justin relates concerning Jesus, as a whole, has a very unhistorical character, since in addition to the virgin birth and the visit of the magi he reports only the crucifixion. From all this, Johnson concludes that Jesus of Nazareth was not an historical figure.

Most interesting now, of course, was what Johnson had to say about *Paul*. For Johnson, the "apostle of the heretics," as Tertullian referred to Paul, and regarded the apostle himself with great mistrust, was also not a historical figure. Apart from the traitorous silence of Justin, he also calls attention to Lucian, who in his *Peregrinus Proteus* mentions this wandering Christian preacher's great theaters of activity without betraying any knowledge at all of the famous apostle to the Gentiles. As Tertullian said, the identification of the sender of a letter as "Paul" and the appearance of Paul's name in the address of a letter is still not sufficient proof for the existence of such an apostle. According to Johnson, there had nevertheless been a *Paul-legend*, which Marcion could approptiate for the benefit of his theology. For Johnson, the inescapable and reasonable conclusion can only be that the Marcionites themselves produced ten apostolic letters of their own. And if they ascribed these to an apostle from early Christian times, this would have been entirely in accord with the practices of Christian theologians at that time.

According to Johnson, it is unthinkable that the mixture of heterogeneous elements represented by so-called Paulinism were united in a *single* historical individual. For Johnson, Paul was the apostle of Marcion, but in a different sense than was usually assumed: he was Marcion's creation! Leaving aside their interpolations, the Pauline letters speak for Marcion. One hears him speaking everywhere — e.g., in the characteristic Marcionite opposition between spirit and flesh, law and gospel, the God of mercy and the God of vengeance, etc. All these concepts that we regard as typically Pauline are, for Johnson, actually Marcionite.[7]

Maybe Marcion himself was the author of the Pauline letters: "Whether this last apostle, the "miscarriage," as he refers to himself, in whose passionate declaration the contour of Gnosis can be clearly recognized... was Marcion himself, or Marcus, or some other student of the great 'shipowner from Pontus,' must still be investigated."[8] In any case, for Catholics Marcion became a heavily loaded fruit tree to which, by plundering it, they must be thankful for their Paul.

By reading the decisive passages from the *Antiqua mater*, what I should have recognized long before became immediately clear to me: There was only one possible solution to the authorship problem of the Pauline letters and that was Marcion! I found it entirely incomprehensible that I had not recognized this until now. Just as unexplainable was the fact that — except for radical criticism — previous research, with downright reprehensible naiveté, had left the figure of the great second-century heretic completely out of view with regard not only to the reception of the Pauline writings but also with regard to their origin — even though, to be sure, many scholars today are nevertheless of the opinion that Marcion was the first person to assemble a canon of Pauline letters.

The First Witness to Paul: Marcion the Heretic

Who was Marcion?

He was certainly the most controversial and, at the same time, the most important theologian of the second century, the person whose real significance for both the *origin* and, as we will see, for the *content* of our present biblical canon, i.e., the collection of the twenty-seven New Testament writings, is still scarcely recognized. For his opponents, the Catholic Christians, Marcion was purely and simply the "chief heretic," the incarnation of evil, the "firstborn of Satan."[9] On the other hand, his friends and followers revered him as the great Christian teacher. When they looked towards heaven, they saw him standing at the left of Christ (the right side was reserved for Paul).[10]

The enmity of the Catholic Church at that time for the archheretic is easy to explain when one considers that in their time Marcion and his followers represented one of its strongest and most dangerous competitors. Marcion was not only a teacher, but was also active as a *founder of his own churches*, which were named after him (as Lutherans were later named after Luther) and were spread through in the entire world from Rome to Edessa (in present-day Syria).

In the second and third centuries the Marcionite church was simply *the opposition* to the Catholic church and for a long time was superior to it in power and influence. "Marcion's heretical tradition has filled the entire world," the Catholic Tertullian (following Justin) still complains at the beginning of the third century, in his mammoth work against Marcion, that had as its only purpose the extermination of the cursed Marcionite heresy.[11] Even the Christian adversary Celsus, who debated with Origen, understood "Christians" to mean primarily *Marcionite Christians* — which permits a significant inference about the spread of Marcionism at this time.[12] As so often in early Christian history, the person of Marcion is more obscured than clarified by the all-consuming polemic of the church fathers. From what they report, however, one can nevertheless gather that Marcion was born around the end of the first century in Pontus in Asia Minor. Some reporters want to be more precise, by making Marcion a fellow countryman of the philosopher Diogenes ("Diogenes in the barrel") and having him make his appearance, like Diogenes, in Sinope, the leading city of Pontus, on the south coast of the Black Sea. Without doubt, the tendency to associate Marcion, who according to Hippolytus was supposedly a follower of Cynic philosophy (which at that time would not exclude being a Christian),[13] with the founder of this philosophical school (Diogenes) plays a role here. Marcion's father was supposedly a bishop. Some church fathers report that the relationship between father and son was very strained and that the father excluded his son from the church because he purportedly seduced a virgin. This could simply be common gossip by the church fathers. But one can nevertheless explain very well how such stories could arise, since Marcion, who remained a bachelor for his entire life and later taught an extreme form of sexual asceticism (so that he even forbade married members of his church to engage in sexual relations), certainly provided sufficient material for all kinds of speculation.[14]

As a ship-owner and merchant, Marcion is thought to have resided a long time in Asia Minor, where he obviously acquired a great amount of money, until finally, "already as an old man" (i.e., presumably around 60), after the death of Bishop Hyginos (140 CE),[15] he came to Rome. Whether and to what extent Marcion was already active as a missionary before he came to Rome is disputed. While Harnack and other investigators think that Marcion began to found Christian churches of his own *only after his stay in Rome*, many scholars represent the view that Marcion already began to build his Church before coming to Rome. On the whole, the latter view seems much more plausible. Since already in the middle of the century the Catholic Justin can already observe that Marcionite churches are spread throughout *the entire world* (*1Apol.*, 1.58), Marcion must have already been active as a missionary and have founded his own churches prior to his residence in Rome, whereby these churches, of course, could have had a loose relationship with the Catholic church in Rome. The enormous spread of Marcionite churches throughout the entire Mediterranean region cannot possibly be explained if this took place in a decade and a half, apart from the fact that one can hardly credit such a gigantic missionary achievement to a man who was already "somewhat old."

In Rome there now takes place an event with great significance for the further development of church history: Marcion is excommunicated (presumably in 144 CE, in July?). From this time on, the Marcionite and the Catholic churches stood in opposition to one another, as in our own time, for example, Protestantism and Catholicism.

Of course, immediately following Marcion's arrival in Rome there was a friendly relationship between Marcion and the Roman church. Marcion had attempted—clearly with some success at first—to win the Roman church for himself by presenting them a splendid sum of money amounting to 200,000 sestercen, which in present day buying-power would represent several million dollars (one sesterse = 2 ½ asses)[16]. Where this money came from is not entirely clear. It is not said whether Marcion had earned it by his profitable work as a ship-owner, as is most often assumed, or perhaps (which I hold as more probable)—like the "Paul" of the letters, who collected money for the church in "Jerusalem"—had asked his own churches for money before he set out for the "Jerusalem" of his own time, i.e., Rome (Rom 15:26; 1Cor 16:1f; 2Cor 9:12). If one considers that in the entire affair the example, or parallel, as the case may be, of *Paul* obviously plays an important role, the latter explanation is in no way entirely improbable. Werner Hörman also notes that here Marcion clearly emulates the apostle Paul as his great example: "His great example becomes visible: Paul. Did he not—and with much labor—plead for money from all his Greek churches for years in order to donate it, as had been arranged, to 'the poor in Jerusalem'? Now, were there not also "poor in Rome.' "[17]

In spite of the impressive gift of money by the Marcionite Simon for the Roman Peter (Acts 8:18ff.), Marcion-Simon was not able to obtain the favor of the followers of Peter in the long run. "Part and lot" (Acts 8:21) in the Roman church can obviously not be purchased either with money or with nice words, which would certainly also not have been missing. The gift of money might have contributed to confusing the minds of the Roman church for a while, but it then came to an open break. In a short time, Marcion got his 200,000 sestercen back again by return mail.[18]

What happened? Obviously, in the meantime, after the initial delight over the welcome improvement of his church endowment, the Roman Peter had sufficient opportunity to consider the matter a bit and to project a clearer picture of the remarkable traveler from the Near East. Even if it was only after a difficult inner struggle, for him it was therefore as if scales had fallen from his eyes. Like Peter in his judgment of Simon Magus, he now recognized: "For I see that you are in the gall of bitterness and in the bond of iniquity".

In the meantime, Marcion had become identified with heresy.

Marcion's Two Gods

The chief reproach made against Marcion was that he taught two Gods. Above all for Jewish Christians, who clearly had significant influence in the world at that time, the Marcionite teaching seems to have made their hair stand on end. By closer examination, Marcion's theology turns out to be an aggressive attack on everything that for Jews was dear and cherished. That includes, above all, the confession of one creator God, the father of Jesus Christ. Marcion claimed that alongside the (Jewish) creator God there was also another God, a second, or "foreign," God. This "other God" is the good and loving God, while that God, i.e., the Jewish God, is the God of the creation and the law. While the good God revealed himself for the first time in Jesus Christ, the Old Testament is the revelation writing of the Jewish God. The Jewish creator God is subordinate to the good God in every way, who dwells above him in his own heaven (the third heaven).[19] The clearest proof of this is his creation, which with all its deficiencies and abominations, above all the loathsome dirt and filth of procreation, birth, putridity, etc., represents lamentable and ludicrous tragedy and shows itself to be entirely the work of bungler, even the Jewish Demiurge. The entire imperfection of this God also finds expression in the fact that he is the God of the Old Testament law, with its unmerciful and primitive demands, e.g., "Eye for eye and tooth for tooth," etc. As a righteous God, with the promulgation of his law he is at the same time a hard and cruel God with an explicit partiality for his chosen people. As the Old Testament also shows, he takes pleasure in wars and bloodshed, he is hot-tempered, changeable, unpredictable, and peevish. For this reason, those persons in the Old Testament who should be regarded as really righteous are not those who do the will of the Righteous (God), as Abel and Abraham, for example, but, on the contrary, precisely those who rise up against him, like Cain, for example, who murdered his brother.

The *good God*, on the other hand, who was often referred to by Marcion and the Marcionites as the *Good* or the *Foreign*, is entirely different from God the creator and giver of the law. He is the creator not of the imperfect, material world, but of the perfect, invisible world. His outstanding characteristic is not righteousness, but *love* and kindness. The love and mercy of this God are so exceedingly large that, in contrast, they themselves disclose those who are foreign to him by nature, who as creatures of the creator God are imprisoned in the transitory cosmos, sighing under the yoke of his tyranny.

But quite unexpectedly, and without any of the prophets inspired by the muffled spirit of the Old Testament God being able to foresee anything about it, the good God released humankind from the dominion of transience and the law of the Jewish God by sending his Son to earth—to be sure, only in what seemed to be a body (phantasma), since the Deliverer could naturally not really enter into the dirty, material world, which of course represented only a concoction of the Demiurge. Since no external compulsion made this step necessary, this was an act of pure *grace*, an outflow of perfect goodness and mercy, pure *gospel*. Through his Son, the good God frees humankind from the power of the righteous God. Or better, one must say he buys him out, in that he delivers to the righteous God as a purchase price the blood of his Son, who had been hanged on the Old Testament tree of shame (Gal 3:13; Dtn 27:26). The goal of the salvation work of Christ is not forgiveness of sins, but liberation from the power of the creator God into the dominion of the good God. People everywhere can be set free when they believe the gospel of the cross of Christ, through which the power of the law has been broken, and where therefore *faith* now stands in the place of obedience to the law, love in the place of righteousness, and hope in an invisible kingdom of God in place of hope in an earthly-messianic kingdom, which the Jews (and many Jewish-Christians) anticipate.

When did Marcion Become a Heretic?

The enormous success that Marcion's message had in the Eastern part of the Roman Empire and would also continue to have—As Walter Bauer showed, the majority of churches in Greece, Asia Minor, and the Near East seem to have been Marcionite[20]—could not be repeated in the West. As his excommunication in 144 CE shows, after prolonged hesitation Marcion received a clear rebuff. A contribution to this was certainly the fact that in the Roman church, where Marcion presented his theology, Jewish Christians had especially great influence. Naturally, they could not accept Marcionite teaching in any way and obviously could only perceive it as one of the worst blasphemies of Israel's God.

After his excommunication in Rome, Marcion soon disappeared from the scene. In a letter that was supposedly still known to Tertullian, he seems to have defended himself against accusations that had been made against him. Unfortunately, however, like so many documents that would have burning interest for us in this instance, this letter has been "lost." We do not know, therefore, how Marcion himself reacted to the accusations that had been raised against him. We only know that the Marcionite church continued to bloom in the second half of the second century and that "synagogues of the Marcionites"[21] and Marcionite churches existed even longer in almost all the large cities of the Roman Empire — to the distress of the Catholic Christians, who still had to wait for Caesar Constantine so that the despised "heretics" could finally be finished off.

Marcion was supposedly in Rome still one more time, where he was offered fellowship with the church under the condition that he "integrate again into the church the others whom he had convinced of his perdition."[22] Marcion purportedly acquiesced before he died. Without doubt, behind this tradition stands hardly anything else than Catholic triumphalism.

A rather important question in this connection is whether Marcion was already a "heretic" when he came to Rome or first began with his "heresy" in Rome. The church fathers attempt to present it as if it was in Rome that Marcion came under the influence of certain Gnostic teachers, Cerdo, the student of Simon, for example, or possibly also the Gnostic Valentinus, who resided in Rome at that time, and in association with them first arrived as his own teaching, which differed from Gnostic teaching above all by its rejection of everything speculative[23]. That is certainly not very probable, especially when one considers that according to a tradition mediated by Irenaeus (after Papias), Polycarp, the bishop from Asia Minor, identified Marcion as the "firstborn of Satan."[24] That allows only the conclusion that Marcion already represented his "heresies," the "two God" teaching and the rejection of the Old Testament, in his pre-Roman phase and so also that the Roman church certainly could not have been entirely ignorant of this teaching when Marcion arrived in Rome. Marcion was certainly not an unknown quantity for them. Then the gift of money that Marcion offered the Roman church first takes on a proper meaning, when one recognizes that Marcion thereby wanted to obtain something *for himself and his teaching*. In this way, Marcion wanted to stir up sympathy for his theology, which he knew very well would not be uncontroversial in Rome. It was doubtless already a tactical maneuver, with which Marcion attempted to scatter sand in the eyes of his (already at hand) critics and to win those who were wavering for himself, to be sure, without success, as we saw. The influence of the Jewish-Christian faction in Rome and their clientele was stronger.

Now it is certainly clear that in later times — at least on the Roman side — people did not want to acknowledge all this. Especially the memory that they had received a Christian teacher with open arms and had accepted money from him must have been painful, if not unbearable, since — seen in retrospect — his heretical tendencies were already generally known. Only after Marcion's Roman publicity campaign miscarried and his (Jewish-Christian) opponents were able to carry out his excommunication did he better understand everything. Now it was clear that the Roman church accepted the 200,000 sestercen so readily only out of ignorance of Marcion's actual character, and that it was not that they perhaps wavered for a while, but that *he* had disguised himself.

Marcionism and Gnosis

With regard to Marcion's theology, this fits together, by and large, with a religious movement in late antiquity referred to as Gnosis. In the opinion of the church fathers, we have to do here with a teaching going back to the Samaritan Simon Magus — according to statements of the church fathers, Marcion's spiritual (grand-)father! (see below) — which we encounter in the entire Mediterranean region from the first century on in differing forms by different representatives. In addition to the Samaritan Simon, for example, Valentinus, the respected "star" among Gnostics at that time, would also be a representative of Gnosis, as well as Cerdo, the disciple of Simon, who resided in Rome at about the same time as Marcion.

A characteristic feature of Gnostic as well as Marcionite teaching would be especially its *dualism*, which certainly finds its radical expression, above all, in Marcion's teaching of two Gods. Like Marcion, Gnostics also make a distinction between the creator God and the foreign, or, as he is usually referred to, the *unknown* God. As with Marcion, contempt for the creator God is connected with ascetic, world-denying, and sometimes also libertine elements. (Slogan: "In order to give the creator God a cold shoulder, we do what we like.") Like the Gnostics, Marcion also struggled with an ancient human problem: the question *Unde malum?* What is the origin of evil? How did suffering come into the world? And he solved this problem in a way similar to theirs, although a simpler way, less complex, and thus also more effective and more popular. He made a clear separation between *creation and the creator God*, on the one side, and the *good God* (who, according to his conception of God, as the "loving God" could not be made responsible for the misery on earth), on the other. It was a neat resolution of the theodicy question, at the cost of the unity of God. We might interpret Marcion to say that the question as to why God allows evil to exist is misplaced, directed to the wrong person. The real God has nothing to do with this world. It is not *he* who allows that, but his subordinated colleague. For the suffering of the world is the responsibility of the one who created it, the Demiurge.

One could say that in his way Marcion popularized Gnosticism and made it a mass movement. That also finds expression in the fact that he reinterpreted the central Gnostic concept of *Gnosis*, i.e., the saving knowledge (*Gnosis* = knowledge), through whose mediation the gnostic person is set free from all earthly ties. Marcion turned the saving knowledge, that is reserved for only a few elite persons with understanding, into the (saving) *faith*: the faith in the gospel of the cross of Christ, through whom the foreign God set humankind free. This message, which Marcion moreover proclaimed in public, not in secret circles like the Gnostics, could be understood by everyone. His immense success showed that Marcion was right.

An aggravating objection can be made to what was just said. It can be said, on the contrary, that this singular conception of faith was not at all the invention of Marcion, but already goes back to Paul, and that in other places as well Marcion links up with Paul again and again.

As a matter of fact, in the presentation of Marcion's teaching, the similarities not only with Gnosis but also with the decisive, fundamental ideas of Pauline theology must be taken into consideration. It is an old debate whether Marcion was more Pauline or more Gnostic. In the same way as for Paul, so also for Marcion the concepts of *law and gospel (of the cross), grace, freedom, faith, redemption* and/or *deliverance* certainly play a central role, whereby the crucial difference only seems to be that the theology of Marcion is dualistically imprinted in a much more powerful way through the teaching of two Gods, so that impression arises that as a student of Paul, Marcion sharply radicalized his theology.

Marcion did in fact represent himself as a student of Paul. It is known that Paul was highly revered in the Marcionite churches, and even had actual religious features. The high position that Paul occupied (next to Marcion) in the Marcionite churches can be explained from the fact that this was Marcion's best authority and security, the firm foundation-stone, from which he could wage the battle against what he perceived as a completely Judaized Roman Catholicism.

We will have to ask later how this came about — how Marcion hit particularly on Paul to ground his teaching through the authority of the apostle, and above all in opposition to all those who (from Rome) relied on Jerusalem, Peter and the Twelve, i.e., in opposition to the Catholic Christians. Above all, we must ask who this Paul was, whom Marcion referred as his authority and regarding whom he and his followers claimed that *he alone* (*solus Paulus*)[25] had been granted the full revelation of God.

Here we would only emphasize that it would obviously not have been sufficient if Marcion had appealed to his own discernment as a basis for his theology. In the circles he addressed that would not have been acceptable. "At that time it was necessary to legitimate the developing church and to appeal to documents that derive from Christ and the apostles. The Gnostic so and so did not release a publication, but he had been inspired by Paul, or Peter, or even words of the Lord himself suddenly spoke from his mouth."[26] In the same way as his opponents, if he wanted to achieve something,

Marcion was dependent on *documents from the apostolic past*, and, indeed, obviously to such an extent that one almost has the feeling that if Marcion had not had the letters of Paul, he plainly would have had to fabricate them.

Marcion's "Discovery"

It would certainly be a waste of time if we attempted to elicit an admission from Marcion as to whether he and/or his coworkers forged the Pauline letters, or at least some of them. We can not expect such a thing—i.e., the admission, not the forgery! —from a such a shrewd theologian and churchman as Marcion. He would hardly have been so naïve as to give away his "kündlich großes Geheimnis" (1 Tim 3:16). Nevertheless, there is a hint that should make us listen very carefully: the Marcionites claimed that their master had found a letter of Paul (the one to the Galatians)! Let's turn our attention for a moment to the following highly interesting passage from Tertullian (AM 4.3):[27] In this passage, Tertullian contests Marcion's claim that the sacramentum (= secret) of the Christian religion began with Luke the Evangelist, who for Marcion was the Evangelist. Tertullian points out that, on the contrary, already before Luke there was an authoritative testimony (i.e., going back to the apostles) through which Luke himself first became a believer. Nevertheless, Tertullian continues, Marcion stumbled upon the letter of Paul to the Galatians, in which he vilifies even the apostles for not walking in accordance the truth of the gospel, etc.: *Sedenim Marcion* **nactus** *epistolam Pauli as Galatas...* ("But now, since Marcion discovered the letter of Paul to the Galatians..."). *Nancisci* means "to attain by accident" (e.g., a suitable harbor: *idoneum portum*). Tertullian clearly seems to allude here to the claim by the Marcionites, or Marcion himself, that Marcion had accidentally and fortunately "discovered" the letter of Paul to the Galatians.

As we otherwise know from the history of pseudepigraphy and literary forgery, the publication of such writings, as a rule, tends to be preceded by their "discovery."[28] Some uncertainty remains, however, since from the concept nancisci it is not entirely clear whether the reference is to the discovery of something that was already at hand, which Marcion did not know about until then.

Mouse from Pontus – or Catholic Redactor?

Now comes, to be sure, still a further observation which in fact provides the strongest support for the suspicion that, in addition to the collection of the Pauline letters, Marcion and his circle could have also participated in their origin. It has to do with the form of the canonical and Marcionite texts of the Pauline letters, i.e., the field of literary- and textual criticism.

According to the prevailing conception even today, the form of the Marcionite text represents a version of the original, canonical text that had been abbreviated by Marcion. For his own purposes, on the basis of definite theological interests, the mouse from Pontus (the *Mus Ponticus, A.M. 1.1*), as Tertullian maliciously referred to Marcion, simply "nibbled away" textual passages he didn't like and made numerous abbreviations and changes.

Of course, this accusation against Marcion raised up by the church fathers, which seems to be repeated with reference to the Gospel of Luke being supposedly adulterated by Marcion, has not remained uncontested by scholarship in the past. One could not ignore the fact that in the early church not only did the Catholics make the charge of textual adulteration against Marcion, but, *vice versa*, the Marcionites also made the same charge against the Catholics. Tertullian likened the debate between Catholics and Marcionites to a *tug-*

of-war, in which both he and Marcion tested their strength and "with the same exertion pull back and forth. I say I have the truth. Marcion says he has it. I say that Marcion's is falsified; Marcion says the same about mine."[29]

With regard to the *Gospel of Luke*, The theologians A. Ritschl and F. C. Baur first contradicted the church fathers and advocated an *UrLuke theory*, i.e., the assumption that Marcion had been in possession of a more original edition of the Gospel of Luke than the (Catholic) church. Then this assumption must have soon retreated again — partly for good reasons, which do not need to be presented here in detail[30].

With regard to the *Pauline letters*, for which the problems are constituted somewhat differently, the theologian Adolf Hilgenfeld made the attempt to largely unburden Marcion from the suspicion of having consciously falsified the text[31]. A decisive step beyond Hilgenfeld and Harnack, who was walking in a similar path, was taken by the Dutch New Testament scholar W. C. van Manen, who for the first time carried out a fundamental textual and literary investigation of the letter to the Galatians to examine the possibility that the Catholic church tendentiously reworked the Pauline letters, in which case the briefer Marcionite version would be the more original.[32] The result of his investigation by and large confirmed this suspicion very impressively.[33]

Even if it is objected that from the priority of the Marcionite readings over the canonical one cannot draw direct consequences for a decision regarding the authenticity of the letters, it must nevertheless be said in general that the thesis that with Pauline writings we have to do entirely with a product *fictae ad haresem Marcionis*[34], i.e., pseudepigraphic writings from the school of Marcion, receives an important foundation which elevates it from the sphere of pure conjecture to the level of the (textually) palpable. A more detailed investigation shows that consideration of textual and literary-critical problems can frequently produce important insights regarding the historical and theological (namely, Marcionite) perspective of the author as well as historical situation of the particular letter's origin, which then, in return, has direct consequences for resolving the question of authenticity.

Paul as an Apostle of Circumcision

A striking piece of evidence for the fact that the Pauline letters were reworked from a Catholic perspective is Gal 2:5, where the author of Galatians speaks of the apostle's visit in Jerusalem:

> But not even Titus, who was with me, being a Greek, was compelled to be circumcised. But on account of the false brethren secretly brought in, who slipped in to spy out our freedom which we have in Christ Jesus, so that they might enslave us... to whom we did [not] yield submission for a moment, that the truth of the gospel might be preserved with you.

While in the Marcionite text of 2:5 there is a "not," this is missing in texts of most of the Catholic church fathers. In their view, Paul gave in to the Jewish-Christian "false brethren" (who obviously required circumcision).

In spite of Tertullian's complicated argument, there can be no doubt, and it is generally recognized today, that the Marcionite text cited by Tertullian represents the original reading. The majority of textual witnesses—all the Greek manuscripts, for example, and the Syriac translation—have a "not" at this place.

The omission of the small but crucial word, through which the uncompromising radical of the original text is unawares turned into a compliant pacifier, who for the sake of peace practices circumcision, makes it clear beyond doubt that the text in fact has been tendentiously reworked *from the Catholic perspective*, which in this case served to set aside the differences which existed between Paul and the rest of the apostles with regard to circumcision. In so doing, the Catholic redactor oriented himself on the picture of the conciliatory and compliant pragmatic figure in Acts, who could also calmly look the other way when the issue had to do with placating the somewhat difficult Jewish-Christian brothers:

> Paul wanted Timothy to accompany him; and he took and circumcised him because of the Jews that were in those places, for they all knew that his father was a Greek.

The give and take in the textual tradition shows what often enough remains unobserved or simply denied, namely, that the controversy between Catholics and Marcionites regarding the correct picture of Paul had the utmost relevance for the presentation of the historical course of early Christian events in the theological discussion of the second century. The issue here had to do not with questions concerning the past, but concerning the present, with the question of which party had the greater right to appeal to Paul for their theology. As the example shows, the temptation existed for both sides to resolve the controversy not only by theological discussion and their own writing of church history (Acts), but through massive intervention in the textual form of the Pauline writings. Thereby, however, the temptation also existed to actually produce documents which could be appealed to in defense of their own point of view.

An Initial Visit with the Pope – An Interpolated Trip to Rome

What we have said regarding the significance of the Pauline letters in the confessional disputes between Catholics and

Marcionites in the second century can be illustrated in an exemplary way by the following central passage from the letter to the Galatians. In Gal 1:15ff. the author speaks of the time following his call to apostleship:

> But when he who had set me apart from my mother's womb, and had called me through his grace, was pleased to reveal his Son in me, in order that I might preach him among the Gentiles, immediately I did not confer with flesh and blood, nor did I go up to Jerusalem to those <u>who were apostles before me</u>, but I went away into Arabia; and again I returned to Damascus. Then after three years I went up to Jerusalem to become acquainted with Cephas, and remained with him fifteen days. But I saw none of the other apostles, except James the brother of the Lord. (In what I am writing to you, before God, I do not lie!) *Then I went into the regions of Syria and Cilicia. And I was still not known by sight to the churches of Christ in Judea. They only heard it said, "He who once persecuted us is now preaching the faith he once tried to destroy." And they glorified God because of me.* Then after fourteen years I went up again to Jerusalem with Barnabas, taking Titus with me also. I went up according to a revelation (kata apokalypsin). And I laid before <u>them</u> the gospel which I preach among the Gentiles (and privately before those of repute), lest somehow I should be running in vain, or had run.

As can be seen from Tertullian,[35] who cites Marcion's text, in which only one visit by Paul in Jerusalem is mentioned, the verses in italics seem to have been missing.

Whoever wants to be convinced that the text was *expanded by Catholics* and not shortened by Marcionites only has to take notice of the (underlined) pronoun "them" in 2:2, which in the present context has no clear reference. One must go back to 1:17 to understand that the reference here is obviously to *those who apostles before me*. All attempts to relate the little word to Jerusalem (Schlier), because "according to a well-known use of the pronoun, the residents of a previously mentioned city" could be mentioned in the plural, are not convincing, since Paul hardly laid his gospel before *all the residents* of Jerusalem, but only the leaders of the Jerusalem church.[36]

1. The text in italics thus turns out to be a later interpolation.
2. because the Greek word for "to become acquainted" in 1:18 appears nowhere else in the Pauline letters;
3. the formula *before God, I do not lie* is highly suspicious and otherwise also only appears where one must suspect an insertion (Rom 9:1; 2 Cor 11:31);
4. because after the affirmation by the writer that following his conversion he *did not go immediately* to Jerusalem one would expect a longer period of time than just three years! The reference to *fourteen years* in 2:1 is much more plausible as a continuation from 1:17.
5. Apart from that, one should consider what Bruno Bauer already observed: "If he [Paul] spends fifteen days in Jerusalem, visits with Peter and James, and the presence of the other apostles in the holy city was something entirely taken for granted, as he shows by his oath, it would have been impossible for him not to see them."[37]

How should one explain the insertion? — Obviously, the section reflects a refined attempt to closely connect Paul, whom the Marcionites appeal to, with Cephas-Peter, the leader of the Jerusalem party, whom people in Rome appeal to, and indeed as soon as possible after his conversion, which is clearly interpreted not at all as his own revelation, but only as a *sign by God* that he should go to Jerusalem (as in Acts: see above ⇒ *Two Pauls*).

In other words, *the insertion functions to remove sovereignty from Paul and make him dependent on Jerusalem.* The letter to the Galatians, in whose introduction it is explicitly said that

Paul is an apostle called by God, and indeed "not by men nor through a man," and in which his independence from Jerusalem continues to be emphasized, has been reworked on the basis of the Catholic Acts of the Apostles. The tendency is the same: Paul had *no revelation of his own* (as the Marcionites claim with their *solus Paulus*), but had been with the apostles, or at least Peter. As a representative of the Jerusalem church, *Peter* (and not God) instructed him.[38] Two weeks is a long time. Consequently, the Marcionites could not appeal to Paul (*"solus Paulus"*)! Because they have no independent revelation, they have no right to be an independent Church! As Paul was dependent on Jerusalem, so also they are dependent on Rome (the legitimate follower of the Jerusalem church)! There can be no true Christian without Rome's blessing!

To make this clear was not an easy task for the Catholic redactor, but also not entirely hopeless, since the period of time between Paul's conversion and his first visit in Jerusalem had not been precisely set forth in Acts. Acts 9:23 speaks only of "many days." Now it was certainly impossible to understand this as referring to the fourteen years spoken of in Gal 2:1, nor was it possible to place the journey to Jerusalem all too soon after the conversion, since in Gal 1:16 it is explicitly said that Paul did *not immediately* establish a connection with those who were apostles before him. As between Scylla and Charybdis, the redactor decided for a period of three years, perhaps believing thereby to conform somewhat with Luke's reference to "many days" as well as not to expressly contradict the emphatic assertion in Gal 1:17 that Paul did *not immediately* establish a connection with those in Jerusalem (which he would have done had he taken over the Lukan formulation).

As an objection to the explanation advanced above, one could ask why the redactor emphasizes with great force that in Jerusalem Paul saw *only* Peter and James, when his own interest consisted precisely in connecting Paul as closely as possible with the apostles in Jerusalem? The explanation for this is very simple, if one keeps before his eyes the difficult task that the redactor faced:

In Gal 1:17 Paul expressly denies that following his conversion he made contact with those who were apostles before him. The redactor could have deleted this sentence – or reinterpreted it. As a skillful redactor, who wanted not to write a new text, but rather to modify the existing text, he chose the latter alternative. Therefore, he interpreted 1:17 so that although Paul did see Peter and James, he saw none of the other apostles. This concession was necessary because of the context. This splitting apart, of course, was a rather artificial construction (as Bruno Bauer already saw: had the other apostles then just left on a journey? Did Paul then intentionally avoid them?), but in this way Paul was nevertheless connected with the Jerusalem tradition. Paul had seen Peter and James and was together with Peter for fourteen days! That should suffice to provide proof (for the Marcionites) that the Paul of Galatians, like the Paul in Acts, received no independent revelation.

The Pauline Christ as Son of David

The letter to the Romans begins:

> Paul, a servant of Jesus Christ, called to be an apostle, set apart for the gospel of God *which he promised beforehand through his prophets in the holy scriptures, (namely) the gospel concerning his Son, who was descended from David according to the flesh and designated Son of God in power according to the Spirit of holiness by his resurrection from the dead, Jesus Christ our Lord, through whom we have received grace and apostleship to bring about the obedience of faith for the sake of his name among all the nations, including yourselves who are called to belong to Jesus Christ;* To all God's beloved in Rome, who are called to be saints...

That the prologue to the letter to the Romans seems heavily over-burdened has been noted by many interpreters. This is generally explained today by a citation-theory: At this point the author of the letter, i.e., Paul, cites a formula deriving from tradition.[39] This explains the related overburdening of the entire sentence as well as the eventual presence of tensions in content.

In view of the fact that the citation-theory seems very suitable for explaining the inner contradictions and inconsistencies in the Pauline letters, it is not surprising that it enjoys great popularity today and that New Testament scholars are widely occupied with scouring the Pauline letters for traditions and ferreting out creedal formulas, confessions, hymns, and the like. This tradition-historical orientation has meanwhile even effected the textual structure in newer editions of the Greek New Testament. If today one opens the "Nestle-Aland" (27th edition), one often has the impression, in view of the hymns, creedal formulas, etc., set off and distinguished in print from the rest of the text, that instead of the text of the New Testament, we are reading an operatic libretto.

The attractiveness of the citation-theory is obvious: whoever is of the opinion that the apostle cites tradition can in addition perceive the Pauline letters as by and large a literary unity — and one has no need to concern oneself with the spiritual and mental state of the apostle if he writes this at one time and immediately thereafter the opposite, because one nevertheless knows for certain that at this point the apostle is only quoting.

If one does not want to impute to the self-contradicting apostle a total inability to logically discriminate, the alternative to the citation-theory is the interpolation-theory. With this theory one must assume that passages which, for whatever reasons, are not suitable for the present context or contradict the content of the context do not derive from Paul, but were worked into the text by a later redactor.

It is obvious that this theory has little appeal for many theologians. The picture of the Christian Church would now be quite different, not a confessing, singing, and dancing community, but a quarreling, interpolating, and falsifying community, which seeks to be in the right even if it is contrary to the original author of the holy text. Whoever interpolates wants to cut off the first author of a text, to undertake dogmatic improvements, to stamp the text with his signature — against the author.

All this does not fit the conception of many present-day theologians, particularly those who want to know nothing about conflicts and tensions in early Christianity and instead, in a catholicizing manner, conjure up an apostolic idyll of undisturbed harmony and unity at the beginning of church history. Instead of ominous interpolations they prefer sympathetic, church-friendly citation-theories.

Now, to be sure, even the citation-theory consists not of bright light alone, but also has some dark, shadowy sides — at least for the thinking mind. How is it possible, one asks oneself with great wonder, that the apostle, who came over to the Christian church only a few years after the death of Jesus, could already reach back to such an abundant reservoir of confessional formulas, hymns, and other traditional materials? How could these traditions originate at all in the brief time that the conventional way of looking at early Christian history allows us?

Let's be clear. If Paul's conversion took place around 31/32-35 and the death of Jesus was in 30, and if we must further assume that Paul already knew about the Christians prior to his conversion, since he persecuted them, one must also assume that Paul was familiar with them from their first beginnings on — so can one speak at all of a "pre-Pauline" tradition? But even if one assumes that Paul first came into continuing contact with the earliest church and its Hellenistic branch in Antioch only shortly before the Apostolic Council (c. 48 CE), these churches, which in the opinion of some theologians perhaps first existed only since 40 CE,[40] had scarcely more than ten or fifteen years for the development of traditions which arose independently of Paul's influence. It should be evident to everyone that this time period is hardly sufficient to produce the wealth of fixed creedal formulas and confessions, as well as poems and hymns, which New Testament scholarship today claims to have discovered.

Of course, the observation that the author of the Pauline writings now and then employs citations, and thus makes use of Christian tradition, need not be entirely false. But then one should be clear about the difficulties which arise from this observation and, in such a case, draw the consequences. The only possible and sensible consequence is the recognition that the period of time between the author of the Pauline letters and the earliest Christian church was obviously substantially greater than we previously thought on the basis of our preconceived historical picture.

The existence of established traditions in the Corpus Paulinum thus represents one of the most important arguments for a later time of origin for the Pauline letters.

We would certainly point out, however, that in no way must everything be tradition that is regarded as such today, and that, on the contrary, in many cases we must reckon with the possibility of interpolation. That will certainly always be the case where the contradictions and tensions between the suspicious fragment and the rest of the text are so strong that a use of tradition seems to be excluded, since the author would then have contradicted himself, or interrupted himself. Even if what the author cites need not always be in harmony with his own perspective, one should nevertheless expect, at least where it clearly contradicts him, that he would provide further clarification, commentary, and elaboration. In a great many fragments, however, where present-day theologians see a citation by Paul, an appropriation of tradition, that is not the case at all.

We would like to illustrate this with the prologue from the letter to the Romans cited above:

Scholars today generally begin with the assumption that in Romans 1:3-4 we have to do with a "pre-Pauline" formula. Above all, the "discrepancy between the preexistence-christology of Paul... and the adoptionist christology" is perceived as an "especially clear indication" for this.[41] While in other places in the letter, in a similar way as in the Gospel of John, the Sending of the Son (incarnation-christology) is spoken of (Rom 8:3; cf. Gal 4:4), in Rom 1:4 the writer represents the idea that Christ was first designated Son of God through the resurrection. In itself, one would think that the two different conceptions totally exclude one another, since only one or the other can be correct: either Christ was already the Son of God at the time he became man, or he first became Son of God through the resurrection.

Nevertheless, as a rule, most theologians have no difficulties assuming, with help from their citation-theory, that what logically does not belong together could already be unified by the author of the letter to the Romans (Paul). For Schmithals, by citing the formula, Paul "expresses with deliberation that he recognizes the adoptionist formula as an expression of the common Christian confession: the differences that are evident in the various christological sketches do not harm the unity of the gospel but vary the unchanging kerygma with regard to the horizon of understanding of the respective hearers and in different times and cultures."[42] The Catholic theologian Otto Kuss expresses himself in a sense similar to Schmithals. Kuss speaks in this context of an "archaic" formula and declares: "It must be taken into account, therefore, that Paul is indebted to preceding preaching for this formulation... He obviously regards it important to demonstrate his 'orthodoxy' by an emphatic connection with the tradition of the church in Rome that is unknown to him."[43] Now, in this context the concept "archaic" is certainly very peculiar, especially for a Catholic theologian used to thinking in large historical time-frames. What does "archaic" mean in view of the fact that, according to Kuss, Paul wrote the letter to the Romans in the time between fifty and sixty CE, that the church had existed for perhaps twenty years, and that the formula therefore can be at most only twenty years (!) "old"?

Without doubt, given the presupposition that we imagine Paul to be already a churchman schooled in Catholic both-and theology, who, as is implied by the Catholic interpolation in 1 Cor 9:20ff., became "all things to all people," it would not be impossible that Paul used the adoptionist formula as an expression of the common christological confession, or in order to demonstrate his orthodoxy; but one would not believe the unbending radical, who in Galatians curses everyone who preaches a gospel different from his own (Gal 1:8), capable of such a thing.

There are also other considerations that strongly support the suspicion that in the entire fragment we have to do not with a citation by Paul, but with an interpolation by a later redactor, who wanted to make the theology of the original letter accord with his own.

The interest of the writer in the Davidic descent of his Christ is peculiar, if one considers that in 2 Corinthians the same writer (= "Paul") declares very clearly his total lack of interest in "Christ according to the flesh" (2 Cor 5:16):

From now on, therefore, we regard no one according to the flesh; even if we once regarded Christ according to the flesh, we regard him thus no longer.

The plural in 1:5 — "through whom we have received grace and apostleship" — does not agree with the singular in 1:1 and could be connected with the tendency of the redactor, that we already saw above, to exclude a special revelation to Paul (which was claimed by the Marcionites) and to incorporate him into the succession of the twelve; Verse 1:1 anticipates 1:7 and shows very clearly that the person who wrote this already knew what stood in the following verse. "If he was free to do so, he would have taken care to provide a better transition to verse 7 and would not have spoken of "being called holy" right after his "including yourselves, who are called..."44

All this shows very clearly that no citation is present in Romans 1:3-4, but that a redactor is at work, and indeed it is again our already familiar (Proto-)Catholic interpolator, who this time again takes the opportunity at the very beginning of the "letter" to the Romans to clarify a fundamental dogmatic position regarding which he believed the original (Marcionite) author of the letter to be dubious:

- The gospel preached by Paul was promised beforehand through the prophets in the holy scriptures. *The Old Testament has not lost its importance.*
- Paul received the revelation together with the other apostles ("we" in 1:5); there is no separate Pauline-Marcionite revelation and *no separate church.*
- Even Paul could teach the *adoptionist christology* common in Jewish circles an
- the Davidic sonship of Christ.

His letters, therefore, present no obstacle to an ecumenical fellowship of catholicized Marcionites and catholicized

Jewish Christians. Each may retain their favorite christological conception. Both may dwell under a common Catholic roof.

Paul teaches a Christ with only an apparent body – Paul as Docetist

Once one has become aware of the numerous Catholic insertions in the Pauline letters, and, on the other hand, also the many Marcionite elements in the theology of the original "Paul," one can find, even in the reworked canonical text, a series of concepts and ideas that can only be meaningfully understood in the context of the Marcionite system. This has been referred to as the point of contact that Marcion found in Paul.[45] In truth, however, we have to do here not with a point of contact, but in a certain sense with Marcionite bedrock, that again and again shines through from beneath the Catholic grass that grows upon it. This Marcionite bedrock certainly includes a docetic christology, i.e., the idea, deriving from Gnosticism and present in the Pauline letters, that Jesus was not a real man of flesh and blood, but only had an apparent body (phantasma).

That finds expression, for example, in the peculiar formulation in Romans 8:3, where the writer says about Christ that (in his earthly life) he came "in a form that resembled sinful flesh":

> For (in order to do) what the law, weakened by the flesh, could not do, God sent his own *Son in a form that resembled sinful flesh*, and for sin, and condemned Sin in the flesh.

In a corresponding way, in the Christ-hymn in Phil 2:7 it is said of Christ Jesus, though he was in the form of God, he did not regard it as robbery to be equal with God, but emptied himself, taking the form of a slave, "becoming a likeness of men" (en homoiōmati anthrōpōn genomenos), and "being found in appearance like a man" (schēmati heuretheis ōs anthrōpos).

Why does Paul not simply say that God sent his Son in the flesh? How does Paul, who presumably stands on the creation-friendly ground of Judaism, arrive at such a strange connection between flesh and sin? Why did the Son not become man, but only like a man? Why was he found "in appearance as a man" and not simply "as man"? There is a simple explanation for this: the author of the cited text was most probably not at all Paul the Jew, but rather the docetic Marcion, or one of his students (or teachers?), writing in the name of the apostle. Did not Marcion say that "our Lord [was found]... as a man in form and appearance and likeness, but without our body"?[46]

One has the impression that the terminology which the author of Romans and Philippians employs in these passages was chosen consciously and with great care—presumably to express his opposition to other christological views of his time (those of the Catholic and Jewish Christians).

This also accords with the fact that in 2 Corinthians Paul explicitly describes a knowledge of Christ "according to the flesh" as an entirely false knowledge:

> From now on, therefore, we know no one according to the flesh; even if we once knew Christ according to the flesh, we know him thus no longer.

For the Marcionite author, the knowledge of Jesus "according to the flesh" must naturally also be incomplete and temporary because such a Christ was appealed to in Rome. It had long since been recognized there, with a definite trace of power being at stake, that a religion that wants to assert itself cannot be grounded on some kind of nebulous entity (e.g., the Spirit), but on something solid and positive: history, tradition, etc.

Paul and the teaching of two Gods

The Marcionite bedrock includes, in addition, language concerning the "aeon of this world" (2 Cor 4:4, Eph 6:12), the "ruler of the power in the air" (Eph 2:2), whereby no one else is meant than the Gnostic Demiurge and his subordinate angelic powers (Col 2:15, Rom 8:38f.; also referred to as stoicheia, Gal 4:3, 9; Col 2:8, 20), i.e., the creator of the world, who according to dualistic-Gnostic thought is responsible for the creation of the evil, material world and who stands in opposition to the so-called foreign God, who through Christ wants to free humankind from their entanglement with the material world and their subjugation to the law.

1) A well-known, "notorious" textual modification by Marcion would be the deletion of the tiny word "in" in Ephesians 3:9:

> To me, though I am the very least of all the saints, this grace was given, to preach to the Gentiles the unsearchable riches of Christ, and to make all people see what is the plan of the mystery hidden for ages [in] God who created all things.

Here Marcion supposedly adapted the original conception of the hiddenness of the secret in God to his own two-God theology by simply omitting the little word "in." Thereby an entirely new, Marcionite meaning of Eph 3:9 results, because the secret is no longer hidden in God, but rather hidden from the God who created all things. In this way, Marcion is supposed to have expressed the idea that the salvation work of the redeemer God remained hidden from the Demiurge, since for Marcion he alone could be the "God who created all things."[47]

Here also the shoe should be on the other foot! Marcion had no need at all to introduce the conception of the Demiurge through the textual modification attributed to him in Eph 3:9, since the text before him very probably contained the original wording. It was the *Catholic redactor* who twisted the point of the sentence by inserting an "in" and thus blotted out the conception of a Demiurge so unbearable for Catholic thought — at the cost, to be sure, of the intelligibility of the now totally obscure statement. For anyone who tries to understand the meaning of this peculiar combination of words, the meaning of the "secret in God" will forever remain a mystery, while the Marcionite text, on the other hand, is very understandable.

2) If Marcion, furthermore, perceived the "angels and powers" (Rom 8:38), who are no longer able to separate Christians from the love of God in Christ Jesus, as the *angelic powers* of the creator of the world, he would than also certainly have found therein the original Marcionite meaning of the statement with its negative, even typically Gnostic-Marcionite qualification of the angelic powers so difficult for Jewish-Christian thought to accept.

3) Again, the same thing holds for the "elements of the world" (= *stoicheia*, Gal 4:3, 9; Col 2:8, 20) and the "principalities and powers" (Col 2:15), but also the angels concerning which the writer of 1 Corinthians warns the women in the church (1 Cor 11:10).

In this connection, typical Marcionite conceptions also include the idea of the *hidden work of the Redeemer*, who, unknown to the Demiurge and his powers, suffered death on a cross and thus redeemed humankind from their power. Accordingly, in 1 Cor 2:8 it says that the rulers of this world would not have crucified the Lord of Glory if they had known who he was:

> But we impart a secret and hidden wisdom of God, which God decreed before the ages for our glorification. None of the rulers of this age recognized this; for if they had, they would not have crucified the Lord of Glory.

According to Marcionite understanding, not recognizing the doxa ("glory") of Christ was the presupposition for the success of the work of salvation, whose fulfillment would bring about the downfall of the God of justice by means of his own righteousness. Since the creator of the world and the powers installed by him (there are therefore no political powers in view) did not recognize Christ and allowed him, although innocent, to be condemned to death, on account of their own ignorance they are delivered up to their own unrighteousness and imperfection. Although Christ had the power to destroy them, he gave them his blood as a ransom, so as to redeem humankind from their power. – Cf. Marcion's doctrine as related by Yeznik of Kolb (387-450 CE):

> They [Marcionites] say that the Unknown God, the God of Love, who was in the first heaven, was hurt by seeing so many souls suffering at the hands of the two imposters: Matter and the Lord of Creation. Therefore, the Unknown God sent His Son to work miracles and cure the blind and foresaw that men would be jealous and crucify him. He also knew that once crucified and buried as mortal, His Son would descend into Hell and empty it by freeing the souls which had been cast there by the Lord of the Laws and Creation.
>
> And indeed, after the Son was crucified, he descended into Hell and freed the captive souls and took them to heaven with His Father, the God of Love. Thereupon, the Lord of Creation grew angry and darkened the skies and dressed the world in black.
>
> The second time Jesus descended in the form of God, he opened a case against the Lord of Creation for having put him to death. When the Lord of Creation saw the Godliness of Jesus, he knew that there was a God higher than himself. Jesus leveled his charges against the Lord of Creation and

demanded that the Laws which the Lord of Creation had written be the judge in their case.

When he placed the Laws between them, Jesus asked, „Did you not write, 'And who ever kills, shall die and who ever spills the blood of the righteous, his blood shall be spilled.'?" After the Lord of Creation acknowledged that he had written them, Jesus demanded that he surrender himself to be punished by death. Then Jesus added, „I have been more just than you to your creations," and he began to list the kindnesses he had done them. Seeing that he had been condemned by his own laws for killing Jesus, the Lord of Creation pleaded that he had killed Jesus unknowingly and offered in retribution to give Jesus all those who believe in him to take where he pleased. After Jesus left the Lord of Creation, he appeared to Paul. He revealed to his apostle the compensation, and thereafter, Paul preached that Jesus „redeemed us for a price." This, then, is the basis of Marcion's doctrine as we have come to know it.[48]

4) In Rom 5:6-8 *the righteous one* and *the good one* are antithetically set one against the other:

While we were still weak, at the right time Christ died for the ungodly. Why, one will hardly die for a *righteous one* (dikaios) – though perhaps for a *good one* (agathos) one will dare even to die. But God shows his love for us in that while we were yet sinners Christ died for us.

Whereas for the *dikaios* one will scarcely die, yet for a good one some would even dare to die. Normally the two terms are thought to refer to the (good or righteous) man. The tortuous explanations of the exegetes are rather senseless, though. That is why we should ask whether perhaps the Marcionites who, as we learn from Origen, appealed to this text, were absolutely right when they understood the good one and the righteous one as their Two Gods:

Moreover the error is exposed of those who imagined that this passage is to be interpreted in the way they allege, that what

[Paul] says, 'For rarely will anyone die for the just,' ought to be understood of the god of the law, whom they affirm is just but not good as well. They would however affirm that Christ is good, as if being the son of a good Father. But what will they do about the fact that we find many martyrs even under the law? ... [49]

5) That Christ gave up his blood to the Demiurge and his powers as a ransom was obviously not first fully formulated in words by the Marcionites, but by "Paul": see Gal 2:21, a passage that in English can be translated as follows:

> I do not spurn the grace of God [like my opponents]; for if righteousness came through the law, then Christ indeed died in vain!

The meaning of the "in vain" only becomes fully understandable if one recognizes that in the original Greek (= dōrean) we have to do here with an expression from the language of business, which literally must be translated "without any (service in) return" (cf. 2 Cor 11:7): "For if righteousness came through the law, then Christ indeed died without any return." The return that the law-giving God exchanged for the blood of Christ is that humankind was released from the dominion of his law (Yesnik's "retribution to give Jesus all those who believe in him.").

Paul — the Domesticated Marcion

For all the passages we have discussed (which only represents a small selection; more can be found in my book Paulusbriefe ohne Paulus?) it becomes clear that the Marcionism of the Pauline letters can be ascertained not only terminologically for individual Marcionite sounding words appearing here and there, but resides deep in the system of "Pauline" theology itself. The Pauline teaching about redemption, with its idea of ransom, originally presupposes a dualistic system of thought. One must ask: from where does Christ ransom humankind? From the law, which as "almost a foreign power, standing in only a loose connection with God, is all but personally conceived,"[50] or, which would be most probable, from the "world rulers" (= stoicheia) as the originators of the law (Gal 4:2-3) and so also from their highest commander, the Demiurge.

Without doubt, the original Pauline-Marcionite soteriology (teaching about redemption) is often distorted beyond recognition by Catholic reworking. The obscurity and vagueness of the Pauline doctrine of redemption arose from the fact that the soteriological ideas (relating to the teaching about redemption), originally conceived for a dualistic system and only really meaningful and understandable in this context, were translated by Catholic, Jewish-Christian reworking into a monistic, or monotheistic, system, and moreover united with additional soteriological motifs (the theory of a sacrifice for sin). Its dark secret is truly a "secret in God," with its overflow of motifs, which are incompatible with one another, allusions to ideas not completely thought-out — and which only can be thought-out at the price of heresy.

All in all, it may have become clear, in any case, that the author of the Pauline letters could hardly have been a Jew, not even a Diaspora Jew alienated from the religion of his fathers, but could only have been a Marcionite, or perhaps Marcion (and/or one/some of his students). In many cited passages what elsewhere has been skillfully retouched, corrected, and eliminated through Catholic redaction of the Pauline letters is glaringly evident: the subliminal defamation of the Jewish God, the Creator and Law-giver, by no one other than "Paul," i.e., the original, Marcionite Paul himself.

The passages provide further support for the thesis that Marcion had in no way been a radical student of Paul, but that "Paul" was rather a domesticated (most extensively by Catholic reworking) child of Marcionism, in which the witness to his spiritual origin is still entirely evident. In short: *Marcion is not the radical Paul*, whom until today scholarship holds him to be, *but "Paul" is rather a diminished Marcion* (i.e., catholicized, tied to the Catholic dogma of the *one* God who is both Creator and Redeemer).

Paul – the non-Jew

Corresponding with our thesis that the Pauline letters originally derived from Marcionite circles (which would mean, first of all, Gentile Christian circles) is the observation that the actual writer of the letters (as well as the redactor) again and again expresses himself in ways that lead to the conclusion that—contrary to the claim he himself advances—he is not at all a Jew by birth.[51]

Above all in Romans and the two Corinthian letters it can be shown that the author thinks and writes not from a Jewish consciousness, but from that of a non-Jew. For example, while a faithful Jew (similar to a Muslim today) divides the world into believers and non-believers (= *Goyim*), the author of Romans distinguishes in a good Greek way between *Greeks and barbarians* (Rom 1:14). The concept of a barbarian has a genuine Greek tone, and would have a peculiar ring even in the mouth of a supposedly Diaspora Jew from Tarsus.

In other places as well, one does not exactly get the impression that the author of Romans writes like someone who was raised in Judaism and is familiar with the its customs and practices (1:16; 10:12; 2:9-10; 3:9; 2:17; 2:28, 29; 3:1; 3:29).

Rom 3:9 is especially peculiar, where Paul asks the question: *ti oun; proechometha;* which is usually translated as "What then? Do we have an advantage?" The idea then is that at this point Paul wanted to ask whether Jews, whose advantages he has just discussed at length, have an advantage over the Gentiles because of these prerogatives: "What then, do we [Jews] have an advantage?" (cf. the English RSV). Literally, however, the text says something different: Not "Do we have an advantage?" (active), but, "Are we surpassed?" (passive).

Although this is the only grammatically correct translation, it is not found in present-day editions of the Bible only because it cannot be reconciled with the assumption that the person who wrote this was a Jew. It would presuppose that the writer of this passage was a Greek, or at least a non-Jew, who from such an awareness writes: "What then? Are we [non-Jews] surpassed [by the Jews, whose prerogatives were just discussed in vv. 1-2]?"

The writer of this passage had forgotten for a moment that, according to universal tradition, the person in whose name the letter is written is supposed to be a Jew by birth. If one understands that, the text immediately becomes clear. One need not regard it as corrupted, as many exegetes do; one does not need to give the words any other meaning than they grammatically acquire.[52]

In the Corinthians letters as well one can find tell-tale indications of the real origin of the author. Of course, here also the author appears as a Jew (2 Cor 11:22); but the emphatic way he does this, to be sure, is already somewhat suspicious. In any case, in 1 Cor 14:11 the writer again uses the term "barbarian" in a typical Greek way. In 1 Cor 9:12 Paul the Jew says that "to Jews I became as a Jew." One asks with wonder why he must first *become* what he has already been for a long time!

1 Cor 11:4 is also very remarkable, where Paul instructs the men not to pray with their heads covered, since this is a disgrace:

> Any man who prays or prophecies with his head covered dishonors his head.

If one recalls that even until today Jewish men are obligated wear a head-covering in their worship service, one can perceive this instruction only as an indication that the author of this letter certainly could not have been raised in the Jewish tradition. Alan F. Segal: "Jewish men wore prayer shawls in Paul's time (Mark 12:38). The tallit is the ritual garb that grew out of the command of the third paragraph of the Shema, which demanded the wearing of fringed garments (Deut. 6; see also Num. 15:37-41). Although the ritual of wrapping oneself in the tallit for prayer is ancient, a specific ritual garment developed only later, because in this period many Jews ordinarily wore a tallit or fringed garment, which distinguished them from gentiles ... The custom of wrapping oneself in the tallit, including veiling one's head with it, could itself have been the forerunner of head coverings (kippot) (b. Menachot 39b; b. Baba Batra 98a; especially b. Rosh Hashanah 17b), as piety provided that a tallit could be used to wrap or veil the head. Veiling the head with the prayer shawl is a sign of the holiness of Torah reading, and it is an impressive aspect of orthodox services even today. Some strictly observant Jews always put the prayer shawl over their heads. It might reflect the ritual preparation necessary for divine encounters among Jewish Christian mystics. The context of Paul's polemic can imply that the leaders of the opponents veiled themselves or that the entire opponent community did."[53]

I think, if Paul had really been a "radical Jew" (Daniel Boyarin)[54] and the disciple of Gamaliel, he would have at least paused for a moment here and attempted to justify his regulation. Instead, he connects here with Greek practice: "The free Greek man does not cover his head; he only covers his head in circumstances of great sorrow."[55]

As the citation from the Greek poet Menander (1 Cor 15:33) shows, the author of the Corinthian letter is very familiar with Greek literature. One might believe this could also be true for Paul the Jew. It is nevertheless strange that the Paul who supposedly studied with Rabbi Gamaliel obviously had difficulty with the Hebrew language and was not able to read the Hebrew Bible in the original language, but instead always used the Greek translation (Septuagint), and even a version having a close relationship with an edition first originating in the second century (Theodotion).[56]

In the margin, it should finally be noted that the following anti-Pauline tradition was supposedly circulating in Jewish-Christian Ebionite churches. Epiphanius knows an Ebionite *Acts of the Apostles* in which he says he found many errors, and in which Paul was characterized as a false apostle. Paul was said to have been born in Tarsus *from Gentile parents*, and accepted circumcision in Jerusalem in order to marry the daughter of the High Priest. After the marriage unraveled, he polemicized against circumcision, the Sabbath, and the law:

> Nor are they (Ebionites) ashamed to accuse Paul here with certain false inventions of their false apostles' villainy and imposture. They say that he was a Tarsean - which he admits himself and does not deny. But they suppose that he was of *Greek parentage,* taking the occasion for this from the (same) passage because he frankly said, „I am a man of Tarsus, a citizen of no mean city." They then claim that *he was Greek and the son of a Greek mother and father,* but that he had gone up to Jerusalem, stayed a while, and desired to marry a daughter of the High priest. He therefore became a proselyte and was circumcised. But since he still could not get that sort of girl he became angry,

and wrote against circumcision, and the Sabbath and Legislation".[57]

What use was made of the Pauline letters in the second century?

An argument often advanced in the past against the radical denial of authenticity for the Pauline letters was that the problems addressed by Paul in his letters, e.g., circumcision, freedom from the law for Gentile Christians, etc., presuppose the historical situation in the first century, not the second.

This opinion was occasionally also shared by radical critics, for example, the English radical critic G. A. Wells, who in a series of publications disputed the historical existence of Jesus, but at the same time held fast to the authenticity of the Pauline letters. In a letter he wrote to me, it says that "in the Pauline letters generally regarded as authentic today the writer addresses questions — the question of circumcision, for example — which no longer had any significance at all when the Gospels and Acts were written."

In my opinion, this often-asked question can be refuted with relative ease, and, moreover, a deeper study of the question regarding the historical situation of origin of the Pauline letters must necessarily evolve into one of the most important arguments for their inauthenticity, since all observations lead again and again to the insight that the Pauline letters can only have the historical and theological situation of the second century as the fertile soil in which they are rooted. If one pulls them out and transplants them — heeding their own claim, or that of the pseudonymous writer — into the time of the first century, one falls into a thicket of difficulties and perplexities. In order to keep the tiny plants alive one must support them with many complicated and artificial hypotheses, so as to finally ascertain again and again that all this has been of no avail. On the other hand, if one leaves the letters there where they come from, in the second century, everything becomes clear and intelligible. The plants develop splendidly and in a short time each one has become a beautiful, large tree of knowledge.

With regard to the matter itself, it can be said that the fact that the problems addressed in the Pauline letters were all still very much alive in second century, and even at the beginning of the third, shows, as we have already demonstrated above, with regard to the *history of influence* of the letters, from both a negative and a positive perspective:

Negative: We know nothing at all about the reception of the Pauline letters in the second half of the first century and in the beginning of the second.

We do not know in what way the Galatians reacted to Paul's writing, or whether the simple, war-like mountain people in Galatia would have understood it at all. Neither from that time nor from any later time do we have any kind of documentation as to whether he was granted success or failure. Furthermore, we also do not know what became of the people we meet in the Pauline writings—although some of them obviously had very great importance in the churches—like Apollos, for example, whose name has a suspicious similarity to Apelles, the student of Marcion, and alongside Peter (= Catholic, Jewish-Christians) and Paul (= Marcionism) clearly stands here as a symbolic figure for the stronger Gnostic Christianity.

Everywhere a great black hole opens up, that can be filled in only with a great deal of fantasy and has been until today— with regard to the supposedly Pauline churches, for example, which in the second century must have completely disappeared from the scene; or the Pauline school and Pauline students, concerning which no one has ever been able to say anything about what later developed and what happened, for example, to Timothy and Titus and all the others after the death of their master. Apart from the letters and Acts, or later church legends, in any case, they do not surface again historically.

Positive: If we thus know nothing at all about the immediate reception of the Pauline letters, it should be even more surprising that after an initial phase of absolute silence in the second century the reception history of the letters suddenly takes on a highly dramatic development.

In this regard, the passion with which the Catholic theologian Tertullian battles Marcion and his interpretation of the Pauline writings, and debates with him about precisely those themes which supposedly should no longer be relevant in the second century, like circumcision and the law, for example, shows what was at stake for him – and for Marcion as well. The question regarding the historical Paul, which is answered in the Pauline writings and in Acts respectively in different ways, was in no way merely an academic controversy, but was an existential concern for the Catholics as well as for the Marcionites and Gnostics. It was not simply different pictures of Paul and different conceptions of Paul that stood over against one another here, but, what is often forgotten, also different Christian groups, or churches, each of which appealed to "their" Pauline letters for their own theological conceptions and reclaimed the apostle exclusively for themselves. *In the second century, Paul was the object of a church-political controversy which was a matter of life and death.*

In many exegetical works concerned with the relationship between Paul and Luke, or between Paul and Acts, this is largely overlooked. One has the impression from them that Luke stands here, working on his theological draft, as a solitary man of letters—and they basically do not understand at all what could have moved him to produce such an ingenious, refined, detailed history a good half century after the death of the apostle. Still less, of course, they do not understand how, in this framework, also some letters, which seem to have been almost forgotten until now, suddenly take on great importance, because, even though they were written in a much different time to much different Christians, in a wondrous way they provide precise answers for those problems with which Christians in this century are concerned. If the Marcionites' claim that God had entrusted Paul, and *him alone (solus Paulus)*, their highest patron of the church, with the secret revelation, and that only he knows the truth (Irenaeus, AH 3.13.1), was then decisively rejected by Acts, in which Paul appears as subordinate to the Twelve, as the representatives of Rome-Jerusalem, and thus excluded as a source of "wild tradition,"[58] the Marcionites themselves then could now refer to the letter to the Galatians, where Paul thankfully furnished the most precise information regarding the historical circumstances of his relationship with the Jerusalem apostles before him, and indeed exactly the information the Marcionites needed now to legitimate themselves as the *one true* church.

That the protest in Galatians or even in 2 Corinthians against Luke's picture of Paul is perceived by us today only as peculiarly muffled need not be denied. But that has to do less with the original Paul, or the writer of these letters, himself, and much more with the Catholic redaction, or reaction, which, as I showed above, often regarded it necessary, at decisive places, to stuff a gag in the apostle's mouth. — When all is said and done, also and precisely in the insight that in the second century the Pauline letters were followed by a tendentious, Catholic reworking, as Galatians, for example, unmistakably shows, we have a further indication of their inauthenticity, since the special relevance of the writings in this time can hardly be explained if we had to do with purely historical documents.

Apart from other matters that cannot be pursued here,[59] that with problems addressed in the Pauline letters we have to do with *problems from the second century*, not the first, becomes finally also clear if one investigates the *opponents* battled in the Pauline writings.

The opponents of Paul

Most of the perplexities in which research has often become entangled have to do with the fact that one endeavors to clarify the question concerning opponents in the framework and against the historical background of the first century and not the second, as would be presumed, after all, from the close relationship in content between Galatians and Acts. When one recognizes that the letters were written in the second century, it is immediately understandable that the opposing front that the author of the Pauline letters addresses is not at all one limited in each case by particular local circumstances, but is already universal. He addresses the entire (Marcionite) Church from Rome to Edessa, and has in view Judaizing and Catholic opponents outside as well as spiritual-libertine Christians in his own ranks.

That the writer has *Catholic opponents* in view is clearly indicated by the letter to the Galatians, which we have already mentioned so often. The writer basically does not battle here at all against the rejection of the apostle by Christian churches, unknown to us, in distant Galatia, but against their audacious takeover by Catholic Christians. This is shown, for example, by Gal 5:11, a passage totally bewildering for every reader, where Paul contests the claim that he still preaches circumcision:

But if I, brethren, still preach circumcision, why am I still persecuted? The stumbling block of the cross would [then] be removed.

This is amazing! The opponents of Paul could certainly have made a host of charges against him, but there is one that they in fact certainly could not make, namely, the charge that he pursues the same goal as they do, that he preaches circumcision like they do!

The misunderstanding that Paul fights against cannot have existed either for Paul's opponents or for those who heard Paul's gospel preached in Galatia, and is as fully incomprehensible as this correction is. — In may be then, one sees, that at this point the writer of the letter turns his pen against the appropriation of the apostle, as this takes place in Acts, against his being brought back home into the lap of the Catholic church. Paul also — so it was said in the group that the writer of the letter confronts (and which is articulated then in the Acts of Luke) — is one of ours and had had an attitude towards the law just as broadminded as ours, whereby as proof of this supposed practice of circumcision reference could be made to Acts 16:3 (the circumcision of Timothy). It is clear that the writer of Galatians can not idly watch while someone made the sovereign apostle of Marcion dependent on Jerusalem, a representative of the despised Jewish-Christian reverence for the law, or both-and Theology, for which in Rome one appealed to Peter. For him it was necessary to free the apostle from the frightful embrace of Jewish-Christian Catholicism and to reject the attempt appropriate him in the sharpest way possible, so as to retain him for the Marcionite church as the sovereign protagonist of the law-free gospel, who was called to be an apostle not by men nor through a man — and certainly not at all by the twelve super-apostles appealed to in Rome.

Furthermore, how could the Marcionite author of our letter have better resisted, how could he have better pulled the ground from beneath the feet of his opponents than by allowing his apostle-avatar to be resurrected once more from the past and transferred from the dead to among the living, so that he might be allowed to speak to his church in a very personal way with his very own voice and with all stringency pronounce his decisive No! to every Catholic tendency towards appropriation?

That the writer of the Pauline letters opposed not only the Jewish-nomistic oriented Christianity of the second century and their motto, "We know however that the law is good" (1 Tim 1:8), but also the total rejection of the apostle on the Jewish-Christian side, is shown above all by 2 Corinthians, where the memory of the apostle is defended against posthumous defamation by Judaizers and where the writer explicitly makes known his intention to provide the church with arguments for those who slander him.

> We are not commending ourselves to you again, but giving you an opportunity to boast on our behalf, so that have something against those who boast in outward appearance and not [the condition] of their heart (5:12).

But in Galatians as well the writer seems to have in his ears personal accusations raised up against the apostle, as when he asks—obviously alluding to a designation used by the opponents—whether he has become their enemy by holding up the truth to the Galatian churches.

> Have I then become your enemy by telling you the truth? (4:16)

One wonders whether the founder of the churches in Galatia, the person who a few years earlier was first received as an angel and whom those in Galatia have to thank for nothing less than their existence as Christian churches, from one day to the other could fall into such disrespect that, on account of a few false-teachers who have worked their way into the church, one is even carried away to characterize him as an "enemy" (echthros hymōn gegona)? In the context of the letter and of the relationship of the apostle to his church, this remark is just as incomprehensible as the missing counter-question of the apostle, with which he then earned this harsh designation. All this then becomes understandable when one recognizes that the writer of Galatians obviously does address a concrete situation or a concrete accusation from the churches, but already has before his eyes an established theme from the anti-Pauline polemic of his own time.

In fact, in this connection, whoever is knowledgeable about early Christian literature will remember that the designation of Paul as an "enemy," or "hostile man," is very common in the *Judaistic-Ebionite polemic of the second century* and is found in many places. Thus, in the Jewish-Christian *Epistula Petri*, for example, the "lawless and irrational teaching of the hostile man" is mentioned, whereby, in the opinion of most scholars, by "hostile man" no one other than Paul himself is in view. Peter against Simon (Paul):

> You see how the statements of wrath are made through visions and dreams, but the statements to a friend are made face to face, in outward appearance, and not through riddles and visions and dreams, as to an <u>enemy</u> (ōs pros ton echtron, Hom 17:18)… my precursor Simon. For if he were known, he would not be believed; but now, not being known, he is improperly believed; and though his deeds are those of a hater, he is loved; and though an <u>enemy</u> (ho echthros), he is received as a friend (Hom 2:18) … Peter about Simon (= Paul): For some from among the Gentiles have rejected my legal preaching, attaching themselves to certain lawless and trifling preaching of the man who is my <u>enemy</u> (kerygma tou echthrou anthrōpou, EpPtr 1:2)

The assumption of two, or perhaps three fronts (in addition, there is also Gnostic libertinism on the left wing of

Marcionism, which I can not consider in more detail here) against which the author of Galatians directs his teaching, need not be understood schematically. The transitions between Catholicism and Jewish-Christian Ebionite Christianity were at that time certainly still fluid. Many differences, which first become evident and clear as day from a later historical perspective, obviously must have gradually become crystallized in extended and difficult discussions. In my opinion, that the total Judaizing rejection of Paul and the Catholic reception might not diverge as much as it must appear at first is shown very well by precisely the history of the literature to which H.J. Schoeps refers in his reconstruction of the history and theology of Jewish Christianity, namely, the history of the pseudo-Clementine writings, which originally stemmed from Ebionite/Elchasaite Jewish-Christian circles and could finally be united with a literary romance bearing the title of the man who as no other must be regarded as the symbolic figure for the approaching Roman Catholicism: Clement of Rome! As the bishop in Rome, the Roman Clement is at the same time the (3.) successor of the Jewish-Christian Peter.

In any case, if the observation that the author of Galatians in his writing expresses disapproval of three opposing fronts, against extreme Judaism, or Judaistic anti-Paulinism, Catholic Paulinism, and libertine Gnosticism, is an indication for the writing of the letter in the second century, and not the first, one finds oneself, beyond this, in agreement with what we know about Marcion and his church at this time. The threefold front corresponds in remarkable ways with the battle carried out by Marcion around the middle of the second century, which likewise was directed

    a) against extreme Judaism, on the one side,
    b) Speculative and libertine Gnosis, on the other,
    c) as well as Catholicism in the middle.

Marcion as Author of the Letters?

Can it be concluded from all this that Marcion himself wrote the Pauline letters?

On closer consideration, one will have to say, having once granted the presupposition that the Pauline letters are of later origin and that all clues indicate an origin in Marcionite circles, that the assumption that Marcion himself could be their author, or redactor, not only can not be excluded, but even has the greatest likelihood.

It cannot be denied that Galatians as well as 1 and 2 Corinthians and Philippians display a characteristic profile. The personal character of these letters, for which reason they have been regarded as authentic until today, in fact indicates an author, or collector and reviser, of distinct individuality. At that time, however, there were few such persons in Marcion's close circle. Since we know nothing about Cerdo, apart from Apelles, Marcion's student, who was perhaps responsible for the writings regarded as "deutero-Pauline,"[60] only Marcion remains after all. In my opinion, it is very conceivable that Marcion attempted to resolve the problems in his churches on the basis of documents that drew their authority from Paul, the legendary patron of the church, and that the battle reflected in the Pauline letters and which gives them their supposedly unmistakable and uncontrived character is nothing more that the reflection of those controversies that Marcion fought out in and with his churches.

In my view, that Marcion was the writer of Galatians is indicated by Gal 4:17, where the writer of Galatians charges that the (Catholic) opponents are zealous for the church only in order to *exclude them* (some textual witnesses even read "exclude *us*," i.e., Paul himself[61]), which means, of course, to *excommunicate them*:

They zealously court you, not for good, but because they would exclude you/us, so that you zealously court them.

Now it is difficult to imagine that the apostle Paul or his churches were already in danger of being excommunicated. With regard to Marcion, however, we know for certain about his exclusion from the church in 144 CE. Obviously, the writer (= Marcion) makes reference to his own situation shortly before his excommunication, which then projects back into the life of his apostle. The reader of the letter is obviously supposed to perceive the correspondence between the destiny of the apostle and Marcion's own—and thus be won over for Marcion's cause, that is so closely linked with the apostle's.

Chapter 3

A Legend and its Historical Kernel

A Final Open Question

When I had finished dealing with Marcion, I still had many unanswered questions. If it was true that we have Marcion or one of his pupils to thank for the Pauline letters in their original form (for me there was hardly any more doubt about this), who then was Paul, i.e., that figure *in whose name* the letters were written in the first half of the second century?

I certainly was faced here with question just as difficult as that concerning the author of the letters, and a question as well that for lack of an answer had become the rock on which all previous attempts to demonstrate the spurious character of the Pauline letters had obviously run aground. The question concerning the person in whose name the letters are supposed to have been written is closely connected with another question, which for naïve readers of the Pauline letters still represents the most persuasive argument for their authenticity: namely, the question of how it comes about that a number of passages in the Pauline letters give us the impression, by a host of personal indications, of something that absolutely could not be fabricated.

Fabrication Impossible?

Above all, the writings characterized by F.C. Baur as the primary Pauline epistles contain a number of statements which provide us with hints concerning the person and character of the presumed author. Not only in the historical-biographical sections of Galatians but also in other places, above all in 2 Corinthians, the author steers the reader's attention, consciously or unconsciously, to his own person — or, as the case may be, that person in whose name he authored his writing. In so doing, he seems to often defend himself against false accusations and charges that had been raised up against him. From Gal 1:10, 2 Cor 5:11, and 1 Thess 2:4 it can be inferred that the apostle is accused by his opponents of attempting to please men; 2 Cor 12:16 clearly shows that this was accompanied by the charge of deception. The accusations and insinuations against the apostle could even climax in the assertion that he had become an enemy of the church (Gal 4:16).

On the other hand, the person of the apostle seems to be carefully depicted by the author. The figure of the apostle is recommended to the churches as worthy of imitation (1 Cor 11:1); the kindness, patience, and gentleness of the apostle are strongly emphasized by the author (1 Thess 2:3ff.); the apostle is a visionary, and receives revelations that elevate him over other men (2 Cor 12:1ff.). Long catalogues of perils provide information regarding his numerous tribulations and afflictions (2 Cor 6:4ff.; 11:23ff.). In Ephesus he even fought in the arena with wild beasts (1 Cor 15:32). He bears on his body the marks of Christ (Gal 6:17), for which reason the churches in Galatia could even regard him as an angel of God and receive him as Jesus Christ (Gal 4:14), and indeed in spite of the "temptation" in his "flesh" that this represented for them and which seems to be associated in some way with his external appearance or with a mysterious suffering, which may be related to the "thorn in the flesh" mentioned by the author of 2 Corinthians (12:7f.).

In the past, alongside the particularities concerning the life of the churches that we learn from the letters, precisely such remarks and details relating to the person of the apostle were very often regarded as the most certain confirmation of the authentic, unmistakable, and unfabricated character of the primary Pauline letters. For William Wrede and many other scholars this constituted the primary argument against the radical rejection of the authenticity of the entire collection of Pauline writings. For them "the forger capable of inventing such unintentional, individual, purely personal, momentarily-born remarks, as are found here in abundance, and, moreover, to simulate thereby in all the letters a uniform, original personality as the author is still to be born."[1] Nevertheless, this argument, newly advanced again and again until today in different formulations and expressions, on the basis of which it is thought, for example, that the Dutch radical criticism of the Pauline letters might be seen as a "grave aberration of criticism,"[2] seems to me, on the contrary, much too general and all-inclusive to seriously set aside the doubts concerning the Pauline authorship of the letters, and indeed for the following reasons:

1) It is a mistake to think that by contesting the authenticity of the Pauline letters the "original personality" of their author is also denied. The letters could be inauthentic — and at the same time have an original author's personality with its own style and unmistakable profile. To put this another way, no one would deny that in the letters of the young *Werther* we have fictional prose, but there can nevertheless be no doubt that in the case of their author, Johann Wolfgang von Goethe have to do with an original personality.[3]

2) What one understands by a "uniform, original personality" is still far too dependent on the subjective feeling of

individual scholars. Instead of speaking in a general way of an "original personality," it is far more important, in my view, to first give an account of the "personal items" we encounter in the letters of Paul by systematic collection and sifting of individual passages as well as by their differentiation. The references to the person of the apostle in the letters, mentioned above at the beginning of this section, should rather already make one skeptical. Whether a man who recommends himself to others as an example to be imitated and who, among numerous other severe afflictions and adventures, also survived a battle with wild animals (1 Cor 15:32) unscathed can be accepted as a historical person without further examination seems very questionable.

To deduce from personal remarks the original personality of the author, and thereby the "authenticity" of his writings, is by no means compelling, and it is especially inappropriate where on closer observation the "personal items" underhandedly show themselves to be literary devices. In the Pastoral Epistles we also encounter a picture of Paul with a definite, characteristic stamp, and indeed a picture that, as most scholars recognize, is not identical with the person of the author but which serves the pseudepigraphical author as a literary device to tie together the myriad moral and doctrinal statements in the letters as the self-testimony of the apostle and to authorize them at the same time.

To be sure, in comparison with the picture of Paul in the rest of the letters, it is frequently observed that the picture in the Pastoral Epistles exhibits greater formality and idealization. But apart from the fact that, as we already noted, the picture of Paul in the letters generally regarded as authentic at times does not lack a certain schematizing and idealization, it does not yet follow from this that, in contrast to the Pastoral Epistles, the remaining letters must be authentic. One must also consider the possibility that the picture of Paul offered by the writer of the primary letters was more complex and differentiated than that available to the author of the Pastoral Epistles. Finally, one must also consider the possibility that the author of the primary Pauline letters was a more a sensitive and more distinguished man of letters than the person who wrote the Pastoral Epistles—even an "original (authorial) personality."

3) Just as the authenticity of a Pauline letter cannot be deduced from individual personal remarks, so also its authenticity cannot be inferred from the personal passion of the author. The personal zeal with which the author of Galatians, for example, or the author of 2 Corinthians, goes to battle against his opponents in no way needs to be feigned, since, as we showed above, it can be understood very well against the background of the second-century theological discussion between Marcionites, Jewish Christians and Catholics.

4) Even the controversy about the figure of the apostle need not be a special artifice of the pseudepigraphical author, who in this way seeks to give his writings the impression of greater authenticity. Rather, this seems much more to reflect the actual state of the discussion in the second century concerning the image of Paul. The author of Galatians and 2 Corinthians obviously only attempts to defend the image of the revered patron of the Marcionite churches against defamations, like those expressed by Jewish Christians, for example, or against appropriations from the side of Catholic Christians (Acts).

Debates about fundamental theological principles are often enlivened with personal questions. As an example, one can point to the discussion between Catholics and Protestants concerning Martin Luther. History has shown that the question regarding characterization of the reformer remained very much alive in confessional polemic long after his death, and the discussion about it was just as controversial as that concerning his teaching. One only has to recall the heated debates still ignited by the books of the Catholic theologians H. Grisar († 1932) and H.S. Denifle († 1905) some centuries after the death of the reformer and in which posthumous accusations were made against Luther, for example, that he had been not only a pornographer, a propagator of dirty stories, a drunkard, a glutton who eats like animals, and grossly ignorant, but also a despicable fabricator and liar.[4]

The image of the reformer, therefore, was contested for a long time after his death — in the very same way as the image of Paul, which was still contested in the middle of the second century by Gnostics, Marcionites, Jewish-Christians, and Catholics. Now we possess sufficient biographical and auto-biographical witnesses to the life of the reformer on the basis of which Protestant scholars could easily refute the defamation of their reformer. What would have happened if this had not been the case and the reformation had taken place in a time in which the fabrication of pseudepigraphic writings was in no way perceived as objectionable, but was entirely an everyday occurrence?

Who would want to exclude the "discovery" of pseudepigraphic letter of Luther in which the deceased reformer once more announces his desire to speak and posthumously counters all the accusations against which he had not been able to defend himself in his own lifetime, or perhaps did not have to.

The Legendary Paul

This is the question: Who then does the figure of the apostle Paul — to whom especially the Marcionites adhered as their church patron and in whose name Marcion and his pupils composed letters for the edification of their churches but also to ward off attacks by opponents — have in view? In other words, what are the historical and literary fundaments, the "foundation stones," from which the image of Paul in Galatians and in the other so-called Pauline letters is constituted?

In theory, we do not need at all to envision a particular historical person (in the modern sense), i.e., a *Paulus historicus*, as the Dutch radical critics called him. It would also be entirely conceivable that the author of the Pauline letters did not begin at all with a historical figure into which he projected himself (as a present-day writer projects himself into a historical person), but with a *legend*, and in particular a legendary Paul (which does not necessarily exclude the possibility that this legend has a historical kernel). In other words, it is possible and even very probable that the (Marcionite) author of the letters came to know his hero, the apostle Paul, exclusively from oral or written legendary traditions of his time and that even in his letters he does not imagine him as a historical person, but as he is portrayed in the legends: as the great hero of the faith in the past, powerful in words and deeds. — At the very least, in a time when everything historical very soon becomes enveloped and absorbed by the legendary this would be possible.

At the same time, this would also explain the presence in the letters of the peculiar and occasionally downright presumptuous self-stylization of Paul, e.g., when he urges his readers to imitate his example (1 Cor 4:16; 11:1; [Eph 5:1] 1 Thess 1:6; [2:14;] Phil 3:17) or boasts of wondrous deeds (Rom 15:18f; 2 Cor 12:12). In these passages the author of the letters actually does not speak about his own person at all, concerning whom he could have hardly said all these things without being accused of human arrogance by his contemporary readers, but about his revered example, as he had come to know him from the legends. The readers expect nothing more from him, and certainly nothing less, than they knew about the Paul of the legends. The splendor of the image of Paul, magnified and transfigured by legend, must necessarily also radiate in the letters that the apostle supposedly wrote in his own lifetime.

That a legend concerning Paul in fact existed in Christian circles in the second century cannot be denied. The best proof of its presence, among others, is Luke's Acts of the Apostles. That from a historical perspective the picture of Paul sketched out in Acts by Luke the "historian" is almost totally unusable has been recognized by most theologians since F.C. Baur. We are told there, as we already heard above, about all kinds of wondrous deeds of the apostle, about healing the sick (14:8 ff.) and raising the dead (20:9ff.), about a miraculous release from prison in the middle of the night (16:23 ff.), about angels who suddenly appear (5:19; 8:26; 10:3, 7; 12:7f, 10; 27:23), etc. With good reasons one is able to say that in Acts we do not have to do with a presentation of history, but that a legend is spun out here, not only about Paul, of course, but about all those who belonged to the earliest churches and their apostles.

The presentation of Paul in Acts, to be sure, is certainly not the only form of the legend about Paul; it represents rather only a very particular version, namely, that of the Lukan (Catholic) church. If we look around outside the canonical literature, we ascertain that stories and anecdotes were also passed around in heretical circles (Gnostics, Marcionites) in which the life and work of the apostle was presented in similar wondrous and legend-embellished ways. This found literary expression in the so-called *Acts of Paul*, to which the *Acts of Paul and Thecla* belong. If we are concerned with the literary and/or tradition-historical sources for the picture of Paul that the writer of our letters could have had before his eyes, then we cannot disregard precisely these apocryphal sources.

Paul and Thecla

The picture of the apostle we encounter in the Acts of Paul is entirely different from that in the canonical Acts. Of course, here also Paul is at work as a missionary; he is active in the entire region of Asia Minor; the stations of his journey are Damascus, Jerusalem, Iconium, Antioch, Myra, Sidon, Tyre, Ephesus, Philippi, Corinth, and finally Rome, where he dies as a martyr. But there are nevertheless a great differences.

The differences have to do with the *external* frame of Paul's work—while Acts reports three missionary journeys of the apostle, the Acts of Paul relates only a single great journey of Paul, which finally leads him to Rome—as well as the content of his preaching. At the center of Paul's preaching in the Acts of Paul stands not the message of the resurrection, as in Acts, but the preaching of (sexual) continence (Greek = *enkrateia*). At the center of Acts stands Paul the Jew. The hero of the Acts of Paul, on the other hand, scarcely makes an appearance as a Jew; he is primarily a (Hellenistic) ascetic and a preacher of an ascetic lifestyle and piety.

We can best clarify the differences between Luke's picture of Paul, that we know from canonical Acts and which we have already characterized in more detail above, and the picture in the Acts of Paul if we take a look at the Acts of Paul and Thecla, which represents the most famous piece of this apocryphal literature and was transmitted independently.

The Acts of Paul and Thecla is a peculiar mixture of religious edification literature and ancient adventure and love stories. They relate how the apostle comes to the city of Iconium (today *Konya* in Turkey) and wins a virgin named Thecla for the Christian faith. In the middle of Paul's sermon, which Thecla follows from the window of her house, stands the requirement of (sexual) abstinence. A beatitude enunciated by Paul, which reminds on Jesus' sermon on the mount, goes:

> Blessed are the pure in heart, for they shall see God. Blessed are they that keep the flesh chaste, for they shall become the temple of God.
>
> Blessed are they that abstain (or the continent), for unto them shall God speak.
>
> Blessed are they that have renounced this world, for they shall be well-pleasing unto God.
>
> Blessed are they that possess their wives as though they had them not, for they shall inherit God…
>
> Blessed are they that have kept their baptism pure, for they shall rest with the Father and with the Son.
>
> Blessed are they that have compassed the understanding of Jesus Christ, for they shall be in light.
>
> Blessed are they that for love of God have departed from the fashion of this world, for they shall judge angels, and shall be blessed at the right hand of the Father.
>
> Blessed are the merciful, for they shall obtain mercy and shall not see the bitter day of judgement.
>
> Blessed are the bodies of the virgins, for they shall be well-pleasing unto God and shall not lose the reward of their continence (chastity), for the word of the Father shall be unto them a work of salvation in the day of his Son, and they shall have rest world (5-6).[5]

The preaching of Paul awakes in Thecla the desire for a life of chastity. Much to the distress of her future husband, Thamyris, who, for understandable reasons feels that his future wife has been deceived by the apostle's preaching, endeavors to stir up the people and the authorities against the apostle. Thamyris blames the apostle, not entirely without justification, of corrupting the women of the city of Iconium through his preaching by dissuading them from marriage. In fact, he thereby soon causes Paul to be arrested and thrown into prison. But a secret meeting nevertheless takes place at night with his devoted Thecla. By bribing the guard, she is able to come to him in prison in order to sit at the apostle's feet, listen to his preaching, and kiss his chains.

After Thecla is discovered in the prison, Paul is brought before the judgment-seat of the governor. In the meantime, Thecla, who remained behind in the prison, rolls about on the consecrated place where Paul had taught while he sat in prison.

> But the governor heard Paul gladly concerning the holy works of Christ. And when he had taken counsel, he called Thecla and said: 'Why doest thou not marry Thamyris according to the law of the Iconians?' But she stood there looking steadily at Paul. And when she did not answer, Theocleira her mother cried out, saying: 'Burn the lawless one! Burn her that is no bride in the midst of the theater, that all women who have been taught by this man may be afraid!' And the governor was great affected. He had Paul scourged and drove him out of the city, but Thecla he condemned to be burned.[6]

Thecla is immediately brought to the theater, where straw and wood have been gathered for the burning. "As she is brought in naked, the governor wept" — obviously less tears of sympathy than of amazement — for he "marveled at the power that was in her." The executioners stacked the wood and ordered her to ascend the pyre. But in that moment when the fire was ignited a powerful rumble beneath the earth shook the theater and, by intervention of the Almighty, great masses of water and hail poured down, "so that many were endangered and died, and the fire was quenched, and Thecla was saved."

The events in Iconium constitute the prelude for a series of further wondrous events involving Paul and Thecla. In Antioch an obtrusive Syrian named Alexander provokes the next mischief when he embraces the virgin on an open street and is rejected by her. Because Thecla ripped away his cloak and knocked the crown from his head, she is brought before the governor and condemned to fight with beasts. Taken to the arena once again, tumultuous events unfold in the course of which Thecla throws herself in a pit filled with water and baptizes herself. All the seals in the water are killed as by a lightning flash. Likewise, the bears and lions fall into a kind of overpowering sleep and do not touch her. Thecla herself is surrounded by a cloud of fire so that she could not be seen in her nakedness. Having been saved once more, Thecla returns again to Iconium. Her fiancée is fortunately no longer alive, so Thecla can now pursue her calling undisturbed and proclaim the word of God. At a great age she finally passes away peacefully.

The *Acts of Paul and Thecla* are only a small excerpt from a great amount of Pauline literature, now partly lost, in which the adventures of the apostle are related in "edifying" legendary ways. The *Acts of Paul* stemming from Enkratite-Marcionite circles are interesting in that a series of connecting points can be ascertained between them and the author of the Pauline letters. I would like to provide the following examples therefor:

The Face of an Angel

In Gal 4:14 Paul relates that the churches in Galatia had received him "as an angel of God."

And you did not scorn or despise the temptation for you in my flesh, but received me as an angel of God, as Christ Jesus.

The Dutch radical critic Loman already wondered about this and asked how the Galatians arrived at this remarkable conception.[7] The passage from the Acts of Paul and Thecla with the familiar portrayal of the apostle could offer an explanation. The picture of Paul presented here has influenced the iconographic representation of Paul until the present:

> And he saw Paul coming, a man of small stature, with a bald head and crooked legs, in a good state of body, with eyebrows meeting and nose somewhat hooked, full of friendliness, now appearing like a man, and now with the face of an angel (3).

As this passage shows, the face of an angel is obviously a common feature of the picture of Paul in the Pauline legends.

The same is true for conception we meet in Gal 4:14 that the figure of Christ appeared in the figure of the apostle. Here also there are remarkable parallels in the *Acts of Paul and Thecla* (21): As Thecla is led into the theatre to be burned "she sought for Paul as a lamb in the wilderness looks around for its shepherd. And when she looked out over the crowd, she saw *the Lord sitting in the figure of Paul.*" This passage shows that the author in fact had the Pauline legends in view from where he knew about the wondrous appearance of the apostle.

Fight with Beasts in Ephesus

What Paul says in 1 Cor 15:32 — "If in a human way I fought with wild beats in Ephesus, what gain do I have?" — has been puzzling for exegetes, first of all because as a citizen of Rome Paul could not be condemned to fight wild beats (ad bestias) in the arena, and secondly because the prospect of surviving such a fight was extremely small. Also remarkable is the unusual emphasis on *the kata anthrōpon*, concerning whose meaning—"according to the will of man" or "in a human way"—exegetes differ, as well as the word "in Ephesus," which one would not expect under the usual assumption that Paul authored his letter to the Corinthians in Ephesus.

One finds the solution for these problems when one again understands what is said in 1 Corinthians against the background of the *Acts of Paul*, in this instance as a reference by the writer to the legendary portrayal found there of a fight with wild beasts that Paul endures under wondrous circumstances. It is reported in the *Acts of Paul* that in Ephesus Paul was forced to fight with beasts in the stadium. When a wild lion, who had been captured just shortly before, was set upon the apostle, Paul recognized it to be that lion for whom he had only shortly before administered the holy sacrament of baptism. A conversation takes place between Paul and the lion, who it turns out can also speak: "Lion," asks Paul, "was it you whom I baptized?" To which the lion answers, "Yes!" But Paul speaks to him again: "And how were you captured?" To which the lion replies, "Even like you were, Paul."

As the spectators, in view of the friendly relationship between the two, begin to become impatient and let still more animals loose against Paul, there takes place—as already in the theater in Iconium at the burning of the beautiful Thecla—a direct intervention of heavenly divine power, who obviously no longer wants to be an idle observer. Like a bolt from heaven, a powerful and violent hail-storm forms over the stadium and pouring forth from heaven assures that most of the spectators are struck down and die or take flight, while Paul and the lion remain undisturbed. Finally, Paul takes leave of his animal companion; he exits the stadium and sails off to Macedonia. "But the lion went away into the mountains" — for further missionary work? — "as was customary for it."

Once one is clear about the fact that the pseudepigraphic author of 1 Corinthians makes reference here to the legendary tradition presupposed by the *Acts of Paul*, which in contrast to the canonical Acts knows nothing about Paul's *rights as a Roman citizen*, it also becomes understandable why it expressly speaks of a fight with beasts "in a human way." The author clearly wants to say that in the fight Paul did not battle in a human way, but that — entirely in accord with the presentation in the *Acts of Paul*, which at this place has the apostle rescued by a *divine miracle* (the talking lion, the hailstorm) — he has only the help of God to thank for his deliverance. If on the contrary, Paul had fought in Ephesus only *in a human way*, i.e., without divine help, only with his own human power, he would certainly have died. For this reason the author of 1 Corinthians can rightly ask what Paul would have gained from this without hope in the resurrection. Even in individual details it becomes clear here that the author of 1 Corinthians connected with the Pauline legend and its wonderful portrayal of the fight with beasts in Ephesus and obviously completely identified with his hero.

From Paul of the Legends to the Historical Paul

Even with the reference to legendary literature of the second century, in which the wonderful deeds of the apostle are related, all the elements of the picture of Paul we encounter in the letters are still not all explained. In addition we have to ask whether the Paul of the legends might not be based on a historical kernel that points to a particular historical person?

Even in the past where the authenticity of all the Pauline letters was contested one could not, and generally did not want to, exclude the view that the letters pointed back to and made reference to a historical figure. Since the radical critics did not regard this figure as identical with the author of the letters, they referred to him in contrast to the author[8] as *Paulus historicus*. As a rule, of course, there was not much that could be said about this person. For the Dutch radical critic Loman, for example, *Paulus historicus* remained only a very schematic figure about which he could say little more than that it had to do with a man "who hellenized Christianity in the Diaspora from Syria through Asia Minor and Greece as far as Rome by his zealous propaganda on behalf of the messianic movement."[9]

We learn somewhat more from Van Manen. For Van Manen the *historical Paul* probably was "a somewhat younger contemporary of Peter and the other disciples of Jesus"; he probably was "a Jew by birth" and had been "a resident of Tarsus in Cilicia." After at first having a hostile relationship with the other disciples, he later joined with them and became a wandering preacher, who on his journeys through Syria, Asia Minor, and Greece, finally came to Italy. Presumably, he was one of the first Christians to proclaim Christianity outside of Palestine to the Gentiles.

The picture Van Manen sketches of the historical Paul, whom he does not regard as the writer of the letters, is therefore by and large identical with the picture of Paul in Acts. In other words, in searching for *Paulus historicus* the radical critic Van Manen, who by rejecting their authenticity had lost the Paul of the letters, finally ends up with the Catholic Paul of Acts! To be sure, Van Manen expresses the reservation that Acts contains "truth and fiction at the same time"; but with regard to the relationship between Paul and the other apostles Van Manen esteems the historical value of

Acts more highly than Galatians. Van Manen can go so far as to say that there is no indication of decisive opposition between Paul and the other apostles.[10] In view of the fact that the picture of Paul in Acts is regarded even by conservative scholars as Luke's own fabrication without any claim to historicity, Van Manen's discussion of the historical Paul can hardly still be convincing. Moreover, the question arises as to why a letter like Galatians, for example, could ever have been attributed to precisely the person Van Manen described as a "faithful attender of temple or synagogue."

If with regard to the historical Paul Van Manen knows *too much*, Loman's description of *Paulus historicus* remains unsatisfactory because he knows *too little*. It must be granted, to be sure, that he and other radical critics do not go so far as to throw out the baby with the bath water and entirely deny the existence of a historical Paul. But the historical rubble that is left over by criticism is merely a schematic figure. What we finally learn from them about the historical Paul is only *that* he had lived and worked as a missionary, and that at a later time letters were written in his name. The question arises as to why, in spite of his obviously successful missionary work, apart from the letters written in his name, hardly more than a weak reflection of the historical Paul was left behind in the consciousness of his churches and/or contemporaries, and how he could be regarded as *apostolus haereticorum* (Tertullian AM 3.5.4) if those persons who took care to preserve his memory after his death are to be found precisely in the Catholic and Jewish-Christian storehouse (Acts).

In their search for the historical Paul, Loman and Van Manen landed in a blind alley because they let themselves be guided too much by the picture of Paul in Acts. Although they recognized more clearly than other scholars that the

Pauline letters stand in a suspicious proximity to Marcion and Marcionism, with regard traditions relating to the historical Paul they still began with the picture of Paul in Acts and sometimes very uncritically took those traditions as a basis without posing anew the question of their origin. So there arose the paradoxical picture of the "orthodox" Jewish apostle and wandering preacher who was misused by later heretics to legitimate their theology, a picture that understandably could not be very convincing.

What Loman and Van Manen did not yet recognize was, as we indicated above, that the picture of Paul that Luke sketches is already *derived*, a reaction to the Pauline legends circulating at about the same time in Marcionite and Gnostic churches (in Asia Minor), and that, in spite of their often reworked and catholisized final form, the latter seems to contain at the core older and more original material than Acts.

If the Pauline legend was originally at home in Marcionite circles and Acts represents only a Catholic reworking of this legend, then clues leading from the legendary to the historical Paul can point only to the Marcionite churches, not the Catholic. For the question concerning *Paulus historicus* this obviously means that he must be sought only within the Marcionite, or Gnostic, movements of the first and second centuries, not in the "orthodox" churches. In other words, the Marcionite-Gnostic picture of the apostle comes closer to the historical Paul than the picture of the Catholic Jew in Acts.

The Doppelgänger: Paul and Simon

At this point in our investigation a surprising possibility, never before considered in previous research,[11] comes into view: from the writings of early Christian commentators we know that the Church fathers regarded the Samaritan

Gnostic Simon Magus as the spiritual father of the Gnostic-Marcionite heretics. This was especially true for the Marcionite heresy, which the Church fathers connected with Simon in different ways, some direct and some indirect. According to Irenaeus (AH 1.27), Marcion was indirectly connected with Simon through his teacher Cerdo.[12]

> A certain Cerdo, who was associated with the Simonians (ab his qui sunt erga Simonem), came to Rome under Hyginus, the ninth bishop in apostolic succession... Marcion from Pontus, who followed him (succedens), extended his teaching... At this point we must mention him [Simon] in order to show you that all those who in any way corrupt the truth and contravene the preaching of the church are students and successors of Simon the magician from Samaria (Simonis Samaritani magi discipuli et successores sunt). Although they do not mention the name of their teacher, in order to deceive others, what they teach is nevertheless his doctrine. They set forth the name of Christ Jesus in a deceptive way, and in various ways introduce the impiety of Simon, thus destroying many by spreading false teaching under a good name.

Marcion is then directly associated with Simon by Clement of Alexandria. In Clement's *Stromata* (7.17) we read in what is certainly a "very controversial passage, which if taken literally leads to the nonsense that Marcion was a contemporary of Peter,"[13] that Marcion had been *a student of Simon*, who himself had heard the preaching of Peter. This testimony is peculiar, above all, because, as far as we know from his writings discussed by the church fathers, Marcion himself never mentioned Simon at all; Simon's name appears nowhere in his writings! If Marcion is in some way "connected" with the Samaritan Gnostic Simon Magus (which there is no reason to doubt), it must seem odd that he refers to this nowhere in his writings.

Against this, one should not object that his writings are only transmitted to us very incompletely. For it can hardly be doubted that the church fathers would not have hesitated to transmit to us such information about Marcion if they had found only a single reference to this in the writings of Marcion himself.

When Marcion speaks of his spiritual father, he speaks nowhere of Simon, but exclusively of Paul! How can this be explained?

Perhaps because Simon and Paul were one and the same person for Marcion? Is it possible that in Paul perhaps nothing else is to be seen than the transfigured image of the one who preceded Marcion and his students as a spiritual father and who, according to the unanimous opinion of early church commentators, was the head of all heretics and heresies in early Christianity, even and especially the Marcionite: namely, the Samaritan Simon Magus, with whom, as Irenaeus relates, Marcion was connected through Cerdo.

Without doubt, against the identity of Simon and Paul seems to stand, first of all, the banal circumstance that "Paul" certainly does not mean "Simon," or that "Simon" does not mean "Paul," and that the different names seem to refer to different persons. However, precisely with regard to Paul and Simon this argument is of very dubious value, since it is generally known that already within early early Christian literature itself there is a branch where this distinction, indeed, is not carried out and where Simon in fact stands in place of Paul, i.e., is identified with Paul. This would be the so-called Pseudo-Clementines and the Kerygmata Petrou associated with them, coming out of Jewish-Christian, Ebionite circles. The complete identification of Simon-Paul found there — one of the most difficult problems for New Testament scholarship working until now with the assumption of authenticity for the Pauline letters — certainly represents one of the strongest arguments for the identity thesis presented here.

One certainly should not over simplify the problems associated with the pseudo-Clementine literature, which is significantly named after Clement the Roman bishop, the third follower of Peter in Rome. Nevertheless, I believe that the basic problem here can be fairly well stated with the following formulas:

1. In the Pseudo-Clementines Simon is known and opposed by name.
2. The heresies ascribed to him are Marcionite, and
3. —even more strange—the words that are placed in his mouth are those of Paul!

There are a number of solutions for this problem. In my book *Paulusbriefe ohne Paulus?* I described in detail the Tübingen solution, which saw Simon as a characterization of Paul; and today the problem is usually solved in complicated, literary ways. However, there is still another, much simpler solution, which one can only maintain is one is prepared, first of all, to give up the authenticity of the letters, which is certainly the primary reason why, in spite of its simplicity, it has not been considered until now: Why do we not understand the Pseudo-Clementines in a completely literal way? Why do we not take seriously the fact that for the writer of this Jewish, anti-Pauline literature Paul is in fact no one else than Simon?

If words from Galatians are placed there in the mouth of Simon,[14] or if he is portrayed as a missionary to the Gentiles like Paul,[15] who converted Gentiles to Christianity before Peter, if in the Epistula Petri (2.3f.) reference is made "in a hardly concealed attitude" to the "lawless and foolish teaching of a hostile man"[16] (i.e., Paul), all this obviously means, first of all, nothing other than that the author knew the preaching of Paul only under the name of Simon and that for him Paul and Simon were in fact identical. With regard to Simon and Paul, therefore, we have to do with two names for the same person, whereby the Roman word Paul = the Small need not be understood as an additional proper name, but rather as a surname or nickname (supernomen),[17] like, for example, Albert the Great or—an example nearer at hand—Simon Peter.

That in addition to a person's actual name one can attach still more names which in some way express something about the person's character or outward peculiarity is a practice also attested elsewhere in antiquity. It can even go so far that the actual name is no longer known. In the work of the well known satirist Lucian, for example, we meet the figure of the ancient wandering philosopher Peregrinus Proteus. Both names, Peregrinus as well as Proteus, are personal surnames: Peregrinus = "one who is nowhere at home," Proteus = "one who is always wandering." In this example, the real name of the man, who at the same time was a Christian, can no longer be determined.

Moreover, that the name Paul could already be conceived in an figurative sense by the writer of the Pauline letters can be clearly seen in 1 Cor 15:19, where "Paul" speaks of himself as the last and the smallest, like a "miscarriage" as it were. Bruno Bauer correctly commented about this: "He is the last, the unexpected, the conclusion, the dear nestling. Even his Latin name, Paul, expresses smallness, which stands in contrast to the majesty to which he is elevated by grace in the preceding passages of the letter."[18]

Bauer rightly calls attention to the theological significance in the concept of smallness. In fact, beyond Bauer, who did not yet have this connection in view, one must consider that precisely for the Marcionites—and obviously already for the Simonians as well, to whom this goes back—the word "Paul" expressed everything that constituted the core of their theology and for which the "letters of Paul" provide continuous testimony. Where is the freely occurring, unannounced and unconditioned, election by grace better illustrated than precisely by the inferior, the incomplete, by a child, by a small one?

So while Paul, like Peter, was originally nothing more than a surname for Simon, which was first employed only in the Marcionite churches (not in the least because of the theological associations just mentioned which the name could awaken), the name Simon seems to have been more common primarily in Jewish circles. This explains the gradual separation and division of the names in the course of time, which finally led to the division of the person of Simon-Paul himself.

One could say that *Paul* is the transfigured image of Simon among the legitimate disciples and followers of Simon, Marcionites, Gnostics, etc. (recall that the name "Simon" significantly appears nowhere in all the works of Marcion!); [and Simon, on the other hand, stands for the picture of the same person [Paul], more and more consumed by polemic, even as the Antichrist, for the opponents of Simon, the Judaizers.

Accordingly, Simon meets us in the Marcionite-Gnostic literature as Paul, while in extreme Jewish-Christian circles Paul is represented as Simon, or even as the Antichrist or "enemy" and "hostile man." Finally, the separation of the names and the separation of the persons was completed in that moment when the Catholics definitively took possession of patrons of the Marcionite church in doctored them up in their own way, which took place in Acts. After Simon-Paul had once been officially established as Paul in the pantheon of great figures from early Christian times, and thereby a more moderate, even more Catholic Marcionism found entrance into the Catholic church, the continuing polemic against Simon-Paul fermenting in Ebionite, Jewish-

Christian circles, in so far as it related to the Catholic Paul, became a heresy and was no longer tolerated. The moderation of the continuing Jewish polemic directed against Simon-Paul did not take place in such a way that it was simply rejected or combated as false, but

1. in that Simon became expressly distinguished from Paul, and Simon alone, or Simon Magus, as he was now called, was represented as the bearer of all negative attributes, i.e., in a certain sense was built up as the "bogeyman" in place of Paul; and

2. through the Catholic redaction of the Pauline letters, following very soon, which made their far-reaching Jewish-Christian reception possible and took the edge off the polemic (still directed against the Marcionite Simon-Paul).

The process of separation was already completed in Acts and can be observed with ostentatious clarity in chapter eight where in direct connection with the first appearance of Paul Luke immediately speaks of Simon Magus. As the Tübingen scholars already correctly observed, Luke thereby rejects an identification of Paul and Simon, as this takes place in the Pseudo-Clementines, for example.[19] In that Luke depicts Paul and Simon as two entirely different people, the anti-Simonian polemic now has no relationship with the Catholic Paul and thus beats the air.

The Sinful Woman

Against the theory of names just set forth, it could be objected that there are no parallels at all in the history of Christian tradition for such a division of a person. But that is not correct: the division of one person into two different persons, which obviously serves the express (polemical) purpose, in the face of contrary views, of excluding a particular identification, is a literary technique for Luke observable in other passages as well, and which is employed once more in the story of the sinful woman (Lk 7:37ff.). Luke is plainly concerned here to counter the speculation current in Gnostic circles concerning Mary Magdalene as the (fallen) female companion of Jesus Christ and to show that there is no relationship at all between Mary Magdalene and the sinful woman mentioned in the story of the anointing in 7:37ff. This is clearly the reason why immediately after the anointing story he attaches a short list of the female disciples of Jesus, in which Mary Magdalene, Joanna, and Susanna are explicitly mentioned by name:

> ...some women who had been healed of evil spirits and infirmities: Mary, called Magdalene, from whom seven demons had gone out...

For the reader the conclusion—desired by Luke—necessarily follows that at least none of the women named is identical with the sinful woman (not mentioned by name) in the anointing story. In fact, however, from the perspective of tradition history there can be no doubt about the Gnostic origin of the anointing story (with a wealth of erotic motifs and variations on the theme of the fallen Ennoia, Helena, or Sophia, in the form of a historical account).[20] Contrary to Luke, later church tradition clearly recognized this and—as the Gnostics had already done, but now, to be sure, in a time when Gnosticism had been excluded as a danger for Catholic Christianity—again identified the sinful woman with Mary Magdalene.

Historically, therefore, the various features of the picture of Paul represented by the author of Galatians go back to the figure of Simon Magus in the first century. The figure of Paul himself, therefore, is first of all nothing other that the transfigured picture of the legendary founder of religion and patron of the church to whom the Simonian-Marcionite churches were indebted and whose teaching they preserved as the legitimate spiritual successors and heirs.

This explains the peculiar circumstance that in the Jewish-Christian polemic of the second century Simon, who was denounced (by Jews and Jewish-Christians) as the Antichrist, or Beliar, etc., exhibits characteristics of the apostle Paul, and conversely why the figure of Paul, who meanwhile has become revered by the church, exhibits characteristics Simon Magus, the Heresiarch and Antichrist. We have to do here basically with one and the same person. While in the second century both Jewish-Christians and Marcionites were naturally still conscious of this, through the Catholic separation of Simon Magus from Paul and through the usurpation and catholicizing of Paul (who by the surname Saul was also tied to the Old Testament tradition; see Tertullian, who could only trust his Paul after he found him prefigured in the Old Testament)[21] this consciousness gradually passed away and by the beginning of the third century (leaving Tertullian aside, who seems to have still maintained a faint memory or the actual origin of the apostle) was almost completely gone.

Who was Simon Magus?

For our further historical search for traces of the origin of the Christian picture of Paul, who the (Marcionite) author of the letters had in mind in his work, it is necessary that we still occupy ourselves somewhat more deeply with the figure of Simon Magus, or Simon from Samaria, as the case may be. As we have already implied and as we will see still more clearly below, we have to do here with one of the central figures in earliest Christianity, if not even the central figure as such. The immense significance of this Simon, later stigmatized by the church as the Heresiarch and Antichrist, can scarcely be overestimated.

If the emphasis on his great significance seems inappropriate and out of place to a reader who in his or her journey through the world of early Christianity possibly encounters the figure of Simon for the first time, one should consider that the *picture of early Christianity* that has been normative until today is determined by *the church's picture of early Christianity*. The primary sources employed by scholars for this are still Christian: The Catholic Book of Acts, the catholicized letters of Paul, the Gospels, etc. Christian sources that could provide us with a different picture of the situation in the first century either do not exist or were done away with by the Church, for it is self-evident that in a time when Paul and the letters written in his name became accepted as church documents every writing in which Paul was (correctly from a historical perspective) identified with Simon the Heresiarch must be disparaged as satanic. It probably not entirely accidental that the Jewish writings in which this identification is still made (after corresponding Catholic reworking and tranquilizing) have been preserved for us. In any case, in the picture the church produced of its own beginnings, which still imprints us today, the person of Simon became painted over with dark colors for such a long time that, contrary to his real significance, he stood in the shadows of history.

As a dark, insignificant figure, the magician also meets us then in Luke's Acts. When we previously spoke of the close religious-historical relationship existing between the figure of Paul in the Christian legends concerning Paul and those concerning Simon Magus, we already encountered the reference to the magician in Acts 8:9-24:

> But there was in the city a man named Simon who had previously practiced magic and amazed the people of Samaria,

saying that he himself was someone great. And they all gave heed to him, from the least to the great, saying, "This man is the power of God that is called great." And they gave heed to him, because for a long time he had amazed them with his magic. But when they believed Philip as he preached the gospel of the kingdom of God and the name of Jesus Christ, they were baptized, both men and women. Even Simon himself believed, and after being baptized he remained with Philip. And seeing the signs and powerful deeds taking place, he was amazed. Now when the apostles at Jerusalem heard that Samaria had received the word of God, they sent them Peter and John, who came down and prayed for them that they might receive the Holy Spirit; for it had not yet fallen on any of them; but they had only been baptized in the name of the Lord Jesus. Then they laid their hands on them and they received the Holy Spirit. Now when Simon saw that the Spirit was given through the laying on of the apostles hands, he offered them money, saying, "Give me this power also, that any one on whom I lay my hands may receive the Holy Spirit." But Peter said to him, "Your silver perish with you, because you thought you could obtain the gift of God with money! You have neither part not lot in this matter, for your heart is not right before God. Repent therefore of this wickedness of yours, and pray to the Lord that, if possible, the intent of your heart may be forgiven you, For I see that you are in the fall of bitterness and in the bond of iniquity." And Simon answered, "Pray for me to the Lord, that nothing of what you have said may come upon me." And when they had testified and spoken the word of God, they returned to Jerusalem, preaching the gospel to many villages of the Samaritans.

Most scholars agree that the picture of the Samaritan Simon Luke presents here is once again a tendentious characterization. While Luke portrays Simon only as a great sorcerer, who amazed the Samaritans with his sorcery, there is wide agreement today that Simon was certainly more than a successful magician. In the claim to be *the great power of God* is still reflected the prophetic self-consciousness of one of the most influential spiritual leaders of heretical Gnosticism.

In Christian teachings against heresy, the origin of Gnosticism is generally traced back to Simon Magus. Thus, even Irenaeus saw Cerdo and his student (or colleague) Marcion as offshoots of Simon the Samaritan. But not only Gnostics characterized (in the narrow sense) as Simonians, but also Valentinians, Basilideans, Marcionites, etc. were regarded by the church fathers, directly or indirectly, as followers of Simon. Even if "modern research in Gnosis," as Kurt Rudolph, one of its most important representatives, writes, "no longer holds the conviction that Simon Magus has to be considered the ancestor of all gnostic religion,"[22] one nevertheless certainly recognizes that Simon Magus is of decisive significance for the origin of heretical Gnosticism.

Apart from Acts, whose picture of Simon we have already determined, by and large, to be historically worthless, and setting aside Acts 8:10, which could contain an echo of a corresponding Simonian saying, there are a number of other sources in which we meet the Samaritan magician: in Justin, whom we have already often mentioned, in Irenaeus, Hippolytus, the Pseudo-Clementines, and the Alexandrines (Clement and Origen). According to the theologian Beyschlag, we have to do here with the five "pillars" of the patristic Simon Magus tradition.

In non-Christian sources we have a notation of Josephus in his *Jewish Antiquities* (20.7.2), where a "Jew named Simon (*Atomos*), who comes from Cyprus and calls himself a magician" is mentioned. Also in the Jewish Apocalyptic writings and the Sibyllines (Oracles), where an Antichrist appears, many scholars believe this figure to have the features of Simon Magus.

If one attempts to make a rough picture of the figure of Simon Magus from the sources at hand, it would be something like the following:

The author of the Pseudo-Clementines, which certainly represents a very late stage of the Simon legend, reports that Simon came from the village of Gitta in Samaria and that he obtained a Greek education during his stay in Egypt, to which he also brought "extensive knowledge and skills in magic." Simon appeared with the claim to be a "mighty power" of God, and occasionally also referred to himself as the Messiah or as the Standing One, whereby he intended to imply that he would endure forever and that "it is not possible for his body to be subject to corruption" (cf. Clem Hom 2.22ff.)

The writer of the Pseudo-Clementines characterizes Simon's teaching as follows: Simon denies "that the God who created the world is the highest God, nor does he believe in the resurrection of the dead. He turns away from Jerusalem, and sets Mount Garizim in its place. In the place of our true Christ he claims that he is the Christ. He interprets the content of the law according to personal whims. He does speak of a future judgment, but does not take it seriously: for if he were convinced that God would make him accountable, he would not have dared in his wantonness to turn against God."

Here we have the same, or very similar, ideas as we later meet in Marcion. They archetypically exhibit the already familiar features of the Gnostic system, whose basic principle includes—as Marcionism does later—the crass separation between the creator of the world (Demiurge; Jewish God) and the highest God (the unknown, or foreign, God).

Remarkably, the writer of the fictional pseudo-Clementine work regards John the Baptizer to have been Simon's teacher. Simon was among the thirty pupils of the Baptizer. A woman named Helena, or Luna, is also mentioned as a pupil of John (we must also consider her later). Although Simon was regarded as the most important and most capable pupil of John, he was not able to install Simon his successor, because at the time of his death Simon was in Egypt, and another pupil of John, named Dositheos, succeeded in taking over the leadership of the baptism sect.

After his return, Simon at first pretended friendship and contented himself for a long time with second place after Dositheos. Only when Simon began to claim that Dositheos did not correctly transmit the teaching of John did it come to a break. When Dositheos noticed that "Simon's well-calculated slanders were weakening his own authority among the great crowd so that they no longer regarded him as the Standing One, he struck out at him in anger one time when Simon came to the usual meeting. But the stick seemed to pass through Simon's body as if it were smoke. Shocked by this, Dositheos cried out to him: 'You are the Standing One, so I will pay homage to you.' "

The expression "the Standing One" (Greek = *hestōs*) is especially known from the work of the Jewish philosopher Philo. For Philo it refers to God (conceived in the categories of Greek philosophy) as eternally standing still, unchanging[23]. If Simon is referred to as the Standing One, it seems therefore to be a form of honorific title elevating Simon, clearly an expression of his very special nearness to the highest *hestōs*. Even for Philo, the one who draws near to God must himself become a *hestōs* (Philo, Post 23)[24].

It is possible that it was from conceptions of this kind, created from the world of Hellenistic philosophy and mysteries, that the impression arose for later church reporters that Simon had regarded himself as God. The Catholic Christian Justin, in any case, writing around the middle of the second century, knows of three heresiarchs who incurred this (even for Christian heretics somewhat strange) accusation: the already well-known Marcion, Menander, and their common ancestor Simon from Samaria. Justin further reports that, through the influence of evil demons, Simon also practiced his arts in Rome during the time of Emperor Claudius. According to Justin, in the same way as in his homeland, Samaria, where almost everyone had become his follower, here also Simon was held to be a God. Justin relates that on the Tiber river a statue had been erected that bore his name: *Simoni Deo Santo*.[25]

According to Justin and other church reporters the aforementioned Helena was at Simon's side. In contrast to the Pseudo-Clementines, we meet Helena here not as a pupil of John the Baptizer, but as a prostitute, whom Simon became acquainted with in a brothel in Tyre. According to Irenaeus, Simon and the Simonians perceived this as an allegorical event with central significance for the teaching of Simon:

> He led a woman named Helena around with him, a prostitute from the Phoenician city of Tyre whom he had purchased. He called her the first Ennoia (thought) of his mind, the mother of all, through whom, in the beginning, he decided in his mind to create angels and archangels. After this Ennoia sprung forth from him she recognized what her father desired, and she descended into the lower spheres and brought forth angels and powers, by whom also he said this world was made. After she brought them forth, she was held captive by them because of jealousy, because they did not want to be regarded as descendents of someone else. He himself (Simon) is completely unknown to them; but his Ennoia was held captive by the powers and angels that came forth from her, and she had to suffer many humiliating things, so that could return to her father above. And it went so far that she was even enclosed in a human body, and in the course of time, as from one vessel to another, wandered in ever changing bodies of women... For this purpose Simon came, to take her as the first to himself, and also to bring salvation to other people who recognize him (Irenaeus, AH, 1.23.2-3).

In the teaching of Simon and his followers, the Helena-event obviously symbolized the relationship of human souls to

God, or their redeemer. The brothel, in which Helena is held captive, is usually interpreted as the world, in which the souls are imprisoned and in which—far from their heavenly home—they become defiled. The heavenly "fiancé" Simon, then, is no one else than the divine redeemer himself, who frees the souls from their prison and takes them with him back to their heavenly home. In the Exegesis of the Soul, a later Simonian-Gnostic writing, we again meet these ideas, which, as we already said, constitute the core of the Simonian salvation drama and in their significance for Gnostic religiosity and spirituality can hardly be overestimated (one thinks, for example, of the Gnostic sacrament of the "bridal chamber").

> As long as she [= psyche, soul] was alone with the father, she was a virgin... But when she fell down into a body... there she fell into the hands of many robbers... She [lost her] virginity and prostituted herself in her body, and gave herself to one and all... She gave up her former prostitution... and cleansed herself in the bridal chamber. She filled it with perfume; she sat in it watching out for the true bridegroom."[26]

Whether Simon himself wrote down his teachings is a debated question. Hippolytus knows a writing with the title Great Proclamation (Megalē Apophasis), from which he cites a few fragments.[27] In the opinion of Rudolph and other scholars, "this text is hardly to be considered Simon's work"; rather the entire writing "is probably a kind of philosophical-speculative interpretation of sayings attributed to him by his school in the second century."[28] For Leisegang, on the other hand, who saw in Simon the model of the Hellenistic prophet (Empedocles) and regarded him as a "renewer of the ancient Hellenistic prophetic message," the Apophasis largely derived from Simon's pen: "In its basic elements, it is really to be traced back to Simon."[29]

Remarkable about this work is the *apophatische* style, the majestic "I"-tone with which the writer, like a mystagogue, proclaims his teachings as supreme revelations. The introductory words already give this impression: "This writing — a proclamation, a voice, and a name — stems from the decree of the great, unlimited Power. For this reason, it should be sealed, hidden, cloaked, deposited in the abode where the roots of the All are found." Here again, one is reminded of the writer of the Pauline letters, who now and then employs a very similar way of speaking (Gal 1:1.11; 1 Cor 15:51; Col 1:26; Eph 3:4; etc.), which, to be sure, in comparison with the *Great Proclamation* seems only like a weak imitation.[30]

The content of the *Proclamation* presents a complex religious-philosophical system, at the center of which stands an elaborate cosmology and theology. Like many other scholars, Leisegang was reminded by these teachings, which again and again characteristically unfolded in three steps (for example: "The one, who [once] stood, stands, and will stand [again]."), of the German philosopher Hegel with his "Spirit in itself, Spirit for itself, Spirit in and for itself." Thus, in the trinitarian system of Simon one could see an ancient Gnostic prologue to Hegel's philosophy.[31]

We have only legendary reports concerning of Simon's end. The *Acts of Peter* relates that in Rome, where Peter, his stereotypical antagonist, has followed him, he attempted to fly, in order to demonstrate his wondrous power. Peter, of course, by calling upon Christ, is able to have him crash, so that Simon's leg is broken. His followers finally take him to Aricia (South of Rome), where he dies.

According to Hippolytus, Simon had his students bury him, in order to show that he could be resurrected on the third day. The resurrection did not take place, however, because Simon was certainly not the Messiah, as he himself had claimed.[32]

In Jewish and Jewish-Christian writings Simon is finally portrayed as a true pariah. In Jewish Apocalypses, as well as the so-called Sibyllines, the figure of Simon is styled by his opponents as the Antichrist and portrayed in the blackest colors.

In what follows, we will attempt to verify our thesis that the particular elements from which the writer of the Pauline letters constituted his picture of Paul go back to the figure of Simon by means of a comparison of the pictures of Simon and Paul.

The flatterer

Simon attempts to please men, or flatter them – he is sincere, gentle, and peaceable – he accepts no gifts – he feigns sincerity.

In an apocryphal Acts of the apostles it is said concerning Simon: "With the help of his father, the Devil, this man pleases all people."[33] One can see very clearly that the Marcionite author(s) of the Pauline letters often pick up this feature of the Simon-Paul picture. In Galatians the writer asks his readers:

> Am I seeking to win over men or God? Or am I seeking to please men? If I still wanted to please men, I would not be a slave of Christ (Gal 6:10).

In 2 Corinthians he asks in a similar rhetorical way:

> Since we now know the fear of the Lord, do we seek to win over men?

The writer of 1 Thessalonians also expressly emphasizes:

> So we speak, not to please men, but to please God who tests our hearts.

The visionary, miracle worker, and Missionary

Simon has visions — He performs miracles — He is a successful missionary.

Simon the visionary is the central theme of a passage in the pseudo-Clementine literature where Peter disputes Simon's claim that it is possible to experience the same thing by means of a dream or a vision as on the basis of direct eyewitness.[34] As Simon hears this, he interrupts with the words:

> You have claimed that you came to know the teaching of your master very accurately because you heard and saw him directly when he was present, and that, on the other hand, it is impossible for someone else to experience the same thing by means of a dream or a vision. I will show you that this is false... On the contrary, the vision provides, together with the appearance, certainty that what is seen comes from God.

In addition, the Pseudo-Clementines report an attempt by Simon to fly, ending in failure (with a deathly crash). This seems to be a parodistic variation of the Simon as visionary motif.

The author of the primary Pauline letters also portrays Paul as a visionary. Paul is called to his task as an evangelist through a revelation (Gal 1:16), and his trip to Jerusalem for the apostolic council is brought about by a revelation (Gal 2:2). Above all, however, one naturally thinks here about the well-known passage in 2 Cor 12:1ff, where "Paul" reports his having been caught up into the third heaven where he heard unspeakable words (words which Marcion could say that *he* had heard).[35]

> I know a man in Christ who fourteen years ago was caught up into the third heaven—whether in the body or out of the body I do not know, God knows. And I know that this man was caught up into paradise—whether in the body or out of the

body I do not know, God knows—and he heard words which cannot be spoken, which a man cannot utter.

All this shows—not that the author of Galatians and 2 Corinthians himself had visionary experiences, but—that he knew how great a role revelations and visionary-ecstatic experiences played in the biography of his hero in whose name he wrote the "letters"—i.e., Simon-Paul.

The same is also true for *signs and wonders*, which play a large role in the historical reports concerning Simon Magus, or as the case may be, Simon the heretic, referred to as Antichrist/Beliar. Consider the following passage from the Sibylline writings (3.63ff), where it is said concerning the coming of Beliar, which most scholars believe relates to Simon Magus:[36]

> From the Sebasternines Beliar will come afterward, and will make high mountains rise up and make the sea stand still, the great fiery sun and the bright moon, and he will raise up the dead and perform many signs for people. But fulfillment will not be in him, but [only] deception, and he will thus lead many people astray, faithful and chosen Hebrews as well as other lawless persons, who have still never heard the speech of God. But when the threats of the great God draw near, and a fiery power comes through the billowing water to land and consumes Beliar and the arrogant people, all who have put their faith in him...

Other texts relating to the Antichrist (= Simon) also refer again and again to his miraculous deeds.[37] The miracle-working activity of Simon is extensively portrayed in the Pseudo-Clementines, and Acts also reports that Simon, who was referred to as great power (Acts 8:10),[38] had "amazed" the Samaritan people for a long while.[39]

Corresponding with this, in 2 Corinthians, as evidence for his apostolic legitimacy, "Paul" can appeal to the fact that "the signs of the apostle were performed among you... with signs and wonders and mighty works" (12:12).[40]

In the passage from the Christian Sibyllines it is said that Simon misled many people [through his preaching], and indeed not only Hebrews but also "other lawless people, who had never heard the speech of God." It can be inferred from this that Simon had also turned to the Gentiles and carried out missionary activity here as well. Even the Pseudo-Clementines could not avoid mentioning Simon's great missionary success; through him, even before Peter, many Gentiles were supposedly converted to Christianity. Peter is speaking:

> While I am going to the Gentiles, who believe in many gods, to proclaim through my preaching the one God, who made heaven and earth, and everything that is therein, so that they might come to love him and be saved, evil has anticipated me, according to the law of the syzygies, and has sent Simon ahead, so that people who reject the gods who supposedly dwell on earth, and speak no more of their great number, should believe that there are many gods in heaven... I must quickly follow him so that his lying assertions will not gain a footing and establish themselves everywhere.[41]

In the same way, Paul is also called by a revelation to preach the gospel to the Gentiles (Gal 1:16), and at the end of the letter to the Romans he can look back on a preaching mission that reaches over the entire world from Jerusalem to Illyricum (Rom 15:19). Since he no longer has any more room for work here (15:23, 24), it is necessary for him, after the visit in Rome, to go further to Spain. — The situation which Peter refers to in the Pseudo-Clementines seems to be identical with the situation reflected in the Pauline letters: The mission of Simon-Paul is followed by the Judaizing counter-mission.

The Son of Lawlessness

Simon as the "Son of Lawlessness" — Simonian Soteriology — Simon as "Libertine" — Simon as Persecutor of the Saints — Simon as "Enemy"

The primary accusation made against Simon by the Jewish anti-Simonian polemic as well as by Catholic Christian polemic was that he had rejected the Law. The Simonian antinomianism was grounded in the Simonian doctrine of redemption (Soteriology), in which a theologian of the last century already perceived "a magical prelude or counterpart to the freedom from the Law proclaimed by Paul..."[42] To be convinced of this, one should compare the teaching of Paul with the following brief summary of the Simonian teaching by Irenaeus:

> Whoever, therefore, placed their trust in him and his Helena no longer needed to be concerned about them [the angels who made the world], but, as a free persons, could live as they pleased. The were saved by his grace, and not by works of righteousness. The works are not good in themselves, but only by accident. The contrary teaching was devised by the angels who made the world in order to enslave people by means of precepts. He promised them, however, that when the world decomposes they would be set free from the dominion of those angels.[43]

The teaching represented by Simon, according to which the law is abrogated by grace (the spirit) is, as the Gnosis scholar Kurt Rudolph correctly remarked, "a formulation familiar also to Paul which Marcion then extended into a reformation of the gospel, without however paying homage to libertinism."[44] Indeed, that Simon ever paid homage to libertinism at all, as some church fathers asserted, is very doubtful, and is contested by Rudolph. We seem to have to do here rather with Jewish or Jewish-Christian defamation. Much of what was represented as "licentiousness" and "debauchery" by Jews in the first century or by observant Jewish-Christians in the second century was certainly not always the same as libertinism. The author of the seven letters in Revelation can mention the eating of meat sacrificed to idols and "fornication" in the same breath (Rev 2:14). And one should not forget that Protestantism was also often represented in Roman Catholic polemic as libertine blundering.[45]

The Antichrist (Simon) also meets us as the Son of Lawlessness in the Jewish *Apocalypse of Elijah*. Here it is also said that he persecuted the saints with extreme agony.[46] To a certain extent, it seems like this has to do with Simon-Paul prior to his conversion to Catholicism! Indeed, this feature of the picture of Simon-Paul (Paul as persecutor) seems to have been consciously ignored by the Marcionite author of the Pauline letters. He had no reason to report this because his hero did not need to justify himself for the persecution of the saints (i.e., the earliest Jewish-Christian churches), which for him, as an early representative of the Jewish-Christian church, was a matter of indifference. It was the Catholic redactor who first introduced the persecution passages into Galatians, presumably on the basis of the presentation in Acts. For Paul had now become a church patron for Catholics as well. And as long as the memory of the persecution activity of Simon-Paul was present among Jewish Christians, this had to be appeased and compensated for by the introduction of a conversion experience. The conversion of Paul, therefore, is most probably not a biographical fact at all, but only historical in so far as it reflects the beginning of Catholicism with its fraternization of Paul and the twelve. Only now did it first become possible for Jewish-Christians and Marcionites to live peacefully with one another under a common Catholic roof. The historical Simon-Paul was most probably not a convert, but a renegade! — As a lawless Gnostic, Simon is finally identical with the enemy, or the hostile man, who is spoken of not only in the Pseudo-Clementine literature, but also in the Jewish writings directed against Simon, among others, the Epistula Petri, where the "lawless and senseless teaching of the hostile man" is mentioned, namely the teaching of Paul. Even Paul asks the Galatians: "Have I then become your enemy by telling you the truth [of the gospel]?" (Gal 4:16).

The *Match*-Maker

Up to now, in our search for historical traces of Simon Magus we had be satisfied primarily with the distorted picture of the Antichrist and the hostile man in Jewish, or Jewish-Christian, polemic. But the magician did not frequent only the confused fantasies of the apocalyptic writers; the Jewish historian Josephus also mentions him in a brief but highly informative note in his Antiquities.

Moreover, for this reason every doubt regarding the existence of the Samaritan Simon, which was once expressed here and there, should be excluded. The passage from the pen of the worldly historian Josephus irrefutably shows that the Samaritan Simon is not a figure of fantasy. And apart from this, the energy of the hatred which the Jewish and Jewish-Christian writings concentrate on the figure of the *Antichrist* and *hostile man* testifies positively that the object to which they relate has a historical basis. No one polemicizes against a phantom.

In the passage from *Jewish Antiquities* (20.7.2) Josephus attests that the historical Simon was a contemporary as well as a confidant of the Roman governor Felix (51/51-ca. 60 CE). Josephus reports that the Roman governor made use of the Simon's magical abilities, or special persuasive skill, in a delicate situation by employing Simon to mediate a marriage for him.

Felix had fallen head over heels in love with Drusilla, the granddaughter of Cleopatra and Antonius (Tacitus, *Historiae*, 5.9), and also a sister of Bernice, and wanted to marry her. Although Drusilla was already married to King Azizus of Emesa—or had become married to him through her brother Agrippa—and even though Felix, who was famous for his cruelty, having had a "multitude of revolutionaries" crucified daily in Palestine, was a highly questionable specter, from both a human and a political perspective, so that even the Roman historian Tacitus could characterize him as a person "indulging in every kind of barbarity and lust," (5:9) Simon, being called upon here, obviously had no moral reservations about helping prepare the way for the contemplated marriage.

> Felix, the Governor of Judea, had scarcely seen Drusilla, who was distinguished for her beauty, when he was enflamed with great love for her. He sent to her, therefore, a Jewish friend of his named Simon (Atomos), who came from Cyprus and represented himself as a magician, to attempt to persuade [!] her to leave her husband and marry him [Felix]. He had him tell her that if she did not reject him, he would make her a happy woman. In order to avoid the envy of her sister Bernice, from whom she had to suffer many things because of her beauty, Drusilla acted badly, let herself be persuaded to transgress her native laws, and married Felix (Jos Ant 20:142).

The episode related by Josephus is very interesting because we meet both leading protagonists once more in Luke's Acts—although, to be sure, here it is not Simon who converses with the now married couple, but the imprisoned Paul:

> After some days Felix came with his wife Drusilla, who was a Jewess; and he sent for Paul and heard him speak about faith in Christ Jesus. As he spoke, however, about righteousness and [sexual] continence (!) and the future judgment, Felix was filled with fear and answered, "Go away for now! when I have an opportunity I will summon you." At the same time he

hoped that money would be given him by Paul. So he sent for him often and conversed with him (Acts 24:24ff.).

Against the background of the prevalent way of looking at this today, according to which Simon and Paul still represent two different historical persons, one could perceive the passage in Acts as a further extension of our knowledge about the Roman governor and his wife. After the two were married, with the help of Simon, they met the apostle Paul. On this occasion, he appealed to their conscience in a fundamental way by preaching to them about sexual continence, which could be related to the fact that Felix had married a divorced woman. In his relationship with Felix, Paul appears then as preaching a kind of prophetic warning, comparable to John the Baptizer in his relationship with Herod.

So far, so good. Since in the meantime, however, we have become wary, and know that Simon and Paul are not so different, as Luke would like us to believe, but that in the Jewish-Christian polemic of Luke's time the two rather flow into one another in an undifferentiated way, so that words spoken by Paul can be placed in the mouth of Simon, and conversely the picture of Paul exhibits all the features of Simon, we therefore view the entire passage in a somewhat more critical way.

Could it not rather be the case that Luke, as indeed otherwise conforms with his manner, once again engages in apologetic? Could it not be the case that for Luke the entire passage only pursues the goal of removing once and forever the suspicion, that seemed plausible for some, that Paul and Simon Magus were one and the same person? That Paul preaches sexual continence to the freshly-baked married couple could indeed have and entirely different basis than the fact that Felix had just married a divorced woman. With this portrayal of Paul preaching a prophetic warning Luke could have attempted to set aside another picture of the apostle very well known to him, namely, that of the matchmaker spoken of in Jewish and Jewish-Christian circles.

A similar apologetic intention seems to also underlie Acts 24:26. Luke remarks that Felix hoped for a bribe from Paul. This remark as well, which in view of the financial situation of the hardly wealthy tentmaker makes no sense, and for which exegetes have been unable to provide any reasonable explanation, can only be understood when one recognizes that Luke engages here in apologetics. Johannes Kreyenbühl rightly observes in this regard: "The motif of money is… only introduced here to counteract the slanderous accusation by Jews that, as match-maker for Drusilla, Paul had often visited with Felix and was paid for his service." Luke blunts this accusation "by attributing the motive of avarice to the procurator and making Paul the source of money. If Felix hoped to get money from Paul, the relationship between the procurator and Paul invented by the Jews would be relegated to the realm of fable."[47] In other words, the absurd supposition that the governor expected money from Paul, the wandering preacher and tentmaker, obviously serves to refute the accusation (known to Luke) of a close personal relationship between Felix and Simon-Paul.

From Paul to Saul

According to a common conception, that has also become a figure of speech, the effect of the conversion at Damascus was that out of Saul emerged a Paul. This conception is widespread, but is nevertheless incorrect. "The name," as Ben Chorin correctly writes, "has nothing to do with this transformation." In the vision Paul is addressed by Jesus in Hebrew as Schaul, and in Damascus the message is brought to Ananias that Schaul from Tarsus has arrived. Ananias addressed the guest as 'brother Schaul.' It is not true at all, therefore, that here from Saul a Paul came into being; rather, precisely in this vision and directly after it Paul is addressed with his Hebrew name Schaul, with which he also appeared previously."[48]

The name change from Saul to Paul thus takes place in Acts not in direct connection with the conversion, but on the first missionary journey of Paul, while he was on the island of Cyprus, together with his companion Barnabas, and there converted the governor *Sergius Paulus* to the Christian faith. In 13:9 the reader is parenthetically informed that Saul also means Paul ("But Saul, who is also called Paul"). It was not at all uncommon for Jews to take a Roman name alongside their own Jewish name, and the practice is attested elsewhere. This need not occupy us further here. We should rather pursue the question of what the fact that the author of Acts knows about a second name for Paul signifies for our theory. The fact as such could indeed be conceived as a serious argument against our Simon = Paul thesis. In contrast to Paul, the name Saul cannot be understood as a *supernomen* (i.e., as a nickname of Simon's). If Paul's Jewish name was Saul, our Simon = Paul theory would collapse. Now, we already observed above, of course, that Tertullian, in settling accounts with Marcion, had remarkable interest in finding the figure of the apostle, whom he viewed with great mistrust—which many exegetes today could well take as something to emulate—, already prefigured in the Old Testament.

> Because even the book of Genesis so long ago promised me the Apostle Paul. For among the types and prophetic blessings which he pronounced over his sons, Jacob, when he turned his attention to Benjamin, exclaimed, 'Benjamin shall ravin as a wolf; in the morning He shall devour the prey, and at night he shall impart nourishment.' He foresaw that Paul would arise out of the tribe of Benjamin, a voracious wolf, devouring his

prey in the morning: in order words, in the early period of his life he would devastate the Lord's sheep, as a persecutor of the churches; but in the evening he would give them nourishment, which means that in his declining years he would educate the fold of Christ, as the teacher of the Gentiles. Then, again, in Saul's conduct towards David, exhibited first in violent persecution of him, and then in remorse and reparation, on his receiving from him good for evil, we have nothing else than an anticipation of Paul in Saul – belonging, too, as they did, to the same tribe--and of Jesus in David, from whom He descended according to the Virgin's genealogy(AM, 5.1ff.).

What is peculiar here is that only when he sees Paul already signified in the person of the Old Testament king Saul can set his mind at rest with regard to the apostle whose legitimacy has been questioned in a kind of cross-examination over several paragraphs [!].

What does this mean? If we consider in addition that the author of the letters speaks only of Paul, and never of Saul, and that the use of the name Saul is thus a *peculiarity of the Catholic Acts* which we find nowhere else[49], this could mean that Tertullian and the Catholic tradition, as whose representative he appears, obviously had a strong *dogmatic* interest in tying the apostle Paul (in the same way as the twelve apostles) into the Jewish tradition. In view of the fact that in early Christianity dogmatic concerns as a rule preceded historical concerns and surpassed them in importance, it could mean that the Jewish name Saul was later attached to the apostle Paul, and indeed for the purpose of indicating in an unmistakable way the Jewish roots and origin of the apostle. In other words, the name Saul was very probably given to the apostle not by his parents, but by the Catholic church of the second century — presumably for the first time by the resourceful Catholic who wrote Acts! It is not the case, therefore, as one often assumes, that the name Paul was derived from Saul (which moreover is not convincing in itself because there is only a tonal connection between Saul and Paul, and no connection with regard to content: i.e., Paul = "the small one" is not a translation of Saul = "the requested one"!)[50], but, on the contrary, with regard to tradition-history, the name "Paul" took on the Jewish name "Saul" as a later attachment.

The intention of the person who attached the Jewish name Saul to Paul was *to integrate the apostle into the Jewish tradition*. Through the name, the figure of the apostle could thus be tied forever with the Jewish tradition, in which until the present day nothing is known about a student of Gamaliel by the name of Saul. In such a way, the ground could effectively be cut from under rumors, like those spread, for example, in extreme anti-Pauline circles, in which it was said that the apostle was never a Jew at all.

Simon the Leper and Paul's Sickness

Simon and the cross — his outer unsightliness — his illness

In the Apocalypse of Elijah it is said that at the coming of the Antichrist (= Simon) he will be preceded by a cross. For Paul as well, the preaching of the cross is of highest importance: one thinks of the familiar passages in 1 Corinthians:

> For the word of the cross is folly to those who are perishing, but to us who are being saved it is the power of God (1:18).

Now and then, the "Paul" of the letters emphasizes his outer unsightliness, as in Galatians, for example, where he points out that the Galatians responded to the temptation for them in his flesh neither with disgust nor disdain (Gal 4:14); and in 2 Cor 12:7 he speaks of a "thorn in his flesh," which refers, as has correctly been observed, to a sickness that seems to have left behind some kind of marks. This corresponds with the picture of the Antichrist (= Simon) sketched — to be sure, in skewed polemic — by the Jewish apocalyptic writer. The Apocalypse of Elijah describes him as follows:

> He has skinny legs; at the front of his (bald?) head there is a tuft of white hair; his eyebrows (?) reach to his ears, while leprous scabs cover his hands. He transforms himself before those who see him; he becomes a child; he becomes an old man. He will transform himself in every sign; but he cannot transform the signs of his head. By this you will recognize him, that he is the son of lawlessness."[51]

As E. Preuschen correctly determined, the portrait presented here is that of a person smitten with leprosy disease.[52] In addition to the unmistakable reference to the "leprous scabs" on the hands, this is indicated by the reference to "clump of white hair" on the front of the head, which is likewise related to this sickness and belongs to its manifestation. Preuschen is also able to persuasively demonstrate that Paul's sickness too, which the author of the letters repeatedly mentions, seems to be leprosy. "Paul suffers from leprosy. In Hebrew, leprosy is called hebräisch צָרַעַת from צָרַע, whose basic meaning is 'to strike,' or 'strike down.' ... The leper is actually 'one stricken (by God),' which is the meaning of צָרוּעַ in Lev 13:44; 22:4, etc. One now sees what horrible truth the *kolaphizein* [κολαφίζειν = 'to strike'] has for the apostle, and that with the 'thorn in the flesh' he was bloody serious. Since leprosy attacks the skin and builds abscesses in it, Paul was justified in speaking of 'thorns' or 'goads.' Since the head is affected first of all, the expression 'slap in the face' is a very drastic euphemism for this malady."[53]

It becomes clear here that when the author of the letters speaks of Paul's malady he obviously has the sickness of "Simon the leper" in view. Finally, attention should be called to the remarkable parallels in the *outward appearance* of Simon, on the one hand, and Paul, on the other. One should compare the portrait of the Antichrist (= Simon) just cited with the picture of Paul in the *Acts of Paul and Thecla* already given above:

> He saw Paul coming, a man small of stature, with a bald head and crooked legs, in a good state of body, with eyebrows meeting at the nose, very small and projecting somewhat, full of friendliness, now appearing like a man, and now with the face of an angel.

Although in the Apocalypse of Elijah the externals of the portrayal are a caricature and in the Acts of Thecla an idealization, as Preuschen already showed, even after the fantastic exaggeration is removed, there can be no doubt that one and the same person is portrayed: the Antichrist (Simon) is none other than Paul — Paul is none other than the Antichrist (Simon).

Simon and Helena — Paul and Thecla — Jesus and Mary Magdalene

In contrast to the Simon legends and the Acts of Paul, in the Pauline letters there is no figure who plays a leading role here and whose destiny is closely linked with that of Paul (or Simon, as the case may be) — like Helena, as the companion of Simon, or the virgin Thecla, who in the Acts of Paul and Thecla becomes a symbolic figure for the chastity preached by the Paul of the Acts of Paul. The close connection of the Thecla legends with conceptions of ascetic-chastity[54] could also be the reason why, if the figure of Thecla was ever mentioned in the letters, which in my opinion is certainly not improbable, she was deleted by Catholic redaction.

The English radical critic Johnson already called attention to the fact that the relationship of Simon and Helena seems to be reflected in the relationship of Paul and Thecla, if only in a broken way. It is very probable that Thecla was a (tradition-historical) pendant to the Simonian Helena. As Helena, who in symbolic disguise serves as the representative of the human soul, was set free by Simon from the brothel in Tyre (= the world, in which she defiled her soul; cf. the Simonian writing *The Exegesis of the Soul*[55]), so Thecla is set free by Paul for a life in purity and continence.

Apart from all the other parallels that could be mentioned here, one common element is particularly interesting. It is said that Thecla listened to preaching of Paul day and night, and indeed from her window[56]. The mention of the window is in no way accidental. The window motif also appears with regard to Helena, where it is said that "once, in the middle of a great crowd of people, she look out of all the windows of a tower at the same time."[57] In this regard, the theologian Beyschlag rightly observes that "the prurience of Helena is probably alluded to" here, "for to peer out of a window was regarded in the ancient world as a *gestus meretricius*, i.e., as a wanton gesture."[58] Reflected here is the motif of the psyche looking around out the window of the body (= prison), which includes the "uninterrupted watching for the bridegroom,"[59] of which this is a variation. Thecla and Helena are obviously only different names for the same figure: embodiments of the human soul as the object of the Gnostic process of redemption.[60]

In his book about *Gnosis als Weltreligion*, the Dutch theologian Quispel, of the school of C.G. Jung, occupied himself intensely with the figure of the Simonian Helena. In his view, the story of Helena was interpreted allegorically by the Simonians. This is especially the case with the motif of the window, as well with the motif of Helena standing over the castle with a torch. This reflects Gnostic cosmology, the Gnostic conception of the origin of the world. "The story wants to suggest that at the beginning of the genesis of the world the goddess Helena... showed the lower archons of the chaos the higher original light (Epiphanius, [Pan] 23.3). That is the Gnostic myth par excellence, which is found in innumerable variations and can be very briefly summarized. In the beginning were the world of light and the world of darkness; then a hypostasis, usually called the original man or sophia, showed the demons of the world of darkness the original light. These archons, usually conceived as the seven planets, became lustful and pursued the light, which attempted to flee. How the light then becomes mixed with the darkness is portrayed in various ways. It soon comes to pass that the light figure itself becomes lustful and peers down with curiosity (*spectandi libido*), and sacrifices itself to prevent the demons of darkness from gaining entry."[61] Thus, for Quispel the Simonian Helena was "originally... the cosmological potency, which standing on the towering house of the world lets the original light to shine forth..."

In addition to Helena, Quispel regards a series of other ancient female figures as so-called "tower virgins," i.e., as a tradition-historical reflection of the Helena myth, in which the same basic pattern is reflected once again under different names in other, often much stronger historicizing, ways.[62] He also regards the figure of *Salome*, who appears primarily in Gnostic traditions, as a "tower virgin." At this point, one could also call attention to the book of *Joseph and Asenath*, which derives from Jewish circles, but which contains the same motif, further developed, of course, in a more romantic way. It is also said about the beautiful Asenath that her father Pentepheres made here live in a garret on a tower with ten rooms and that no man was ever able to see her, until one day Joseph saw her sitting *in the window* of the garret and finally married her. As has often been rightly perceived, Asenath also represents here the human soul, who is shut up in the body (the tower) and who is set free by Joseph, her savior of souls, who is also referred to as "Messiah" and "Son of God" (4.7; 6.6).

Finally, there is still another motif-historical version of the same material, found in the anointing story of the New Testament, which we already met above. As Quispel also suggested, *Mary Magdalene* obviously belongs in the series of tower-virgins we just mentioned.

We have already indicated that in the figure of the woman whom we meet in the anointing story of the synoptic Gospels (Luke calls her a "sinner," which in the language of that time meant a prostitute) we most probably have a tradition-historical reflection of the (revered above all in Christian-Gnostic circles) Mary Magdalene (presumably from the Hebrew "Migdal" (= the tower). The tradition-historical origin of the entire account, which all the evangelists reflect in very different ways, is still visible in the name of the host, with whom Jesus stays. While Luke cleverly concealed this name (for good reasons), and only relates that Jesus was eating in a house of a Pharisee, we learn from Mark that it was *Simon the leper.*

> And while he was at Bethany in the house of Simon the leper, as he sat at table, a woman came with an alabaster flask of very costly ointment of pure nard, and she broke the flask and poured it over his head (14:3).

As we have seen, however, Simon the leper is none other than Simon Magus, who was also stricken with leprosy. The Aramaic word מצרע, from which the Greek *lepros* (λεπρός) probably derives, has a double meaning. In and for itself, it means "leprous." Since it has tonal similarity with מצרה, however, one could also think of the Aramaic "from Tyre." Simon the leper, then, would be none other than Simon from Tyre. And here also the name Simon Magus immediately comes to mind, who ransomed his wife Helena from a brothel in Tyre.

After what has been said, there is no doubt that the Tyre-Helena motif, that obviously stood at the center of the Simonian doctrine of redemption, in a secondary, tradition-historical process, was carried over to (the "savior of souls") Jesus. We suddenly begin to understand the *erotic motifs* of the entire story, which, to be sure, were mostly eliminated by Mark and Matthew, but still clearly shine through (ointment/perfume, foot-washing) in Luke's version (Lk 7:36ff.).

Finally, it could become clear to us that Gnosis was not a Christian heresy, but that Christianity represents a heresy, a "by-product" of Gnosis — and certainly the most successful.

At the end of our investigation of the remarkable similarities between the Gnostic Simon and the Paul of the New Testament, which led us to the conclusion that we obviously have to do here with one and the same person, I want to once again emphasize that the Pauline letters were indeed *not* written by the historical Paul (= Simon), but by this person's later follower Marcion, or perhaps another Marcionite Christian (Apelles).

Only with this presupposition is the riddle of the Clementine literature solved — which is indeed three-fold, in that in addition to Paul and Simon, there is also Marcion, who is invisibly present in the speeches of Simon — and along with this the question concerning the origin of the Pauline letters.

All in all, given the arguments that have been presented, the thesis that in the case of Simon and Paul we have before us only *one* person, not two, does not seem to me at all too daring. I am certainly well aware that the decisive proof, able to set aside absolutely every doubt, has not yet been produced. But where at all do find such decisive proof in the field of research of early Christian history? Therefore, I would propose that the thesis at least be understood as a working hypothesis and to test it for a while under this presupposition. It could indeed be that even more light will fall on the darkness of early Christian history. Where this is not the case, as far as I am concerned, one may safely forget it again. But as long as the problems that I have attempted to identify remain unanswered, the question at least remains: does Simon = Paul; and does Paul = Simon?

Chapter 4

WHAT REMAINS?

Plato's Allegory of the Cave and the Investigation of Earliest Christian History

In his famous allegory of the cave, the philosopher Plato compares people with prisoners, who have been chained in a cave since birth.[1] Unaware of the cave itself, all that prisoners become aware of in the cave is only their own shadows thrown on the wall of the cave and the echoes of sounds which reach their ears. Since the prisoners have never seen or heard anything different in their lives, they must regard the shadows and echoes as reality, not the people and the things from which they derive. If they were set free from their imprisonment in the cave and had the opportunity to view the true reality in the dazzling light of the sun, they would at first regard this only as an unreal dream and continue to attribute greater reality to their shadows. If on their return, however, they told the prisoners who had remained behind in the cave what they had seen and experienced outside, they would hardly find belief, but instead would only bring forth derisive laughter. And nevertheless, Plato concludes, in spite of all the toil and trouble, it is necessary to being people from appearance to actuality, from the apparent reality into the true reality of their existence.

Although what the philosopher says relates to his own particular theme of philosophy, concerning its wondrous power to free people from appearance and to transfer them from the world of mere opinion into that of true existence, it can also be applied to the theme of this book: the history of earliest Christianity and its scholarly investigation.

It may be that the experience of the reader who has followed the expositions of this book resembles that of the people in the Platonic allegory. It may be that the more he attempts to draw nearer to the colorful and graphic figures of early Christian history relied upon since childhood — Jesus, Paul, Peter, etc. — by means of historical criticism, the more he ascertains that they are historically out of reach and emerge as phantom figures. Perhaps he experienced that what he once regarded — also without closer scientific determination — as immediately illuminating, plausible, and settled turned out to be in truth only shadow-figures.

Just as every shadow makes reference to that which throws the shadow, however, so also those figures in early Christian history, which until now we assumed we saw before us in full reality, and which we now understand to be mere images, make reference to the real forces and leading figures who determined the history of early Christianity. The disappointment that so much was not the way we thought, and the way it had been presented to us, becomes outweighed by the fact that our insight into early Christian history gains depth and plasticity, that we perceive with fewer illusions, but so also more clearly and distinctly, the real historical forces in their battle for the truth, as well as for power and dominion. The loss is compensated for by the fact that we come to know other figures in early Christianity, unknown until now, in whom it becomes clear to us what immense spiritual forces, still entirely free and unhampered by any orthodoxy, were present in the cradle of Christianity, in comparison with which present-day Christianity seems like an extinct volcano.

Finally, however, our loss will be compensated for by the experience of a previously unknown freedom in dealing with the rudiments of our Christian faith. In place of rigidly holding fast or dogmatically adhering to so-called "facts of salvation," a literal understanding of the biblical words, and dogmas thousands of years old, and in place of defending the reality of the shadow-pictures, stands the serene composure of one who has learned to look at the ground of things, and in, with, and beneath the so-called historical facts of salvation to perceive the entirely unhistorical essence of the Christian faith existing beyond time and space, which is substantiated not from the distant past, but from the living moment in the here and now.

The Church and her Heretics

Whoever has reached the conclusion that all the Pauline letters are pseudepigraphic writings from the first half of the second century will then have to view the entire world of early Christianity from a different, changed perspective. For such a person, the trusted figures of early Christianity are no longer what they once were. From a historical perspective, there remains scarcely anything more of the great heroes of early Christian times than a distant reflection, hardly more than a shadow.

On the other hand, those figures who until now had only a shadowy existence in church traditions — the early Christian nonconformists and heretics — begin to gradually step forward from the darkness of history and come nearer to us, with their spirit and even with their writings, which for centuries, without knowing it, we have regarded and revered as the sacred works of apostolic founding figures.

As we have seen, what we can observe again and again in the later church history, namely, that the best and most creative powers have flowed to the Church from its heresies and that the actual role of the Church toward them has only been their ordering, selecting, dogmatizing, and reworking, was obviously already true for the earliest beginnings. The actual intellectual impulses, the great "inspirations," the decisive theological ideas, came from the heretics. In this field, the Church has never been particularly rich or remarkably gifted in original ideas—and this has been the case until today.

The Church's (certainly genial) contribution lay rather in the refined appropriation of what was basically not its own and which it proclaimed as its possession only by means of a few clever artifices, small changes here and there. Thus, just as the Church understood how to "underhandedly take away" the Hebrew Bible from the Jews by declaring it to be *their* Old Testament, the forerunner to their New Testament, thereby taking possession of one of the most important documents in the literary and religious history of humankind, so also the Church treated their heretics. It watched them for a while and quietly left them alone, allowing the heretics to do their intellectual work for them—so then, at the right time, to make an appearance, appropriate the fruit of this work, and declare it to be their own. The Church's relationship with its heretics, therefore, was always ambivalent: from them came the ideas that one did not want to renounce and could not. But instead returning to them the necessary thanks for this, one saw in them a source of great insecurity and trouble. The threat for the Church that emanated from the heretics on account of their simple presence and mere existence is comparable with the irritating threat a thief feels who is constantly confronted by his victim and thus is not allowed the freedom to take undisturbed pleasure in his booty. With an English proverb one could say: "Stones are never thrown but at the fruit-laden tree."[3]

But we should not draw a black and white picture here. The heretics should not be glorified, nor should the men of the

Church be demonized. That would be an unhistorical way of thinking and observing. The point is not to make moral judgments, but only to understand an intellectual-historical process.

From this perspective, one must say that the work of the Church redactors, which began in the middle of the second century to rework in Catholic ways the world-denying, ascetic Marcionite-Pauline message of a foreign God, carried out an important historical and intellectual-historical mission. By connecting freedom with the law, what is above with what is below, and today with yesterday and tomorrow, they tied the message of the Marcionite Paul with this earth again and in this way prevented Christianity from slipping into a world-denying asceticism, or mysticism. At the same time, with regard to Gnosticism, they dammed the vast flood of Gnostic fantasies, and cultivated, tended, and straightened the embankment, to make it possible for the Church-ship to have smooth sailing through the rough currents of the time.

In these ways they made Christianity commensurable with Western culture. And at the same time they may have prevented Europe from being overcome by Asian culture.

Al this is the direct consequence, a direct result, of the Catholic genius empowered by the "heretical" writings, which served as catalyst and break at the same time.

Paul and Jesus

In our deliberations thus far, one figure, from whom all occupation with early Christian history originates, and to whom we return again and again, has still not been considered: namely, Jesus of Nazareth.

Until now, we have met him only now and then, in the story of the anointing of Jesus at Bethany, for example, where we thought we could see for a brief moment the face of the ever-present Samaritan magician flare up behind his name and person.

In order to forestall misunderstanding, I would expressly emphasize that I in no way make the claim here that the Jesus of the New Testament received his life breath from that Samaritan magician whose all-powerful and over-towering person stands at the very beginning of Christianity. Even if there are indications that the figure of Jesus does in fact bear some marks of the Samaritan Simon, which can be well explained from a tradition-historical perspective, and even if it can be seen here and there how the builder of both persons sometimes allowed the two figures to curiously flow together, we have to do nevertheless with two entirely different persons. Without doubt, the Gnostic Simon from Samaria, and the apocalyptic Jesus, stemming from the house of Judah, have entirely different origins.

But — did a historical figure named Jesus exist at all?

In itself, the thesis that the letters of Paul are inauthentic, and that the letters of Paul are thus excluded as a witness to the existence of a historical Jesus, could very well lead to the supposition that there had never been an historical Jesus. With the exclusion of the Pauline letters as the supposedly most important witnesses for the historicity of Jesus, many things do in fact look very different, and many things are possible which until now did not seem possible. In itself, in view of the complete absence of non-Christian sources, doubt in the factual existence of the man Jesus of Nazareth lies close at hand. No person with a sound mind would suppress such doubt, if he or she were not hindered by church tradition and socialization and by a theological consensus that declares every doubter in the past and present to be a "fantasizer." What then should we think about a man who surfaces nowhere except in the writings of his followers and even concerning whose origin and years of birth and death there is no agreement? Obviously, we must doubt his existence.

And nevertheless the theories put forward until now radically disputing the historicity of Jesus seem insufficient to me. As Albert Schweitzer rightly recognized, one of the greatest problems for a consistent-symbolic interpretation of the Gospels is, above all, the *apocalyptic* Jesus with his (disappointed) expectation of a soon end of the world, which can be adapted as the hero of a temporally-transcendent Gnostic salvation story only with difficulty.[4] It is obvious that involved here is not only literary design but also tradition-historical memory, the river of tradition here flowing through time, which on its slow current drags along what in the meantime has long since become out of date and unusable.

So the solution of the entire problem obviously cannot be to *fully* delete a man named Jesus from history. Rather, one must investigate from a tradition-historical perspective the individual components and building blocks from which the New Testament picture of Jesus was constructed — which, like corpuscles and waves, floats back and forth between historical and kerygmatic existence.

Without doubt, we are confronted here with an exciting task, that we can only solve, to be sure, if we do not imagine that from the beginning we already fully possess, as *Beati possidentes*, the only beatific historical knowledge regarding early Christianity. Instead, we should rather recognize — as shameful as this might be after more than ca. two centuries of historical-critical research — that basically, with regard to the most important things, we still know nothing at all, or much too little to be able to accept the *historically grounded* claims of the Christian religion (we would be glad to discuss the other claims).

Instead, we should happily admit our own curiosity and in addition admit — as unpleasant as it might be — that the naked historical truth is better than the most beautiful illusion.

The Foundations of the Christian Faith

In many bestsellers trumpeted as sensational the authors attempt thereby to give an added drama that promises their readers that their new theses and discoveries will shake the fundaments of the Christian faith. If the authors instead of the Christian faith, would speak rather of the Church, or the faith of the Church, one might be able to even affirm them, provided that their theses were valid. For history in fact plays a great role for the Church as the basis for (what is in its eyes) right belief. Thus, we have seen, for example, that for the Church — i.e., for the Catholic great church emerging in Rome in the middle of the second century — it was of decisive importance, in debate with other Christian groups, that it could represent itself as the legitimate historical heir of the early church in Jerusalem. The Church needed history, and in accordance with its own self-understanding still needs it today in order to represent itself as the original (= true) Church and its faith as the original (= true and correct) faith, from which all other churches and heresies are derived.

The notion that the Church can present itself, like everything that comes into being historically, only as something "derived," namely, a form of Gnostic heresy, is thereby excluded. Strictly speaking, as has already been conceded in the meantime by a number of theologians, the historical claim of church is a fiction. The fundaments for the faith of the Church and for what later constituted Catholic orthodoxy were defined in the second century, not the first. That is decisively shown by the fact that, according to current opinion today, the New Testament contains only seven authentic writings, i.e., writings deriving from apostolic times—and in my view consists exclusively of pseudepigraphic writings. Tracing and projecting these fundaments back into the apostolic age only functions as a historical legitimization, which, as one can still observe, has a great significance in human legal affairs. Whether it should also have such significance in religious affairs is very doubtful. Nevertheless, over against the Gnostic currents of the time, institutionally less defined and trusting more in the Spirit, it provided the Church with a powerful advantage, which finally made them victors in the historical struggle for Christian sovereignty.

It was history, therefore, or, better, *the fiction of history*, that placed the Church on a firm foundation, so that it could survive for hundreds and even thousands of years. When and so long as the Church makes its authority, its existence or non-existence, dependent on this history, it must defend this claim with whatever means necessary, or its foundations will be shaken by the discovery that what is claimed to be history is only pseudo-history—unless it prefers, instead, to change its own self-understanding and to ground its authority in spiritual power instead of history.

Now the Christian faith, nevertheless, cannot be identified with the faith of the Church, and certainly not any one church, even if the Church representatives, as a matter of course, more or less hold fast to this claim. Strictly speaking, for the Christian believer, who in his or her faith seeks comfort and support for the crises of life, who would like to be stimulated, comforted, or "edified" by the biblical writings, by the stories in the Old Testament about ancient people, the marvelous parables in the Gospels, by the teaching of the Sermon on the Mount, or by the spiritual fervor of freedom in the Pauline letters (to be sure, sometimes greatly dimmed by Catholic insertions) — for such a person, whether or not these writings come from the hand of a Moses, or a Paul, or any of the other apostles, is a matter of relative indifference. In his or her view, what grants authority to the writings, indeed, is not the *person*, in whose name they were written, but the *spirit* that speaks to him therefrom for hundreds and thousands of years. If the authority of the writings were based on the authority and the name of their author, i.e., on a historical fundament, he would be next to despair. For now his faith would be dependent on the results of historical research, and with such a faith, if one really takes seriously the constantly changing results of historical scholarship, he must soon give up. The very next newspaper report that reaches him at breakfast about a new manuscript found in the desert of Palestine or Egypt could collapse his well-constructed edifice of faith. In contrast to the faith that grants the calm security of a deep, existential trust and comfort and support for one's life, this kind of faith is a restless, unsettled to-and-fro that has no end and leads the believer, as if he were hooked on drugs, to continually require new assurances.

I am certainly well aware that there are many Christians for whom the connections I have attempted to sketch make little sense. For them, in the same way as for the Church, faith is simultaneously *faith in history*, i.e., it is based on specific data, which are sometimes accepted as historical on trust (the so-called "obedience of faith") and sometimes simply accepted as historical without reflection on the matter. It cannot be disputed that these persons can find therein support for their lives, i.e., in a faith that provided a center of meaning for many people for more than fifteen hundred years. On the other hand, however, it likewise cannot be denied that since the awakening of historical consciousness and the beginning of historical inquiry regarding the fundaments of faith much has changed and that since then there are many people who experience very intensely the great uncertainty that has taken hold of faith (as faith in history) since then. They can no longer be satisfied with a faith that still stems from the phase of human history prior to historical consciousness. In their criticism of the foundations of the old faith, which is basically only the reverse side of their search for a new foundation, they are often in danger of throwing overboard the baby with the bath water, i.e., faith along with history, and thereby Christianity as such.

In spite of this danger, it seems to me that this crisis of faith is both necessary and unavoidable. One does not deal with it, as most theologians today do, by making light of, glossing over, or obscuring, but only by pushing the crisis to the extreme limit. Its extreme limit takes place in *radical theology*. Only a radical (i.e., going to the roots) questioning of the foundations of Christianity is able to bring about the crisis, whose absence makes the Christian faith suffer, and, after faith is no longer able to withstand historical criticism, is perhaps also able to provide a look at what is really at stake.

In this sense, radical historical criticism poses no danger for faith. Radical criticism of the foundations of the Christian faith necessarily leads, in a first step, to the destruction, the demolishing, of what has come before, and in this sense to absolute zero. And nevertheless, from the crisis of the Christian faith in history something new necessarily proceeds, i.e., a faith that no longer requires historical fundaments for its confirmation. Christianity would thus have finally become a *religion of the Spirit* — as it once was at the beginning of its history, when there was not yet any (Catholic) church at all, in the Churches of the "heresiarch" Marcion or Simon and all the other Gnostics.

The poem about *The Lost Church*, by Ludwig Uhland, whose opening lines I found as a hand-written remark in the book *Antiqua Mutter*, from the estate of the radical critic Bolland, had a continuation, as I learned when I returned home, picked up an edition of Uhland's work, and read:

> The forest's depths I lately sought,
> From every track of man retired;
> To quit the ills this age hath wrought
> And yearn for God, my soul aspired.
> Where silence all around was poured,
> I heard this pleasant chime again;
> The more my aspirations soared,
> The nearer, louder seemed the strain.
>
> My soul was so absorbed in dreams,
> My mind so ravished by the sound,
> That still a mystery it seems
> How I such heights of fancy found...[5]

With the words of the poet Friedrich Rückert (1788-1866), one could also say:

> Wenn man, was man glauben soll,
> Nicht mehr glauben kann,
> Ist die Zeit eines Glaubens voll,
> Und geht ein neuer an.[6]

> ET: If what one should believe
> One can no longer believe,
> The age of one faith is complete
> And another begins.

The Pope, the Christian and "Fortunate Hans"

In his Introduction to Christianity, Joseph Ratzinger (now Pope Benedict XVI.), in view of the development of the theological movement of the last years and decades, was reminded of the story of "Fortunate Hans." As everyone knows, in the story we are told how Hans, who served his master honestly and faithfully for seven years, received a gold nugget as a reward. Because on his journey the lump of gold became to heavy, however, he traded it for a horse. Over time, however, he was not pleased with the horse either, so he traded it for a cow. Later the cow was exchanged for a goose, and the goose for grinding stone. Hans first finds true fortune, however, when he sees the stone sink into the water and is now entirely free and relieved of every burden. Ratzinger comments: "Has our theology in the last few years not taken in many ways a similar path? Has it not gradually watered down the demands of faith, which had been found all too demanding, always only so little that nothing important seemed to be lost, yet always so much that it was soon possible to venture on the next step? And will poor Jack, the Christian who trustingly let himself be led from exchange to exchange, from interpretation to interpretation, not really soon hold in his hand, instead of the gold with which he began, only a whetstone that he can safely be advised to throw away?"[7]

Although I like very much the comparison Ratzinger makes between modern theology and the fortunate Hans, I cannot agree with the conclusions the Catholic theologian draws from this—to begin with, only because the story is obviously not correctly interpreted. With reference to modern theology, with which he compares the destiny of the figure in the story, Ratzinger is critical of the loss of the gold (i.e., pure and uncorrupted Catholic dogma) and remarks uneasily: "How long his intoxication lasted, how somber the moment of awakening from the illusion of his supposed liberation, is left by the story, as we know, to the imagination of the reader."[8]

But here the worried Catholic churchman reads something into the text of the story that is not found there. In the story, the loss that Hans suffered is really seen in a positive way. With a wink of the eye, the story leaves the decision to the reader to either to take delight in the great foolishness of Hans (in which case, of course, the reader's own cleverness would not have brought him very far), or to perceive the deeper truth behind the apparent foolishness, that nothing more is required for true freedom, for real fortune, than — precisely nothing at all; and that the person who is most free and most fortunate is one who, as the ancient mystics already knew, is free and relieved of all things. For obvious reasons, this point fully eluded the worried churchman. If the story were understood as it intended to be, the conclusion for modern theology that Ratzinger would like to make from the comparison would backfire and apply to himself.

It has precisely to do with the "foolishness" of the matter, one must now say — i.e., one who has learned to lead his life free from and unburdened by external dogmas and authorities, instead of tying his freedom and spiritual health to the golden luster of doctrines transmitted from ancient times. Whoever has enjoyed this freedom will never again long for the gold of the ancient authorities. Nor will he allow anything else to take the place of the lost gold. The places of Jesus and Paul will not be taken by Mohammed, nor Moses, nor Buddha, so highly valued at present, no Koran, no Bhagavad-Gita, and not the rattling of Tibetan prayer beads, as interesting and exotic as all these might be, but he will let it rest that what he once had in his hand he has now lost, or, better, that what he once possessed he still has only as something recalled deeply within. Like the fortunate Hans in the story, the Christian will finally "spring away from all that with a light heart and free from every burden."

The basis for this freedom is not, as Ratzinger presumes, the rashness and hubris of modern man who has thrown everything overboard, but rather the deep recognition that the treasures of the past can be made useful for the present not by desperately and fearfully holding on to them and preserving them, but only by criticism and new interpretation.

Only that person has this freedom, however, who, like the radical critics, is prepared, in certain circumstances, to give up the "fixed formulas of the past" and leave them behind, because they constrict his or her questioning and critical spirit, and threaten to suffocate it. The peculiar paradox is that precisely this freedom over against the traditional Christian faith, which should not be confused with a hostile and negative attitude with regard to the Christian faith, can have as a consequence a much narrower and more intensive tie with the individual contents of the tradition than the conserving (conservative) desire to possess and preserve. Only those persons who are prepared, in certain circumstances, to relinquish traditions that they haul around without understanding, and which really represent life-threatening ballast, are able to experience that what they just thought they had given up returns to them as a refined inner possession, no longer as an authoritative demand, but as a freely won insight. So what still encounters them as the external authority of faith (letter, law, history) returns to them again inwardly (Spirit), so as from then on to constitute a indispensable component of their individual religious lives.

The Letter Kills...

In an essay in which the Dutch radical critic Van den Bergh van Eysinga discussed the importance of Christianity for present-day people, he sketches the development and the course of the education of a child until full maturity., the child is interested first of all, often even before he begins school, in only the mere letters of the alphabet, which he comes to know and learns until he himself can read and write. Afterward comes a time when he is interested not only in reading as such, but where there is a choice and he is concerned with different facts and events. After that comes a further phase of development, where the maturing adult begins to be interested not only in historical facts, but also in their spiritual content. Now it no longer seems important for him whether what is written really took place, but he reads it to suck out for himself the spiritual content — like bees suck honey from blossoms. It occurred to Van den Bergh van Eysinga that the parable stories in the Gospels were good examples, since here also whether what they report actually took place is irrelevant for understanding them, but only the written content. The parables are not devised "to make the hearers believe something, but to make the believer wise. Whether all these things took place far from us a long time ago is not the issue; but the issue has very much to do with whether, on the basis of what took place or what was written, something happens in us, whether the Spirit bears witness to our spirit — then we know that it is true... But the parable itself may never stand in place of its significance, in place of the truth itself."[9]

If one transfers the picture of the maturing child to the present-day situation of Christianity, one would have to say that many Christians still find themselves in the phase of learning the alphabet and learning to read. Even today, for a great number of Christians it still seems more important to militantly defend the letters of one statement of faith or the other than to inquire about the spiritual truth contained therein. Their passion, and not seldom their fanaticism, is ignited by the question as to whether there was "really" a resurrection, an ascension, or a miraculous birth from a virgin, i.e., as historical events, and less often by the question as what significance this then has for their life. It is not surprising that, in view of this sad picture that the discussion carried out among Christians sometimes provides for them, that precisely the free spirits feel repelled and turn away with horror from Christianity and the Church as a whole.

"What value are all the arts of reading and criticism," Friedrich Nietzsche, who came from a pastor's family, already complained, "if afterwards as before, the Church's interpretation of the Bible, the Protestant as well as the Catholic, must be upheld! One does not sufficiently account for the barbarity of ideas in which we Europeans still live. That one can still believe that the salvation of the 'soul' depends on a book! ...And someone tells me people still believe that today. What value is all the scholarly education, all criticism and hermeneutic, if the kind of absurd biblical interpretation upheld by the Church has not yet made shameful red the color of its body."[10] In his rejection of a Christianity degraded to a religion of mere letters and books, Nietzsche was not alone. In a remarkable way, with his criticism of letters and of the common argument among theologians, "It is written...." he stands shoulder to shoulder with the author of 2 Corinthians (3:6): "The letter kills, but the Spirit gives life."

For the person from whom this beautiful statement derives, the decisive criterion for the Christian faith is not whether something is in accordance with scripture; rather, the one and only thing that mattered to him was the Spirit as the ground and source of religious life. One can question whether the Church has given this Spirit sufficient room in its history, or whether the fact that churches today are often so empty is not related to the fact that in its history the Church has depended primarily on the letter instead of the Spirit.

Of course, it is more comfortable to rely on letters: one risks nothing; one never needs to make his own decision; the letter meets our natural need for security and order. Even today, in both the Protestant and Catholic churches, with the words "It is written" one appeals to particular biblical statements in the same way as to legal declarations. The only danger in this is that the security that the letter seems to mediate will finally turn out to be an illusion; that the peace that it seems to provide for our Christian faith when it is disturbed by all kinds of doubt will turn out to be a peace of mind like that of a graveyard.

The letter kills. Not only the letter kills faith, but closely related to it, *history* as well, which the letter relates, can kill faith — at least so long as it is conceived only in a literal way.

Against an all-too-free "spiritual" interpretation of the biblical writings, which in the history reported there sees only pictures and symbols in historical clothing, it is often objected that, in contrast to Asian religions and in common with Judaism, Christianity is a kind of historical religion. The Christian religion, it is said, is based on salvation history, on the facts of salvation. A Christian lives from the facts of salvation.

When one considers the author of 2 Corinthians, for whom the historical side of the destiny of a man named Jesus was of no consequence at all, one may have to relativize these statements somewhat. Moreover, one must ask what is meant here by the so-called facts of salvation. What is the birth in Bethlehem, the ascension, the crucifixion on Golgotha, seen in and for themselves, if we know them only as historical facts, but they signify nothing for us and have no relationship with our personal life? As the Mystic Angelus Silesius said:

> Were Christ a thousand times
> reborn in Bethlehem's stall

And not in thee, thou still
art lost beyond recall.

All so-called Christian facts of salvation are nothing and, in spite of their claimed factuality, would be essentially nonexistent *for us* if we did not make them our possession, if we did not make our own the ideas on which they are based and which have as their basis only the *one* fundamental idea that God is present among us and within us—not as the "wholly other," but as Spirit—and that in our midst and within us God wills to become reality and that we make a place for him.

And what is remarkable is that in the moment when we have understood what should be said to us in the clothing of pictures and parables, which very often also bear the character of historical events, the facts themselves begin to become entirely immaterial, a matter of indifference, and recede into the background.

Then under certain circumstances we can even do away with them—as someone who has learned to walk can throw away his crutches. Then it no longer matters whether this or that "really" took place, i.e., as an historical event; then we also do not need to doubt our faith and despair simply because we cannot reconcile something or another with our scientific world-view. Because we have understood the history, or "stories," as *ideas*, we no longer need to understand them as facts. We grasp that Christian faith does not represent faith in some historical event that took place in one way or another in the distant past, but that this Christian faith can have no other "object" and no other content than that which, according to Christian understanding, is present and active among us in Spirit and in Truth, not only once upon a time 2000 years ago, but here and now.

Again, as the Dutch theologian Van den Bergh van Eysinga wrote: "The written gospel is picture and parable, a shadow of the true gospel, that is not written on yellowed, holy pages, but on the table of our heart. No fact from the past: no birth in Bethlehem, no cross on Golgotha, no resurrection in the garden of Arimathea, no ascension, no outpouring of the Holy Spirit in Jerusalem, not one of all these facts of salvation, so-called facts, can save us."

What can "save" us, according to Van den Bergh van Eysinga, who employs here a decidedly mystical terminology, is a decisive factor deep within ourselves: "The union with God through the delivering up of our own I."

The Role of the Church

The story of the fortunate Hans is a beautiful parable for the way in which modern theology must be transformed into radical theology, with its final and most sincere consequences, in order provide freedom, identity, and personal fortune in life for people today. Using another picture, one could say that our Christian religion is like a school, like the home of our parents in which we grew up, who raised us, and, in the moment when we had become grown up and mature, gave us our freedom. Our future relationship to the Christian religion, therefore, is no longer one of dependence, but one characterized by an interested, critical sympathy and affection. We are and remain true to our origins, of course, and in this sense continue to remain Christians — but, as people who have now set off on our own way, with the necessary critical distance which complete freedom and independence includes.

Does that mean that in the future we no longer need the Church? Yes and no. The Dutch radical theologian Frater Smid explains:

„The Church must terminate itself as a Church. If it does not do this, it betrays its calling, for what it must promote is not the Church, but religion. And Religion as such has no need of the Church. At most it can make use of the Church as a resource, as a shelter, a wayside inn, where one may well stop for refreshment, but cannot remain. For the religions person there are no limits, no resting place or quiet place. His religion is an adventure of his spirit, which at all times and places pours into the universe of the Spirit, so as in this way, without doubt or fear, to attain the true security of 'faith.' This is the adventure that the Church must prepare and make possible. It cannot regard its task as completed until it has guided every last person to this adventure. In every person whom the Church brings to religion in this way, it terminates itself. That is its task and its destiny."[11]

General Index

200,000 sestercen ...109, 110, 115
Abel 111
Abraham 4, 55, 102, 111
Acts of Paul 21, 163, 164, 167, 168, 169, 170, 204
Acts of Paul and Thecla 163, 164, 204
Acts of Peter 189
Adoptionist christology 130, 133
Albert the Great 177
Alexander 167
Alkibiades 62
Allegory of the cave 210
Ananias 19, 72, 73, 199
Angels 136, 163, 165, 187, 194
Antichrist 178, 181, 182, 184, 190, 192, 195, 196, 202, 203, 204
Antinomianism 194
Antioch 20, 69, 73, 86, 94, 96, 129, 164, 167
Antiqua mater 101, 103, 106
Apelles 146, 154, 208
Apocalypse of Elijah x, 195, 202, 203, 204
Apophasis 188
Apostle's Creed 49
Apostolic Council 129
Aposynagogos 64
Arabia 5, 19, 62, 69, 123
Aretas 16
Arimathea 229
Aristides 80, 85
Asenath 206

Asia 34, 68, 79, 87, 94, 95, 107, 108, 112, 114, 164, 171, 173
Atomos 184, 197
Aurelius 54
Bar Kochba 64
Barnabas 19, 123, 200
Basilideans 184
Bauer, Bruno 50, 51, 52, 53, 54, 55, 58, 74, 124, 126, 177, 259
Bauer, Walter 112
Baur, F.C. 50, 51, 53, 59, 120, 157, 163
Beliar 181, 192
Bergh van Eysinga, G.A. van den vi, 55, 56, 57, 94, 224, 229
Bethany 207, 215
Bethlehem 227, 229
Beyschlag, K. 184, 205
Bhagavad-Gita 223
Bolland, G.J.P.J. 55, 101, 102, 103, 221
Bornkamm, G 4, 13
Boyarin, D. 144
Brox, N 29, 33, 36
Bruns, H 82
Buddha 223
Bultmann, R. 82
Caesarea .... x, 20, 21
Caligula 16
Campenhausen, H 32
Canon ix, 25, 26, 28, 29, 47, 64, 77, 79, 106
Caravaggio 18
Carrol, L 12

Catholic redactor 122, 125, 136, 195
Cephas 4, 123, 124
Cerdo 114, 115, 154, 174, 175, 184
Christophoros 96
Church 2, 3, 11, 19, 23, 24, 26, 28, 29, 30, 31, 33, 40, 41, 44, 50, 59, 60, 62, 64, 68, 71, 72, 73, 74, 78, 80, 81, 82, 85, 86, 87, 90, 91, 92, 93, 94, 96, 97, 101, 102, 103, 107, 108, 109, 110, 113, 115, 117, 119, 120, 121, 122, 124, 125, 128, 129, 131, 133, 136, 147, 148, 150, 151, 152, 153, 154, 155, 157, 161, 163, 174, 175, 178, 180, 181, 182, 184, 186, 187, 194, 195, 201, 212, 215, 217, 218, 220, 259
Cicero 60
Citation-theory 127, 128, 130
Claudius 187
Clement x, 82, 86, 87, 88, 89, 90, 91, 93, 94, 96, 98, 153, 174, 176, 184
Cogito ergo sum 100
Companion of Paul 10
Constantine 113
Conversion 17, 18, 19, 22, 24, 69, 71, 72, 73, 124, 125, 126, 129, 195, 199, 200
Corinth 36, 46, 60, 86, 90, 91, 92, 93, 164
Cowley, A 102
Cynic philosophy 108
Cyprus 18, 20, 184, 197, 200
Damascus 5, 9, 16, 17, 18, 19, 66, 69, 123, 164, 199
Damascus Document 17
David 4, 62, 126, 127, 201
Davidic descent 132
Davidic sonship 133

De omnibus dubitandum 103
Demiurge 111, 112, 116, 135, 136, 139, 140, 185
Denifle, H.S 161
Descartes, R 100
Deschner, K 30
Diogenes 107
Dionysius episode 19
Discovery 7, 17, 31, 119, 161, 218
Domitian 64
Dositheos 186
Doubt 99, 101, 103
Dr. Jekyll 52
Drusilla 197, 199
Dualism 115
Dürer, A 22
Dutch radical criticism xiv, 55, 57, 58, 158
Dutch radical critics xiv, 56, 162
Ebionite/Elchasaite Jewish-Christian circles 153
Ebionites 28, 144
Edessa 107, 149
Egypt 63, 185, 186, 219
Eichhorn, G 32
Eisenman, R 17
Enemy 16, 151, 152, 157, 178, 195
Enkrateia 164
Enlightenment 100
Ennoia 180, 187
Ephesus 20, 40, 41, 44, 63, 65, 76, 79, 87, 94, 157, 164, 168, 169, 170
Epictetus 67
Epiphanius .... x, 144, 206
Epistula Petri ...... x, 152, 176, 196
Euripides 19
Eusebius .... x, 44, 64, 259
Evanson, E 48, 49, 50
Exalted Christ 5, 71
Excommunication 113, 114, 155
Exegesis of the Soul 188, 205

General Index

Fairy-tales 12
Felix 21, 196, 197, 198, 199
Festus 21
Fictae ad haresem Marcionis 120
Firstborn of Satan 107
Fortunate Hans 221, 222
Frater Smid, E .... vi, 229
Fuchs, E 82
Galatia 46, 60, 76, 146, 150, 152, 157, 167
Galilee 1, 4
Gamaliel 13, 22, 144, 202
Gellius 67
Gentile Christians 41, 42, 145
Gentile parents 144
Gnosis 38, 78, 106, 115, 116, 154, 184, 194, 205, 208
Gnosticism 54, 78, 116, 133, 153, 180, 183, 184, 214
Gnostics 28, 78, 115, 116, 147, 161, 163, 178, 180, 184, 220
God of Love 137
Goethe, W 158
Golgotha 4, 227, 229
Gospel of Matthew 26
Gospels 2, 4, 8, 24, 25, 26, 145, 182, 207, 216, 219, 225
Goyim 141
Grace 36, 97, 112, 117, 123, 127, 132, 135, 139, 177, 178, 194
Graham, B 82
Great power of God 183
Great Proclamation 188, 189
Grisar, H 161
Hadrian 54, 85
Haller, J 88
Hapaxlegomena 32
Harnack, A 89, 98, 108, 120
Hebrew Bible 144, 213
Hegel, G.F 51, 189
Hegesippus 44
Heidemann 46

Helena 180, 185, 187, 194, 204, 205, 206, 207, 208
Hestōs 186
High Priest 16, 144
Hildebrandt, D 14, 15
Hilgenfeld 120
Hippolytus. x, 108, 184, 188, 189
Historical Jesus 1, 215
Hitler, A 46
Hostile man ... 152, 176, 178, 196
Hyginos 108
Ignatius 68, 82, 86, 87, 88, 94, 95, 96, 97
Illyricum 66, 193
Irenaeus x, 114, 148, 174, 175, 184, 187, 194
Israel 4, 63, 70, 113
Jacob 27, 200
James. 4, 15, 27, 84, 123, 124, 126
Jeremias 35
Jerusalem 5, 9, 16, 19, 20, 50, 62, 63, 65, 69, 71, 72, 73, 74, 76, 87, 109, 117, 121, 123, 124, 125, 126, 144, 145, 148, 150, 164, 183, 185, 191, 193, 217, 229
Jerusalem pillars 73
Jesus 1, 2, 3, 4, 5, 9, 16, 18, 21, 24, 27, 28, 36, 38, 52, 55, 56, 57, 60, 62, 65, 66, 67, 71, 72, 73, 76, 95, 97, 104, 110, 121, 126, 128, 129, 133, 134, 135, 136, 138, 139, 145, 157, 165, 168, 171, 174, 180, 183, 197, 199, 201, 204, 207, 208, 211, 214, 215, 216, 223, 227
Jews 20, 21, 41, 42, 50, 63, 66, 69, 70, 76, 104, 110, 112, 122, 142, 143, 181, 195, 199, 200, 213
Johannine school 44, 45
John the Baptizer 4, 185, 187, 198

234 General Index

Johnson, E. 100, 103, 104, 105, 204
Joseph 4, 206, 221
Joseph and Asenath 206
Josephus x, 66, 67, 184, 196, 197
Judaea 16
Judaism 70, 79, 85, 134, 142, 153, 154, 227
Justin x, 64, 80, 81, 82, 83, 84, 85, 104, 105, 107, 108, 184, 186, 187
Käsemann, E 68, 79
Kerygma 2, 131, 153
Kerygmata Petrou 175
King Azizus of Emesa 197
Kippot 143
Klein, E 72, 73, 78, 82, 83
Koran 223
Kreyenbühl, J 199
Kujau, K. 46
Kümmel, W.G 58
Kuss, O 131
Laodicea 79
Leiden 55, 99, 100, 101
Leisegang, H 188, 189
Leprosy 203, 207
Letter to the Germans 84
Letter to the Laodiceans 42
Lightfoot, J.B 89
Lindemann, A 29
Lion 169, 170
Little red riding hood 13
Loman, A.D 55, 56, 57, 79, 100, 168, 171, 172, 173
Lucian 67, 105, 177
Luke ix, 9, 10, 11, 13, 14, 15, 17, 18, 19, 21, 26, 54, 70, 71, 72, 74, 77, 78, 83, 118, 119, 120, 125, 148, 150, 163, 164, 172, 173, 179, 180, 182, 183, 197, 198, 199, 207, 208
Luther, M 107, 160, 161
Maccoby, Hyam 16

MacDonald, M.Y. 40
Macedonia 10, 20, 50, 170
Magnesia 94
Manen, W. van 55, 103, 120, 171, 172, 173
Marcion 42, 64, 68, 81, 82, 85, 105, 106, 107, 108, 109, 110, 111, 112, 113, 114, 115, 116, 117, 118, 119, 120, 123, 133, 134, 135, 136, 137, 138, 139, 140, 141, 146, 147, 150, 153, 154, 155, 156, 161, 173, 174, 175, 178, 184, 185, 186, 191, 194, 200, 208, 220
Marcionites 28, 105, 111, 113, 118, 120, 122, 123, 124, 125, 126, 132, 133, 137, 138, 139, 147, 148, 160, 161, 163, 177, 178, 181, 184, 195
Mark ...... ix, 21, 26, 143, 207, 208
Marx, K 51
Mary 3, 4, 88, 180, 204, 207
Mary Magdalene 180
Masada 66
Matill, A.J 74
Matthew .... ix, 26, 90, 208
Megalomania 37
Menander 144, 186
Migdal 207
Moses 21, 70, 219, 223
Mount Garizim 185
Mus Ponticus 119
Muslim 141
Myra 164
Naber, S.A 55
Nazareth 1, 2, 3, 4, 24, 25, 105, 214, 215
Nazarite 70
Neapolis 11, 80
Nero 63, 94, 104
Nestle-Aland 127
New Testament ix, xv, xvi, xvii, 7, 10, 12, 23, 24, 25, 26, 27, 29,

30, 31, 32, 35, 39, 43, 44, 47, 50, 51, 55, 57, 58, 64, 66, 67, 68, 72, 77, 79, 80, 86, 90, 98, 104, 106, 120, 127, 129, 175, 207, 208, 213, 215, 216, 218
Nicene Creed 49
Nietzsche, F 45, 226
Old Testament 14, 42, 70, 111, 112, 114, 132, 181, 200, 201, 213, 218
Overbeck, F 45
Palestine. 3, 13, 80, 171, 197, 219
Pastoral Epistles 25, 29, 32, 33, 34, 35, 36, 37, 38, 39, 44, 46, 50, 159
Pauline school... 44, 45, 103, 147
Paul-legend 105
Paulus historicus xv, 162, 171, 172, 173
Pausanias 67
Pentepheres 206
Pentheus 19
Peregrinus Proteus 105, 177
Pergamum 79
Pervo, R. 13
Peter x, 4, 20, 26, 27, 56, 77, 80, 87, 110, 117, 124, 125, 126, 146, 150, 152, 153, 171, 174, 176, 178, 183, 191, 193, 211
Pharisees 4
Philadelphia 79, 94
Philippi 11, 22, 43, 65, 164
Philo .... xi, 186
Pierson, A 55, 56, 76
Pliny the Younger 104
Plutarch 67
Polycarp 94, 97, 114
Pontius Pilate 3, 4
Pontus 106, 107, 119, 174
Pope Benedict XVI. 221
Preuschen, E 203, 204
Prisoner 9, 34, 37, 60, 94, 95

Pseudepigraphic writings 27, 45, 120, 161, 212, 218
Pseudo-Clementines 175, 176, 179, 184, 185, 187, 191, 192, 193
Pseudonymity 27
Quispel, G 205, 206, 207
Qumran 17
Radical theology 220, 229
Ranke-Heinemann, U. 13, 19, 30
Ratzinger, J 221, 222, 223, 224
Redeemer 136, 141
Revelation to John 79
Ritschl, A. 120
Robinson, J.A.T 57
Roman citizen 21, 63, 66, 170
Rome 9, 21, 23, 34, 36, 42, 50, 62, 63, 79, 80, 82, 86, 88, 90, 91, 92, 93, 94, 96, 107, 108, 109, 113, 115, 117, 123, 124, 125, 127, 131, 135, 148, 149, 150, 153, 164, 168, 171, 174, 176, 187, 189, 193, 217
Rückert, F 221
Rudolph, K 184, 188, 194
Ruge, A 52
Sabbath 11, 144, 145
Samaria 174, 181, 182, 185, 186, 215
Samothrace 11
Samson 70
Sanhedrin 16
Sardes 79
Saul 9, 14, 15, 16, 17, 18, 19, 66, 181, 199, 200, 201, 202
Schleiermacher, F 32, 50
Schmidt, J.E.C 32
Schmithals, W. 35, 37, 72, 82, 130
Schoeps, H.J. 15, 153
Schweitzer, A 216
Secondary literature 6
Secretary 33, 40

Segal, Alan F. 143
Seneca 67
Septuagint 144
Sergius Paulus 18, 20, 200
Sermon on the Mount 4, 56, 219
Shema 143
Sibyllines 184, 190, 193
Sidon 164
Simon 54, 110, 114, 115, 152, 173, 174, 175, 176, 178, 179, 180, 181, 182, 183, 184, 185, 186, 187, 188, 189, 190, 191, 192, 193, 194, 195, 196, 197, 198, 199, 200, 202, 203, 204, 207, 208, 215, 220
Simoni Deo Santo 187
Sinope 107
Smyrna 79, 94, 96
Socrates 62
Solus Paulus 117, 125, 148
Sophia 38, 180
Standing One 185, 186
Steck, R. 84
Stephen 14, 15
Stoicheia 135, 136, 140
Suetonius 104
Syria 17, 88, 94, 96, 107, 123, 171
Tacitus 104, 197
Tallit 143
Tarsus ... 1, 13, 141, 144, 171, 199
Tertullian xi, 64, 105, 107, 113, 118, 119, 120, 121, 123, 147, 172, 181, 200, 201
Testament of the Twelve Patriarchs 27
Thamyris 165, 166

The Gospel of John 26
Thecla 164, 165, 166, 167, 168, 169, 204, 205
Theodotion 144
Theophoros 96
Thyatira 79
Timothy ix, 8, 32, 34, 70, 122, 147, 150
Titus ... ix, 8, 32, 34, 121, 123, 147
Torah 143
Tower virgins 206
Trajan 64, 96, 104
Tralles 94
Troas 11, 34, 35, 94
Tübingen 50, 88, 89, 176, 179
Tyre 164, 187, 205, 207, 208
Uhland, L 102, 103, 221
Unde malum 115
Unknown God 115
Ur-Luke theory 120
Valentinians 184
Valentinus 38, 114, 115
Vergil 102
Vermeer 100
Vielhauer, Ph. 10, 11, 259
Volkmar, G 92
Völter, D 96
Vrije Gemeente 57
We-accounts 10, 11
Wells, G.A 145
Werther 47, 158
Weteringschans 56
Wikenhauser-Schmidt 27, 34, 40
Zahn, Theodor 89

BIBLIOGRAPHY

Adamson, James B. (1989): James. The man and his message. Grand Rapids, Mich.: Eerdmans.

Barnett, Albert E. (1941): Paul becomes a literary influence. Chicago Ill.: The University of Chicago press.

Barnikol, Ernst; Bauer, Bruno (1972): Bruno Bauer. Assen van Gorcum.

Barrett, C. K. (1976): Acts and the Pauline Corpus. In: The Expository Times, Jg. 88, 2–5.

Bartsch, Hans Werner (1968): Urgemeinde und Israel. Die Geschichte der ersten christlichen Zeugen auf dem Hintergrund der alttestamentlichen Hoffnung. Wuppertal: Brockhaus (Neue Studienreihe, 11.).

Baudy, Gerhard J. (1991): Die Brände Roms. Ein apokalyptisches Motiv in der antiken Historiographie: Olms, Georg, Verlag AG.

Bauer, Bruno (1842): Kritik der evangelischen Geschichte der Synoptiker und des Johannes. Braunschweig: Otto.

Bauer, Bruno (1850a): Die Apostelgeschichte. Eine Ausgleichung des Paulinismus und des Judenthums innerhalb der christlichen Kirche. Berlin: Hempel.

Bauer, Bruno (1850b): Kritik der paulinischen Briefe. Drei Abtheilungen. Berlin: Hempel.

Bauer, Bruno (1879): Christus und die Caesaren. Der Ursprung des Christenthums aus dem römischen Griechenthum. 2. Auflage. Berlin.

Bauer, Bruno (1998): Christ and the Caesars. The origin of Christianity from romanized Greek culture. Charleston SC: A. Davidonis.

Bauer, Walter (1934): Rechtgläubigkeit und Ketzerei im ältesten Christentum. Tübingen: Mohr (Beiträge zur historischen Theologie, 10).

Bauer, Walter; Kraft, Robert A.; Krodel, Gerhard (1971): Orthodoxy and heresy in earliest Christianity. Philadelphia: Fortress Press.

Bauernfeind, Otto (1956): Die Begegnung zwischen Paulus und Kephas Gal l 18-20. In: ZNW, Jg. 47, H. 1, 268–276.

Baur, F. C. (1835): Die sogenannten Pastoralbriefe des Apostels Paulus. Stuttgart, Tübingen: Cotta.

Baur, Ferdinand Christian (1866): Paulus, der Apostel Jesu Christi; sein Leben und Wirken, seine Briefe und seine Lehre; ein Beitrag zu einer kritischen Geschichte des Urchristenthums. 2. Aufl. Zeller (Hg.). Leipzig: Fues's Verl. (R. Reisland).

Becker, Jürgen (1993): Paul. Apostle to the Gentiles. 1st ed. Louisville Ky.: Westminster/John Knox Press.

Ben-Chorin, Schalom (1986): Paulus. Der Völkerapostel in jüdischer Sicht. 5. Aufl. München: dtv.

Bergh van Eysinga, Gustaaf Adolf van den (1912): Die holländische radikale Kritik des Neuen Testaments, ihre Geschichte u. Bedeutung f. d. Erkenntnis d. Entstehung d. Christentums. Jena Diederichs.

Bergh van Eysinga, Gustaaf Adolf van den (1927): Inleiding tot de oud-christelijke letterkunde. Amsterdam: Holkema & Warendorf.

Bergh van Eysinga, Gustaaf Adolf van den (1946): De oudste christelijke geschriften. Den Haag: Servire (Servire's encyclopaedie in monografieën, 2 : Afd. B4b, Bijbelwetenschap en theologie).

Bergh van Eysinga, Gustaaf Adolf van den (1947-52): Christendom voor nu. In: Bergh van Eysinga, Gustaaf Adolf van den (Hg.): Godsdienstwetenschappelijke studien. Haarlem Willink, Bd. 14, 3–18.

Beyschlag, Karlmann (1974): Simon Magus und die christliche Gnosis. Tübingen: Mohr (Wissenschaftliche Untersuchungen zum Neuen Testament, 16).

Boccaccini, Gabriele (1998): Beyond the Essene hypothesis. The parting of the ways between Qumran and Enochic Judaism. Grand Rapids Mich.: William B. Eerdmans Pub.

Boehmer, Heinrich; Luther, Martin (1918): Luther im Lichte der neueren Forschung. 5., verm. u. umgearb. Aufl. Leipzig & Berlin Teubner.

Bornkamm, Günther (1971): Paul. 1st U.S. ed. New York: Harper & Row.

Bousset, W. (1917): Der Brief an die Galater. In: Weiß, Joh; Baumgarten, Otto; Bousset, Wilhelm (Hg.): Die Schriften des Neuen Testaments neu übers. u. für die Gegenwart erkl. von O. Baumgarten, W. Bousset u.a. 3. Aufl. Göttingen.

Bousset, Wilhelm (1966): Die Offenbarung Johannis. Neudr. d. neubearb. Aufl. 1906. Göttingen: Vandenhoeck & Ruprecht (Kritisch-exegetischer Kommentar über das Neue Testament, 16).

Boyarin, Daniel (2007): Border lines. The partition of Judaeo-Christianity. 1. paperback ed. Philadelphia, Pa.: Univ. of Pennsylvania Press (Divinations).

Braun, F. M. (1955-1957): Marcion et le gnose simonienne Byzantion. In: Byzantion, Jg. 25-27, 631–648.

Brox, Norbert (1969): Die Pastoralbriefe. 4., völlig neu bearb. Aufl. Regensburg: Pustet (Regensburger Neues Testament, 7,2).

Brox, Norbert (1975): Falsche Verfasserangaben. Zur Erklärung d. frühchristl. Pseudepigraphie. Stuttgart: KBW Verl. (Stuttgarter Bibelstudien, 79).

Campbell, William S. (2007): The "we" passages in the Acts of the Apostles. The narrator as narrative character. Atlanta: Society of Biblical Literature (Society of Biblical Literature studies in biblical literature, no. 14).

Campenhausen, Hans von (1951): Polykarp von Smyrna und die Pastoralbriefe. Heidelberg: Winter (Sitzungsberichte der Heidelberger Akademie der Wissenschaften, Philosophisch-Historische Klasse, Jg. 1951, Abh. 2).

Charlesworth, James H. (1983): The Old Testament pseudepigrapha. London: Darton Longman & Todd.

Chester, Andrew; Martin, Ralph P. (1994): The theology of the letters of James, Peter, and Jude. Cambridge: Cambridge Univ. Press.

Couchoud, Paul-Louis (Hg.) (1930): Premiers Écrits du christianisme. Paris: Rieder [usw.].

Deissmann, Gustaf Adolf (1923): Licht vom Osten. Das Neue Testament und die neuentdeckten Texte der hellenistisch-römischen Welt. 4., völlig neubearb. Aufl. Tübingen: Mohr.

Deschner, Karlheinz (1987): Kriminalgeschichte des Christentums. 21. - 27. Tsd. Reinbek bei Hamburg: Rowohlt.

Dessau, H. (1919): Der Name des Apostels Paulus. In: Hermes, Jg. 45, 347–368.

Detering, Hermann (1992): Paulusbriefe ohne Paulus? Die Paulusbriefe in der holländischen Radikalkritik. Frankfurt am Main, Berlin, Bern, New York, Paris, 1991: Lang (Kontexte, 10).

Dibelius, Martin; Bornkamm, Günther; Lietzmann, Hans, et al. (Hg.) (1937): An die Thessalonicher I, II. An die Philipper. 3., neubearb. Aufl. Tübingen: Mohr (Handbuch zum Neuen Testament, / begr. von Hans Lietzmann. Fortgef. von Günther Bornkamm. Hrsg. von Andreas Lindemann; 11).

Dietzfelbinger, Konrad (1991): Apokryphe Evangelien aus Nag Hammadi. Evangelium der Wahrheit; Evangelium nach Philippus; Brief an Reginus über die Auferstehung; Über die Seele; Evangelium nach Thomas; Das Buch Thomas.

Dölger, F. J.: Christophoros als Ehrentitel für Märtyrer und Heilige im christlichen Altertum. In: AuC, Bd. 4, 73–90.

Edelstein, Ludwig (1966): Platos Seventh Letter: Brill.

Eichhorn, Johann Gottfried (1812): Einleitung in das Neue Testament. Leipzig: Weidmann.

Eisenman, Robert H. (1983): Maccabees, Zadokites, Christians and Qumran. A new hypothesis of Qumran origins. Leiden: E.J. Brill (Studia post-Biblica, vol. 34).

Encyclopaedia biblica. A critical dictionary of the literary, political and religious history, the archaeology, geography and natural history of the Bible (1904). London: Adam & Charles Black.

Eznik, Koghbats i.; Samuelian, Thomas J. (1986): Refutation of the Sects. A Retelling of Yeznik Koghbatsi S Apology: St Vartan Press.

Feine, Paul; Behm, Johannes (1950): Einleitung in das Neue Testament. 9. Aufl., Leipzig: Harrassowitz.

Fini, Massimo (1994): Nero. Zweitausend Jahre Verleumdung; die andere Biographie. München: Herbig.

Fischer, Karl Martin (1973): Tendenz und Absicht des Epheserbriefes. Berlin: Evang. Verl. Anst. (Forschungen zur Religion und Literatur des Alten und Neuen Testaments, 111).

Frater Smid, E. (1958): Bevrijdende twijfel. Amsterdam: Becht.

Freedman, David Noel (2008): The Anchor Bible dictionary. New Haven, Conn.: Yale University Press.

Geffcken, Johannes (1902): Komposition und Entstehungszeit der Oracula Sybillina. Leipzig: Hinrichs (Texte und Untersuchungen zur Geschichte der altchristlichen Literatur, Bd. 23,1 = N.F., 8,1).

Gibson, Margaret Dunlop (1903): The Didascalia Apostolorum in English. London C. J. Clay & sons.

Goodspeed, Edgar Johnson ((1927)): The Formation of the New Testament. [Popular ed.] (3. impr.). Chicago Univ. Pr.

Goppelt, Leonhard; Roloff, Jürgen (1978): Theologie des Neuen Testaments. Göttingen: Vandenhoeck & Ruprecht (Uni-Taschenbücher, 850).

Grant, Robert McQueen (1965): The formation of the New Testament. London etc.: Hutchinson University Library.

Griffin, Miriam T.; Nero, Claudius Caesar (1984): Nero. London: Batsford.

Haenchen, Ernst (1982): The Acts of the Apostles. A Commentary: Blackwell Publishers.

Hahn, August (1823): Das Evangelium Marcions in seiner ursprünglichen Gestalt, nebst dem vollständigsten Beweise dargestellt, daß es nicht selbstständig, sondern ein verstümmeltes und verfälschtes Lukas-Evangelium war. Königsberg: Universitäts-Buchhandlung.

Haller, Johannes (1965): Das Papsttum. Idee und Wirklichkeit; Band 1. Die Grundlagen; Band 2. Der Aufbau; Band 3. Die Vollendung; Band 4. Die Krönung; Band 5. Der Einsturz. Reinbek bei Hamburg: Rowohlt.

Harnack, Adolf von (1985): Marcion. D. Evangelium vom fremden Gott ; e. Monographie zur Geschichte d. Grundlegung d. kath. Kirche. Unveränd. reprograph. Nachdr. d. 2., verb. u. verm. Aufl. Leipzig 1924. Darmstadt: Wiss. Buchges.

Hays, Christopher M. (2008): Marcion vs. Luke: A Response to the Plädoyer of Matthias Klinghardt. In: ZNTW, Jg. 99, 213–232.

Hengel, Martin (1976): Die Zeloten. Untersuchungen zur jüdischen Freiheitsbewegung in der Zeit von Herodes I. bis 70 n. Chr. Univ., Diss.--Tübingen, 1959. 2., verb. und erw. Aufl. Leiden: Brill (Arbeiten zur Geschichte des antiken Judentums und des Urchristentums, 1).

Hennecke, Edgar; Schneemelcher, Wilhelm; Wilson, Robert McLachlan (1992): New testament apocrypha. Cambridge: James Clarke & Co.

Henss, Walter (1967, 1967): Das Verhältnis zwischen Diatessaron, christlicher Gnosis und „Western Text". Erläutert an einer unkanonischen Version des Gleichnisses vom gnädigen Gläubiger ; Materialien zur Geschichte der Perikope von der namenlosen Sünderin Lk 7,36 - 50. Berlin: Töpelmann (Beihefte zur Zeitschrift für die neutestamentliche Wissenschaft und die Kunde der älteren Kirche, 33).

Hildebrandt, Dieter (1989): Saulus, Paulus. Ein Doppelleben. München, Wien: Hanser.

Hilgenfeld, Adolf (1855): Das Apostolikon Marcion's. In: ZHTh, Jg. 25 [NF 19], H. 3, 426–484.

Hilgenfeld, Adolf (1890): Der Gnosticismus. In: ZWTh, Jg. 33, 1–63.

Hilgenfeld, Adolf (1903): Die alten Actus Petri. In: ZWTh, Jg. 46, 321–341.

Hörmann, Werner (Hg.) (1994): Gnosis. Das Buch der verborgenen Evangelien. [7., veränd. Aufl.]. Augsburg: Pattloch-Verl.

Hübner, Reinhard (1997): Thesen zur Echtheit und Datierung der sieben Briefe des Ignatius von Antiochien. In: ZAC, Jg. 1, 44–72.

Johnson, E. (1887): Antiqua mater. A study of Christian origins. London: Trübner.

Käsemann, Ernst (1963): Paulus und der Frühkatholizismus. In: ZThK, Jg. 60, 75–89.

Käsemann, Ernst (1969): New Testament Questions of today. (2. ed.). London: SCM Press.

Kippenberg, Hans G. (1971, 1971): Garizim und Synagoge. Traditionsgeschichtliche Untersuchungen zur samaritanischen Religion der aramäischen Periode. Berlin: de Gruyter (Religionsgeschichtliche Versuche und Vorarbeiten, 30).

Klein, Günter (1961): Die zwölf Apostel. Ursprung und Gehalt einer Idee. Göttingen: Vandenhoeck & Ruprecht (Forschungen zur Religion und Literatur des Alten und Neuen Testamentes, 77 = N.F. 59).

Klinghardt, Matthias (2008): The Marcionite Gospel and the synoptic problem 50.2008. In: NovT, Jg. 50, 1–27.

Kreyenbühl, Johannes (1900): Das Evangelium der Wahrheit : Neue Lösung der Johanneischen Frage. Berlin: Schwetschke.

Kümmel, Werner Georg (1977): Introduction to the New Testament. Rev. ed., 2. impr. London: SCM Press.

Kuss, Otto: Der Römerbrief. Regensburg: Pustet.

LeBas, Philippe; Waddington, William Henry (1972): Inscriptions grecques et latines recueillies en Asie Mineure. Hildesheim: Olms.

Lechner, Thomas (1999): Ignatius adversus Valentinianos? Chronologische und theologiegeschichtliche Studien zu den Briefen des Ignatius von Antiochien. Leiden, Boston: Brill (Supplements to Vigiliae Christianae, 47).

Leisegang, Hans (1985): Die Gnosis. 5. Aufl. Stuttgart: Kröner (Kröners Taschenausgabe, 32).

Lietzmann, Hans (1910): An die Galater. [Ausg. in 5 Bden]. Tübingen: Mohr (Handbuch zum Neuen Testament: Die Briefe des Apostels Paulus, hrsg. von Hans Lietzmann; Bd. 3: die vier Hauptbriefe; 1).

Lightfoot, J. B. (1885): The Apostolic Fathers: revised texts with introductions, notes, dissertations, and translations. London: MacMillan.

Lindemann, Andreas: Briefe, Briefliteratur. In: Krause, Gerhard; Müller, Gerhard (Hg.): Theologische Realenzyklopädie: de Gruyter, Bd. 1, 194–196.

Lindemann, Andreas (1979): Paulus im ältesten Christentum. Das Bild des Apostels und die Rezeption der paulinischen Theologie in der frühchristlichen Literatur bis Marcion. Univ., Habil.-Schr.- -Göttingen, 1977. Tübingen: Mohr (Beiträge zur historischen Theologie, 58).

Lohse, Bernhard (1983, c1981): Martin Luther. Eine Einführung in sein Leben und sein Werk. 2., durchgesehene Auflage. München: Beck.

Loman, Abraham Dirk: Het oudste Christendom. In: Stemmen uit de Vrije Gemeente, Jg. 1882.

Loman, Abraham Dirk (1899): Nalatenschap. Groningen: J.B. Wolters.

Lona, Horacio E. (1998): Der erste Clemensbrief. Ergänzungsreihe zum Kritisch-exegetischen Kommentar über das NT: Vandenhoeck & Ruprecht.

Lublinski, Samuel (1910): Das werdende Dogma vom Leben Jesu. 1. und 2. Tsd. Jena: Diederichs.

Lüdemann, Gerd (1996): Heretics. The other side of early Christianity. 1. American ed. Louisville, Ky.: Westminster John Knox Press.

Maccoby, Hyam (1986): The mythmaker. Paul and the invention of Christianity. London: Weidenfeld & Nicolson.

MacDonald, Margaret Y. (2008): Colossians and Ephesians: Liturgical Press.

Manen, W. C. van (1891): Paulus II. De Brief aan de Romeinen. Leiden: Brill.

Manen, W. C. van (1896): Paulus III. De Brieven aan de Korinthiers. Leiden: E.J. Brill.

Manen, W. C. van (1900): Handleiding voor de oudchristelijke letterkunde. Leiden: Van Nifterik.

Manen, Willem Christiaan van; Schläger, Gustav (1906): Die Unechtheit des Römerbriefs. Leipzig.

Moo, Douglas J. (1996): The Epistle to the Romans. Grand Rapids Mich.: W.B. Eerdmans Pub. Co. (The new international commentary on the New Testament).

Muddiman, John; Barton, John (2010): The Oxford Bible commentary. Oxford: Oxford University Press.

Niebuhr, Karl-Wilhelm (1992): Heidenapostel aus Israel. Die jüdische Identität des Paulus nach ihrer Darstellung in seinen Briefen. Univ., Habil.-Schr.--Halle, 1991. Tübingen: Mohr (Wissenschaftliche Untersuchungen zum Neuen Testament, 62).

Nietzsche, Friedrich Wilhelm (1977): Werke in drei Bänden. 8. Aufl. Schlechta, Karl (Hg.). München: Hanser.

Oepke, Albrecht; Althaus, Paul; Fascher, Erich (1960): Der Brief des Paulus an die Galater. 2., verb. Aufl. Leipzig: Deichert (Theologischer Handkommentar zum Neuen Testament: mit Text und Paraphrase / bearb. von P. Althaus ... Später hrsg. von Erich Fascher ...; 9).

O'Neill, J. C. (1970): The theology of Acts in its historical setting. 2nd ed. London: S.P.C.K.

Origen; Scheck, Thomas P. (2001): Commentary on the Epistle to the Romans; books 1 - 5. Washington, DC: Catholic Univ. of America Press (The fathers of the church: a new translation / ed. board: Ludwig Schopp ...; Vol. 103).

Overbeck, Franz; Bernoulli, Karl Albrecht (1911): Das Johannes-Evangelium. Studien zur Kritik seiner Erforschung. Tübingen: Mohr.

Parvus, Roger (2008): A New Look at the Letters of Ignatius of Antioch and Other Apellean Writings: iUniverse.com.

Pervo, Richard I. (1987): Profit with delight. The literary genre of the acts of the apostles. Philadelphia: Fortress Pr.

Pierson, Allard (1878): De Bergrede en andere synoptische Fragmenten. Een hist.-krit. Onderzoek ... Amsterdam: Van Kampen.

Preuschen, E. (1901): Paulus als Antichrist. 2 (1901) 169. In: ZNW, Jg. 2, 169–201.

Price, Robert M. (2000): Deconstructing Jesus. Amherst, NY: Prometheus Books.

Price, Robert M. (2009): The Legend of Paul's Conversion. We Have Ways of Making You Talk. Online verfügbar unter http://www.robertmprice.mindvendor.com/art_legend_paul_conv.htm.

Quispel, Gilles (1995): Gnosis als Weltreligion. Die Bedeutung der Gnosis in der Antike. 3. Aufl. Bern: Origo-Verl. (Lehre und Symbol, 38).

Ranke-Heinemann, Uta (1992): Nein und Amen. Anleitung zum Glaubenszweifel: Hoffmann und Campe.

Raschke, Hermann (1926): Der Römerbrief des Markion nach Epiphanius. Bremen: Schünemann (Schriften der Bremer Wissenschaftlichen Gesellschaft Reihe D, Abhandlungen und Vorträge, 1,8).

Ratzinger, Joseph (2004): Introduction to Christianity: Ignatius Press.

Rengsdorf, Karl Heinrich (Hg.) (1964): Das Paulusbild in der neueren deutschen Forschung. Darmstadt: Wiss. Buchges. (Wege der Forschung).

Robinson, James M. (1988): The Nag Hammadi library in English. 3., completely rev. ed. Leiden: Brill.

Robinson, John A. T. (1976): Redating the New Testament. London: S.C.M. Press.

Rückert, Friedrich; Beyer, Conrad: Friedrich Rückerts Werke. In sechs Bänden; mit literarischen Anmerkungen, Rückerts Bildnis, zwei Gedichten in Originalhandschrift und der Einleitung: Friedrich Rückerts Leben und Bedeutung. Leipzig: Hesse.

Rudolph, Kurt (1975): Gnosis und Gnostizismus. Darmstadt: Wiss. Buchges.

Rudolph, Kurt (1983): Gnosis. The nature and history of an ancient religion. Unter Mitarbeit von R. Mc Wilson und Kurt Rudolph. Edinburgh: T. & T. Clark.

Rudolph, Kurt (1998): Gnosis: Continuum International Publishing Group Ltd.

Salles, A. (1958): Simon le Magicien ou Marcion? In: VigChr, Jg. 12, 197-224.

Schelkle, Karl Hermann (1988): Paulus. Leben - Briefe - Theologie. 2., unveränd. Aufl. Darmstadt: Wiss. Buchges. (Erträge der Forschung, 152).

Schleiermacher, Friedrich; Gass, J. C. (1807): Ueber den sogenannten ersten Brief des Paulos an den Timotheos. Ein kritisches Sendschreiben an J. C. Gass, Consistorialassessor und Feldprediger zu Stettin. Berlin: Realschulbuch.

Schlier, Heinrich (1971): Kritisch-exegetischer Kommentar über das Neue Testament. 14. Aufl. = 5. Aufl. d. Neubearb. Göttingen: Vandenhoeck & Ruprecht.

Schmidt, Johann Ernst Christian (1804/5): Historisch-kritische Einleitung in' s Neue Testament. Gießen: Tasche & Müller.

Schmithals, Walter (1960): Pastoralbriefe. In: Die Religion in Geschichte und Gegenwart. 3., völlig neu bearb. Aufl. Tübingen: Mohr, Bd. 5, 144-148.

Schmithals, Walter (1961): Das kirchliche Apostelamt. Eine historische Untersuchung. Göttingen: Vandenhoeck & Ruprecht (Forschungen zur Religion und Literatur des Alten und Neuen Testaments, 81 = N.F., 63).

Schmithals, Walter (1965): Paulus und die Gnostiker. Untersuchungen zu den kleinen Paulusbriefen. Univ., Habil.-Schr.--Marburg. Hamburg-Bergstedt.

Schmithals, Walter (1971): The office of Apostle in the early Church. Unter Mitarbeit von John E. Steely. London: SPCK.

Schmithals, Walter (1979): Die Berichte der Apostelgeschichte über die Bekehrung des Paulus und die „Tendenz" des Lukas. In: ThViat, Jg. 14, 145–165.

Schmithals, Walter (1984): Neues Testament und Gnosis: Wissenschaftliche Buchgesellschaft.

Schmithals, Walter (1988): Der Römerbrief. Ein Kommentar. Gütersloh: Gütersloher Verl.-Haus Mohn.

Schmithals, Walter (2001): 75 Jahre: Bultmanns Jesus-Buch. In: ZThK, Jg. 98, 25–58.

Schmithals, Walter (2009): Zu Ignatius von Antiochien. In: ZAC, Jg. 13, H. 2, 181–203.

Schneemelcher, Wilhelm; Hennecke, Edgar (Hg.) (1971): Neutestamentliche Apokryphen in deutscher Übersetzung. 4. Aufl., durchges. Nachdr. der 3. Aufl. Tübingen: Mohr.

Schoeps, Hans Joachim (1949): Theologie und Geschichte des Judenchristentums. Tübingen: Mohr.

Schoeps, Hans-Joachim (1956): Urgemeinde, Judenchristentum, Gnosis. Tübingen: Mohr.

Schoeps, Hans-Joachim (1964): Das Judenchristentum. Untersuchungen über Gruppenbildungen u. Parteikämpfe in d. frühen Christenheit. Bern, München: Francke (Dalp-Taschenbücher, 376).

Schweitzer, Albert (1984): Geschichte der Leben-Jesu-Forschung: UTB.

Schweizer, Eduard (1945): Der zweite Thessalonicherbrief ein Philipperbrief? In: ThZ, Jg. 1, 90–105.

Segal, Alan F. (1990): Paul the convert. The apostolate and apostasy of Saul the Pharisee. New Haven: Yale Univ. Pr.

Speyer, Wolfgang (1970): Bücherfunde in der Glaubenswerbung der Antike. Mit einem Ausblick auf Mittelalter und Neuzeit; 24: Vandenhoeck & Ruprecht.

Speyer, Wolfgang (1971): Die literarische Fälschung im heidnischen und christlichen Altertum. Ein Versuch ihrer Deutung. München: Beck (Handbuch der Altertumswissenschaft [Bd.2]).

Steck, Rudolf (1888): Der Galaterbrief nach seiner Echtheit untersucht nebst kritischen Bemerkungen zu den paulinischen Hauptbriefen. Berlin: Reimer.

Talbert, Charles H. (1978): Perspectives on Luke-Acts. Danville VA: Association of Baptist Professors of Religion (Perspectives in religious studies: Special studies series, no. 5).

Uhland, Ludwig; Skeat, Walter W. (1864): The songs and ballads of Uhland. London: Williams and Norgate.

Vandenberg, Philipp (2000): Nero. Kaiser und Gott, Künstler und Narr. Vollst. Taschenbuchausg., 1. Aufl. Bergisch Gladbach: Lübbe.

Verhoef, Eduard (1979): Er staat geschreven ... De oudtestamentische Citaten in de Brief aan de Galaten. theol. Diss.-- Amsterdam, 1979. Meppel: Krips Repro.

Vielhauer, Philipp (1975): Geschichte der urchristlichen Literatur. Einleitung in das Neue Testament, die Apokryphen und die Apostolischen Väter. Berlin: de Gruyter (De Gruyter-Lehrbuch).

Voelter, Daniel E. J. (1892): Die ignatianischen Briefe auf ihren Ursprung untersucht. Tübingen.

Volkmar, Gustav (1856): Über Clemens von Rom und die nächste Folgezeit mit besonderer Beziehung auf den Philipper- und Barnabasbriefe sowie auf das Buch Judit. In: ThJb(T), Jg. 15, 287–369.

Waitz, Hans (1904): Simon Magus in der altchristlichen Literatur. In: ZNW, Jg. 5, 121–143.

Walker, W. O. (2004): Acts and Pauline Corpus Reconsidered. In: Porter, Stanley E; Evans, Craig A. (Hg.): The Pauline writings. London, New York: T & T Clark International, 55–75.

Walton, Steve (2000): Leadership and lifestyle. The portrait of Paul in the Miletus speech and 1 Thessalonians. Cambridge: Cambridge University Press.

Warmington, B. H. (1969): Nero. Reality and legend. London: Chatto and Windus (Ancient culture and society).

Weiß, Joh; Baumgarten, Otto; Bousset, Wilhelm (Hg.) (1917): Die Schriften des Neuen Testaments neu übers. u. für die Gegenwart erkl. von O. Baumgarten, W. Bousset u.a. 3. Aufl. Göttingen.

Werner, Martin (2007): Die Entstehung des christlichen Dogmas. Problemgeschichtlich dargestellt. Waltrop: Spenner (Theologische Studien-Texte, Bd. 19).

Wikenhauser, Alfred (1973): Einleitung in das Neue Testament. 6., völlig neu bearb. Aufl. Freiburg im Breisgau: Herder.

Wilckens, Ulrich; Brox, Norbert; Blank, Josef; Schweizer, Eduard; Schnackenburg, Rudolf (1978): EKK. Neukirchen-Vluyn: Benziger; Neukirchener Verl.

Wildemann, Bernd (1983): Das Evangelium als Lehrpoesie. Leben u. Werk Gustav Volkmars. Zugl.: Berlin, Kirchl. Hochsch., Diss., 1982. Frankfurt am Main, Bern, New York: Lang (Kontexte, 1).

Zahn, Theodor von (1873): Ignatius von Antiochien. Gotha: Perthes.

Zwierlein, Otto (2009): Petrus in Rom. Die literarischen Zeugnisse; mit einer kritischen Edition der Martyrien des Petrus und Paulus auf neuer handschriftlicher Grundlage. Berlin, New York: de Gruyter (Untersuchungen zur antiken Literatur und Geschichte, 96).

NOTES

CHAPTER 1: THE INVESTIGATION OF THE PAULINE LETTERS...

1. Bornkamm 1971, 110.

2. Vielhauer 1975, 391. Becker 1993, 14: "Quite apart from the significant differences between Pauline and Lukan theology, which are almost totally ignored here, the book of Acts is so seriously, unharmonizably different from Paul in its information, as just demonstrated above, that the author cannot have been a student of Paul or a traveling companion of the apostle to the Gentiles. Indeed, he did not even use any of Paul's letters; he was probably not even aware of this correspondence. His knowledge rests on general church tradition ("Paul legends"), which was already developing during the apostles lifetime..."

3. Vielhauer 1975, 391; cf. Campbell 2007, 9ff., who cites Bauer 1850a, 125–132, he suggested that "we" style was a product of the author's imagination.

4. Vielhauer 1975, 393.

5. Ranke-Heinemann 1992, 197

6. Pervo 1987, 3.

7. Hildebrandt 1989, 39.

8. Schoeps 1964, 40.

9. Schoeps 1956, 13; Schoeps 1949, 441ff; cf. Eisenman 1983, 76,b. 144.

10. Eusebius HE 2:23; cf. 2 ApokJk 61ff.

11 Maccoby 1986, 86.

12 Eisenman 1983, 41 n. 17; cf. Boccaccini 1998: "Many scholars take 'the new covenant in the land of Damascus' (6:5, 19; 7:14-15, 18-19; 8:21; 20:12) as a reference to the exile of the Qumran community in the Judaean desert. For Lawrence H. Schiffman, 'Damascus' is 'a code word for Qumran.'"

13 Ranke-Heinemann 1992, 200; cf. Price 2009.

14 "In Damascus, the ethnarch of King Aretas guarded the city of the Damascenes in order to seize me; but I was lowered in a basket through a window in the wall, and escaped his hands." (2 Cor 11:32)

15 The final canonization first took place a century later; see the 39. Easter letter of Athanasius from 367 CE.

16 Cf. van Manen 1891, 204 =Manen, Schläger 1906, 189f..

17 Wikenhauser 1973, 376.

18 Wikenhauser 1973, 583.

19 Muddiman, Barton 2010, 1263: Eric Eve: "Despite 1 Pet 1:1, the author is unlikely to have been the apostle Peter."

20 Edelstein 1966; Speyer et al. 1971, 82f, n. 11

21 Lindemann, 195.

22 Brox 1975, 65.

23 Ranke-Heinemann 1992, 274.

24 Deschner 1987.

25 von Campenhausen 1951, 183.

26 Schmidt 1804/5.

27 Schleiermacher, Gass 1807.

28 Eichhorn 1812.

29 See Wikenhauser 1973, 523.

30 Brox 1969, 47.

31 Brox 1969, 47.
32 Ibid., 50.
33 Wikenhauser 1973, 470.
34 Cited by Brox 1969, 271.
35 Schmithals 1960, 146.
36 Brox 1969, 115.
37 Schmithals 1960, 147.
38 Bauer 1879, 373ff..
39 Wikenhauser 1973, 470, 489
40 Wikenhauser 1973, 470.
41 Ibid., 471.
42 Ibid., 471.
43 See Fischer 1973, 14; Schmithals 1984, 81.
44 MacDonald 2008, 17.
45 van Manen 1900, 47.
46 MacDonald 2008, 18.
47 Bergh van Eysinga 1927, 100
48 Bergh van Eysinga 1927, 105f.
49 See the overview by Schelkle 1988, 125. 1 Thess 1:1 = 2 Thess 1:1f. - 1 Thess 1:2f. = 2 Thess 1:3 - 1 Thess 2:12 = 2 Thess 1:5 - 1 Thess 2:13 = 2 Thess 2:13 - 1 Thess 3:11-13 = 2 Thess 2:16f. - 1 Thess 5:14 = 2 Thess 3:6 - 1 Thess 5:23 = 2 Thess 3:16 - 1 Thess 5:28 = 2 Thess 3:18.
50 Bergh van Eysinga 1927, 111f..
51 Dibelius et al. 1937, 40f.
52 Schweizer 1945
53 Schmithals 1965, 89–157

54 Overbeck, Bernoulli 1911, 98, 104, 206,.

55 See Bergh van Eysinga 1927, 153.

56 Ibid.

57 Idem, 154.

58 Schleiermacher, Gass 1807; Baur 1835.

59 Hahn 1823, 50, 50; cited by, van Manen 1891, 31, Manen, Schläger 1906, 3.

60 Baur 1866, 276.

61 E.g. Holsten and Hilgenfeld, who regarded 1 Thess, Phil, and Phlm as authentic.

62 We have to do here, to be sure, with a piece of self-characterization. But the passage nevertheless discloses something about Bauer's psyche, which at this time seemed in some sense to be "ridden by the devil." In my opinion, the category of the "demonic," that Barnikol, Bauer 1972 quite often employs as a scientific evaluation of the Bauer phenomenon, is not very helpful.

63 Bauer 1842, 314f..

64 Bauer 1850a, I, V.

65 So already Steck 1888, 6f..

66 Bauer 1850b, I, VI: "If the compiler is unveiled, we will determine, first of a ll, the relationship between Romans and the Corinthian letters and their origin."

67 Bauer 1850b, III,8.

68 See also the chapter in Bauer 1879, 371f.: "Der Gnosticismus in den paulinischen Briefen," 371ff.

69 Bauer 1850b, III,118ff..

70 Bauer 1998

71 Bauer 1879, 327.

72 Bauer 1879, 318.

73 See Bergh van Eysinga 1942; 3ff..

74 Bergh van Eysinga 1912, 171.

75 Feine, Behm 1950: "Dutch theologians such as Pierson, Naber, Loman, Van Manen, Van den Bergh van Eysinga, and Steck in Switzerland, also reject the four major letters of the apostle and explain as the fallout of anti-nomistic currents from the time around 140 CE, but in doing so begin with untenable literary presuppositions and an atrocious historical construction." Cf. Kümmel 1977, 250.

76 Robinson 1976.

77 Kümmel 1977, 250

78 Cf. Loman 1899, 15ff.

79 Pierson 1878, 103.

80 van Manen 1896, 159; cf. ⇒ *Paul -- the non-Jew*.

81 Cf. e.g. Griffin, Nero 1984, Warmington 1969, Fini 1994, Baudy 1991, Vandenberg 2000.

82 Cf. Boyarin 2007, 67–73: "Until quite recently liturgy and which was interpreted as a project for driving the Jewish Christians out of the Synagogue and the precipitating factor of the final break between Christianity and Judaism, the so-called parting of the ways. However, there is every reason to doubt that the so-called curse of the heretics was formulated under Gamaliel II at Yavneh or that it existed at all before the end of the second century. The only source we have for this 'Yavnean' institution is a Babylonian talmudic story from the fourth or fifth century of Rabban Gamaliel asking Samuel the Small to formulate such a blessing—'blessing' means curse here —the latter forgetting it a year later and meditating for two or three hours in order to remember it (BT Be-rakhot 28b-29a). This hardly constitutes reliable evidence, or indeed evidence at all."

83 Tert AM 5.1.

84 Josephus, *Ant*. 20.9.4.

85 For a criticism of Lindemann, see Detering 1992, 437ff..

86 Käsemann 1969, 238f
87 Didascalia Apostolorum, 25.20f. Gibson 1903, 109f; Bartsch 1968.
88 See Klein 1961, who in his investigation of the origin of the Christian apostle concept deals in detail with the picture of Paul in Luke; also Schmithals 1961, 269ff.; Schmithals 1971; Schmithals 1979
89 Schmithals 1979, 151.
90 Schmithals 1979, 151ff.
91 Klein 1961, 146f..
92 Klein 1961, 159.
93 Klein 1961, 160f.. The interpolated passage Gal 1:18-24 is excluded from this framework; see the chapter "Entry visit with the Pope – an interpolated trip to Rome."
94 Ibid., 161, n. 771, with reference to the commentaries by Lietzmann 1910, Schlier 1971, and Oepke et al. 1960.
95 Bauer 1850b, I, 17.
96 In Talbert 1978, 88, 98.
97 Bauer 1879, 372.
98 Pierson 1878, 103f..
99 For a helpful summary, see Walton 2000, 14ff.
100 E.g. Walker 2004, 62: "I believe that Luke did know the letters of Paul, some of them at least, and that it is possible to show, with a high degree of plausibility, why he chose not to mention these letters."
101 E.g. Barrett 1976, 4: "Paul's personal friends must have known that he wrote letters — they conveyed them for him; but Luke was not one of these friends."
102 Klein 1961, 215; cf. Lindemann 1979, 164.
103 Kümmel 1977, 469: "In all likelihood, therefore, Rev was in fact written toward the end of the reign of Domitian, i.e., *ca.* 90-95."

104 Hengel 1976, 249; cf. also Weiß et al. 1917, 278, with regard to Rev 11:1-2: "But not only the forecourt should be spared but also those 'who pray therein' ... Who are these? ... They must be those who not only come there now and then, but are constantly there. Now for a long time, during the Roman war, the Temple (apart from the forecourt of the Gentiles) was the primary residence of the Zealots. They used it primarily as a fortress, but like their predecessors ... at the same time they clung to the holiness of the house of God and regarded themselves as invulnerable there ... This faith in the invulnerability of the Temple and the remnant sheltered therein is shared by our author, and with this his time is determined. He knows that the rest of the city is lost, but hopes that the assault of the enemies will be broken on the ramparts of the Temple. That means he had already experienced the Romans' entrance into the city (since May, 70), but not yet their burning of the Temple (August, 70), i.e., he wrote in the summer of 70 CE." Cf. also Bousset 1966, 32f., 32f.; as well as Couchoud 1930: "It (Rev) is the oldest Christian writing."

105 Käsemann 1963, 242

106 See Detering 1992, 264.

107 Vielhauer 1975, 599; Chester, Martin 1994, 144 (between c 100–150 CE)

108 Further parallels:

http://www.radikalkritik.de/Aktuelle%20Texte.htm : Echte und vermeintliche Paulus-Zitate bei den Apostolischen Vätern und Apologeten (ohne Diognetbrief).

109 Cf. Lindemann 1979, 353ff..

110 Schmithals 1969,5, 250, n. 91; cf. O'Neill 1970, 27f..

111 Cf. Bauer 1934, 218f. = Bauer et al. 1971, 216 = http://jewishchristianlit.com/Resources/Bauer/ : "With respect to Paul, not only is his name lacking, but also any congruence with his letters. But for a learned churchman who carried on his work in Rome around the middle of the second century to act thus can only [219] be understood as quite deliberate conduct. And

if pressed to suggest a reason for this, it would seem to me that the most obvious possibility here would also be the reference to Marcion."

112 Klein 1961, 200.

113 It would be represented, for example, by Goodspeed (1927), 55–57; Grant 1965, 136; regory 2003: 189}; cf. Lindemann 1979, 354

114 Barnett 1941, 222.232.247.

115 The Dutch radical critic Loman already made this fundamental argument in an investigation in 1882, to be sure, without finding great response.

116 Apol 3:2 – Rom 1:25; Apol 8:2 – Rom 1:22; Apol 15 – Rom 11:36, 2 Tim 3:13;

cf. http://www.radikalkritik.de/Aktuelle%20Texte.htm :

Echte und vermeintliche Paulus-Zitate bei den Apostolischen Vätern und Apologeten (ohne Diognetbrief).

117 Lona 1998, 75; Laurence Welborn in: Freedman 2008, 1060: "The epistle is customarily dated to the end of the reign of Domitian (95 or 96 C.E.)"; Vielhauer 1975, 540; but cf. Lona 1998, 76.

118 William R. Schoedel in Freedman 2008, 384–385: "Eusebius (*Hist. Eccl.* 3.36) places Ignatius' martyrdom in the reign of Trajan (A.D. 98-117), and a date in the second half of Trajan's reign or somewhat later seems to fit the picture of the conditions reflected in the letters."

119 Haller 1965, I, 347.

120 This was status quo until 1995. But since then the authenticity of the Ignatian letters has been challenged by Hübner 1997, Lechner 1999, Schmithals 2009, Zwierlein 2009 and Parvus 2008.

121 Haller 1965, I, 347.

122 von Zahn 1873.

123 Lightfoot 1885, Vol. 1.
124 As cited in Voelter 1892, iii.
125 A look at Deissmann 1923 is also well worthwhile.
126 Vielhauer 1975, 536.
127 Volkmar 1856; with regard to Volkmar, see Wildemann 1983.
128 Bergh van Eysinga 1946, 172; cf. Detering 1992, 156.
129 Ranke-Heinemann 1992, 252: "So speaks this unfortunate saint shortly before he was thrown to the wild animals. It may be that the impending horror deranges a person..."
130 Dölger.
131 See Detering 1992, 162f..
132 = en tō deuterō biblidiō

Chapter 2: The Historical Origin of the Pauline Letters

1 Cf. Augustinus Confessionum Libri Tredecim (MPL 032: Col 0657ff) 5.19.
2 Rückert, Beyer, Vol. 4, 90.
3 Uhland, Skeat 1864, p. 424
4 Plinius the Younger, ep. 10.96-97.
5 Suet. Claud. 25.4 ; Suet. Nero 16.2.
6 Tac ann 15.44
7 Johnson 1887, 294.
8 Ibid., 287.
9 So supposedly Polycarp from Smyrna according to the testimony of Irenaeus (AH 3.3.4): "Polycarp himself replied to Marcion, who met him on one occasion, and said, 'Dost thou know me?' 'I do know thee, the first-born of Satan'".

10 Origenes, in Luc hom 25. T. III. p. 962 (MPL 26, 0276C-0277A): "Alii enim aiunt hoc quod scriptum est, sedere a dextris Salvatoris et sinistris, de Paulo et de Marcione dici, quod Paulus sedet a dextris, Marcio sedeat a sinistris; von Harnack 1985, 143, 340*.

11 Tert AM 5.19 ("Marcionis tradition haeretica totum implevit mundum"); Justin, *Apol.*, 1.58. It is important to make this clear. We often believe that the picture of Christianity was obviously already established in the second century by the Catholic church, which was constituted in Rome under the followers of the apostles as the one (and only true) church. That is demonstratedly false. In so doing, we unconsciously take over the Catholic picture of the church. The historical circumstances were different. For a long time, the Catholic church was also only one sect among others, that sect, to be sure, which finally proved to be victorious (above all, against the Marcionites); cf. Werner 2007, 85: "To tell the truth, measured by the same standards with which it condemns other groups and orientations as heretical, the developing Great Church itself is nothing else than a heresy, but just the most successful, which finally drove all others victoriously from the field"; so also Bauer 1934, 233 = Bauer et al. 1971, 231: "The form of Christian belief and life which was successful was that supported by the strongest organization -- the form which was the most uniform and best suited for mass consumption -- in spite of the fact that, in my judgment, for a long time after the close of the post-apostolic age the sum total of consciously orthodox and anti-heretical Christians was numerically inferior to that of the 'heretics.'"

12 von Harnack 1985, 325ff.

13 Cf. the example of the wandering Christian preacher Peregrinus Proteus, whose destiny is reported by Lucian in his satire with that name.

14 To be sure, the Marcionite Church had many catechumens who were allowed to marry, or to live in marital fellowship. It seems to have provided a generous institution of repentance; otherwise it could hardly have become a world-wide church:

see the Armenian Eznik of Kolb, *Against the Sects* von Harnack 1985, 379*: "The Marcionite sects reject marriage and eating flesh,... but they make a false vow; for because they do not resist the desire, they (the sinners) are subjected again to repentance." Moreover, the peculiar circumstance should be noted that Marcion accepted a marriage that had once been joined and recognized the prohibition of divorce (deriving from the Creator of the world): von Harnack 1985, 148, n.1. Altogether, the information mediated by the church fathers about Marcion's strict asceticism may be a bit exaggerated.

15 Tert haer 30; Ir AH 3.4.3; Cyprian Ep 73.2; von Harnack 1985, 24f. 18*f..

16 Tert haer 30; von Harnack 1985, 25.

17 Hörmann 1994, 53,; cf. Rom 15:26.

18 The entire incident seems to be reflected in the eighth chapter of Acts. It is transferred here to Simon (the spiritual father of Marcion and the Marcionites) and Peter (the representative of Rome). "Now when Simon saw that the Spirit was given through the laying on of the apostles' hands, he offered them money, saying, 'Give me also this power, that any one on whom I lay my hands may receive the Holy Spirit.' But Peter said to him, 'Your silver perish with you, because you thought you could obtain the gift of God with money! You have neither part nor lot in this matter, for your heart is not right before God. Repent therefore of this wickedness of yours, and pray to the Lord that, if possible, the intent of your heart may be forgiven you. For I see that you are in the gall of bitterness and in the bond of iniquity.' And Simon answered, 'Pray for me to the Lord, that nothing of what you have said may come upon me.'"

19 Eznik von Kolb 4: 7; cf. 2 Cor 12:2.

Bauer 1934, 21= Bauer et al. 1971, 16; about Edessa: "The older portion of the Chronicle certainly comes from the time in which the Abgar legend had not yet taken root in Edessa, and from a person who was still aware that the earliest history of

Christendom in Edessa had been determined by the names of Marcion, Bar Daisan, and Mani."

21 LeBas, Waddington 1972, 8582f., nr. 2558; von Harnack 1985, 341* :

Synagōgē Markiōnistōn kōm(ēs) Lebabōn tou k(yrio)u kai s(ōtē)r(os) Iē(sou) Chrēstou pronoia paulou presb(yterou) – tou λχ′ etous.

ET = *The meeting-house of the Marcionists in the village of Lebaba, of the Lord and Saviour Jesus the Good Erected by the forethought of Paul a presbyter, in the year 630 Seleucid era (c. 318/19 CE)*

Cf. Adamson 1989, 277f..

22 Tert haer 30.; cf. von Harnack 1985, 23*; Hörmann 1994, 57f..
23 Ir AH 1.27.2.
24 Ir AH 3.3.4f.; cf. von Harnack 1985, 3*ff..
25 Ir AH 3.13.1.
26 Lublinski 1910, 47.
27 Tert AM 4.3.
28 Speyer et al. 1971, 67–70; Speyer 1970.
29 Tert AM 4.4.
30 But cf. Klinghardt 2008; Hays 2008.
31 Hilgenfeld 1855.
32 Manen 1887, 612..
33 See Detering 1992, where van Manen's work is discussed at length.
34 Canon Muratorianus 65.

35 Tert AM 4.4: "Denique ad patrocinium Petri ceterorumque apostolorum ascendisse Hierosolymam post annos quatuordecim scribit..."

36 Schlier 1971, 66.

37 Bauer 1850b, I,16.

38 Bauernfeind 1956, 270, who notices this tension, rightly observes with reference to 1:18-1:20: "A remarkable shadow thus lies over Paul's memory of the first meeting with Peter: If the gap in the apologetic proof were not insignificant, then the entire proof, on which everything else depends, could not be derived from such a strong position as Paul obviously thinks he has".

39 Thus, Schmithals 1988, 48 observes with regard to Rom 1:3-4: "It is almost generally recognized today that Paul... picks up a formula that did not originate with him"; Moo 1996, 45, n. 31: "That Paul in vv. 3-4 is quoting an early Christian tradition, or hymn, or creed is widely held, but considerable uncertainty attaches to the original form and meaning of the tradition. Most are convinced that the creed originated in the early Jewish church and that it had a distinctly 'adoptionist' tone."

40 Goppelt, Roloff 1978, 357.

41 Schmithals 2001, 51.

42 Ibid.

43 Kuss, 8.

44 Manen, Schläger 1906, 32.

45 Hilgenfeld 1855.

46 So an unknown Syrian, cited by von Harnack 1985, 362*.

47 von Harnack 1985, 50.

48 Yesnik of Kolb, Refutation of the Sects 4.1 = ET Eznik, Samuelian 1986, 57ff.; see Roger Pearson's helpful website: http://www.tertullian.org/rpearse/scanned/yeznik_refutation.htm

49 Origen, Comm in Rom, IV,10: ET = Origen, Scheck 2001, 294.

50 Bousset 1917, 55: "And indeed in this connection the power which the representative handing-over of Christ summons is not God, or God's wrath, but an almost foreign power, standing in only a loose connection with God, the almost personified, curse-imposing power of the law."

51 The Catholic redactor as well (whose redactional insertion is not specially discussed here) was probably also not a Jewish Christian, but a Gentile. When a Jewish-Christian redactor is nevertheless continually referred to here, this relates to the tendency of the redactional intervention, not the ethnic origin of its author. Justin was also not a Jewish-Christian, in spite of his relative (to be sure tension-filled Catholic) closeness to Judaism (and to the theology of the redactor). The possibility that Justin himself reworked the Pauline letters can certainly not be excluded, and could explain the "Pauline reminiscences" in his work. This thesis, of course, still requires a fundamental investigation. In any case, it can be said, along with Hermann Raschke, that "from the Gnostic Paul, a spirit much like Justin's... created the Catholic Paul of the letters", Raschke 1926, 129.

52 van Manen 1891, 186,Manen, Schläger 1906, 173. Until today, in most commentaries the passage is translated contrary to its language and grammar: e.g., Wilckens et al. 1978, 172: "The reading proexometha; ou pantōs is early and widely attested. It is certainly original since it is clearly corrected in the western text as the *lectio difficilis*. *Proechesthai* (in the middle voice) is only documented with the meaning "to hold up as protection" (*aethHen* 99.3), "shelter," which is just as inappropriate here as a passive understanding (!). All commentators, therefore, assume a meaning corresponding with the active voice: 'to have an advantage' (cf. *Praecellimuc eos?*)."

53 Segal 1990, 152.

54 Boyarin 2007.

55 Bousset, in: Weiß 1917, II,128}.

56 Regarding the entire question, see the dissertation by Verhoef 1979.
57 Epiphanius, Haer. 30.16.8. ET: Frank Williams.
58 Klein 1961, 215.
59 Lublinski 1910, 93ff. rightly points out that in the Pauline letters regarded as authentic there are always two themes in the foreground: "the relationship between faith and law and between Jewish and Greek Christians. The first century was not the least concerned with these things, while the second century was full of such concerns. As long as the Pharisees and the sectarians got along with one another, there was no enmity between faith and law, since even the prescriptions of the law were attributed a magical significance in the sense of 'grace"... When, however, in the second century, as the consequence of powerful historical events a total separation took place between national and mystical Jews, and as the mystical Jews became Christians, a radical element strived to bring about a complete separation from all Jewish tradition. Not only circumcision and food laws should be done away with, but also the entire Old Testament and the prophets, because all this "law" was in opposition to the creative inspiration of faith. This radicalism was met with resistance, and in the resulting battle, that filled the entire second century and the beginning of the third, the relationship between law and faith was passionately discussed and many negotiations were attempted and the definitive determination of the boundary against Judaism as achieved. If we now come upon early Christian writings that deal with such problems at length, we can rest assured that these documents belong to the second century and not the first."
60 Regarding Apelles, we hear from the church fathers that he lived together with "the ecstatic virgin Philumene" – Tertullian refers to her as a "prostitute" (*prostibulum*), cf. Simon-Helen – "a prophetess with whom he worked together as a devoted adept by expounding his ideas to her and receiving here revelations and predictions in return" (von Harnack 1985, 177f.; = ET, 113); Tert haer 30: "If we must likewise touch the

descent of Apelles, he is far from being 'one of the old school,' like his instructor and moulder, Marcion; he rather forsook the continence of Marcion, by resorting to the company of a woman, and withdrew to Alexandria, out of sight of his most abstemious master. Returning therefrom, after some years, unimproved, except that he was no longer a Marcionite, he clave to another woman, the maiden Philumene (whom we have already mentioned), who herself afterwards became an enormous prostitute. *Having been imposed on by her vigorous spirit, he committed to writing the revelations which he had learned of her. Persons are still living who remember them...*" In her visions, it is said that a youth appeared to her, who identified himself one time as Christ and another time as Paul! – Compare with this Lublinski 1910, 47: "At that time it was necessary to legitimate the developing church and to appeal to documents supposedly deriving from Christ and the apostles themselves. It was not the gnostic so and so who published something, but Paul inspired him, or Peter, or even the words of the Lord himself suddenly spoke from his mouth. It need not always have been a case of forgery, but the real and spiritual conception of the poetic or religious inspiration must lead to deceptions that had begun in good faith."

61 hēmas: cum minusc pauc, sed editum potius utvid de coniectura Bezae (Tischendorf)

CHAPTER 3: A LEGEND AND ITS HISTORICAL KERNEL

1 William Wrede, in Rengsdorf 1964, 2.

2 Ibid. Cf. Lüdemann 1996, 264 about my book: "The thesis of Hermann Detering [Der gefälschte Paulus. Das Urchristentum im Zwielicht, 1995), that the letters of Paul come from the second century, is mistaken and is refuted by the existing sources."

3 Cf. Steck 1888, 351f.: "The assumption that the primary Pauline letters do not derive from the apostle but belong in the second century will always encounter the reservation that in form and

content they give the impression of being the work of such an intellectually powerful personality that they could only be hypothesized in the creative milieu of earliest Christianity, in the circle of the apostle himself. There is a basis for this impression. We have no other writings in the New Testament in which such a powerful and original religious thinking finds expression as in these... But the conclusion which is drawn from this impression must be challenged. It says that because these letters are so incomparable they must have an apostle as their author. But who tells us then that only the apostles were such original thinkers?... Is one or more such personalities impossible for later times?"

4   Boehmer, Luther 1918, 61ff..

5   M.R. James-Translation.

6   This and the following citations are from Hennecke et al. 1992, pp. 242-245, 253.

7   Loman 1899, 68; cf. Detering 1992, 297.

8   Referred to by Pierson-Naber as *Paulus episcopus*.

9   Loman, 47.

10 Van Manen, "Paul," in Encyclopaedia biblica, 1904, p. 3632.

11 Hilgenfeld 1903, 326f.supposed that the name Simon was an old, forgotten surname of Paul, which is close to the theory represented here; see Schoeps 1949, 419.

12 In light of Irenaeus' witness, Beyschlag's assertion (Beyschlag 1974, 68, n. 138) that F. M Braun's claim Braun 1955-1957 that the Gnostic Cerdo was a Simonian "is entirely without basis" requires more detailed justification. F. M. Braun regards Irenaeus' note as a heresiological theory, but nevertheless also holds fast to the Simonian roots of Marcionism. For him the Gnostic *Satornil* establishes the connection with Simonism. In light of the grave differences between Marcion and Satornil, however, this assumption seems very questionable to me. In this regard, see also K. Rudolph Rudolph 1975, 360. Rudolph finds it highly "remarkable that the Pseudo-Clementine sources, which according to the discussion by Salles 1958 were

certainly anti-Simonite oriented, later took on a moderate anti-Marcionite dressing." In my opinion, one should consider these and other observations is one speaks of "pre-Marcionism." From an historical perspective what one characterizes as pre-Marcionism is clearly nothing else than Simonism, or post-Simonism.

13 Waitz 1904, 125.
14 Clem Hom 17.19; Gal 2:11ff; Schneemelcher et al. 1971, II, 77.
15 Clem Hom 2.17.3; 11.35.4-6.
16 Schneemelcher et al. 1971, II, 69
17 Haenchen 1982, 399, n.1: "It was in Egypt of the Macedonian period that a fourth name, with which one was addressed by intimates, was introduced: the so-called *signum* or *supernomen*"
18 Bauer 1879, 381.
19 Haenchen 1982, 305: "The Tübingers therefore concluded that Luke intended to protect Paul from such disparaging associations be here depicting Simon as an entirely different person."
20 See Beyschlag 1974, 184, 184; and Henss 1967, 1967.
21 Tert AM 5.1. "Because even the book of Genesis so long ago promised me the Apostle Paul. For among the types and prophetic blessings which he pronounced over his sons, Jacob, when he turned his attention to Benjamin, exclaimed, 'Benjamin shall ravin as a wolf; in the morning He shall devour the prey, and at night he shall impart nourishment.' He foresaw that Paul would arise out of the tribe of Benjamin, a voracious wolf, devouring his prey in the morning: in order words, in the early period of his life he would devastate the Lord's sheep, as a persecutor of the churches; but in the evening he would give them nourishment, which means that in his declining years he would educate the fold of Christ, as the teacher of the Gentiles. Then, again, in Saul's conduct towards David, exhibited first in violent persecution of him, and then in remorse and reparation, on his receiving from him good for evil, we have nothing else than an anticipation of Paul in Saul – belonging, too, as

they did, to the same tribe--and of Jesus in David, from whom He descended according to the Virgin's genealogy."

[22] Rudolph 1998, 294 = ET Rudolph 1983, 294.

[23] E.g. Philo Post 19, 23, 27.

[24] "...for it happens that that which comes near to him who is standing still longs for tranquillity, as being something which resembles itself."

[25] Just 1Apol 26; 56. The dedication inscription was discovered in 1574 on a Tiber island in Rome. It referred, however, not to Simon Magus, but to an ancient Roman God of oaths, Semo Sancus (*Semoni Sanco Deo Fido Sacrum*.... Justin's confusion and that of other church fathers could be related to the fact that "possibly the Simonians themselves were responsible for the identification, since they worshipped their founder as a divine being (as Zeus among others.)," Rudolph 1998, 295.

[26] *The Exegesis of the Soul*, NHC II, 6, in Robinson 1988, 192-198.

[27] Hipp Ref 6.9-18.

[28] Rudolph 1998, 295 = ET Rudolph 1975, 295.

[29] Leisegang 1985, 67.

[30] In this regard, reference should also be made to a puzzling passage in the writing *Philopatris*, by Pseudo-Lucian, in which one generally sees a characterization of Paul. Here also, however, it cannot be said for sure whether we have to do with a characterization of Paul or Simon. Triephon tells Kritias about his meeting "with a certain bald-headed, large-nosed man from Galilee": *Triephon*: "... By the son of the father, the spirit, who proceeds from the father. Out of three, and three out of one! You are Zeus! who is called God! ..." [Simon's trinitarian system!] *Kritias*: "But I don't understand all that well what you want to say with your one three and three one. Do you refer to the Tetraktys of Pythagoras? or the Ogdoad and Triad [of Valentinus]?" *Triephon*: "Be silent, friend, about things that unspeakable!... I will teach you what the All is, and who he is, and, above all, who he was, and according to what plan the All is led out [the beginning of the *apophasis*!]. For then it was no

different for me than for you. But I happened to meet a certain bald-headed, large-nosed Galilean, who while wandering in the air came as far as the third heaven and presumably learned the marvelous things that he again taught us. By water, he made me a new person, freed me from the dominion of the godless, and placed me on the path of the blessed ones, to walk further in their footsteps. And if you will listen to me, I can also make you a new, true person." — According to *Hieronymus*, there was a tradition in which Paul came from *Gischala* in Galilee, not Tarsus (*Ad Philomena* 23, *De Viribus Illustribus* 5): "Paul, formerly called Saul, an apostle outside the number of the twelve apostles, was of the tribe of Benjamin and the town of Giscalis in Judea. When this was taken by the Romans he removed with his parents to Tarsus in Cilicia. Sent by them to Jerusalem to study law he was educated by Gamaliel ..."

cf. Niebuhr 1992, 107, n. 136; (Lublinski 1910, 225).

31 So also Kreyenbühl 1900, 225 and passim.

32 Hippolytus, *Ref.* 6.20.

33 Acta Pt c Sim, 55, ed. Lipsius Bonnet, I, 203, 1f.; cf. also Hom 18.6-10: *areskontōs tois parousin ochlois*. In this regard, see Schoeps 1949, 301, 418ff..

34 Clem Hom 17:13ff.

35 Esnik von Kolb, 180, cited by von Harnack 1985, 377*: "The apostle says: 'The words that I heard are unspeakable,' and Marcion says: 'I have heard them.'"

36 Geffcken 1902; cf. Kippenberg 1971, 1971, 123, n. 148.

37 Preuschen 1901, 184f..

38 In this regard, see Beyschlag 1974, 99ff..

39 Acts 8:9, 11.

40 Cf. also Rom 15:18ff.

41 Hom 3.59.2; cf. Hom 2.17.3: Peter says, "I came after him (Simon) and followed him"; cf. Hom 11.35.4-6: Peter says, "Now

he (Satan) has sent Simon upon us, preaching under pretence of the truth, in the name of the Lord, and sowing error."

42 Hilgenfeld 1890, 8

43 Ir, *AH*, 1.23.3.

44 Rudolph 1998, 255 = ET Rudolph 1998, 255.

45 The Catholic monk H. Denifle, for example, could thus set forth the thesis regarding Luther and Lutheranism that Luther "invented the doctrine of justification, along with the *sola fide* and the *sola gratia*, only for the purpose of pursuing his dissolute life with all the more indifference and assurance" (Lohse 1983, c1981, 242).

46 ApkElj 4.20-23 = Charlesworth 1983, I, 748. That in the portrayal of the Antichrist we in fact have to do with the (polemically skewed) picture of Simon is shown by the remarkable agreement in the sun and moon miracles ApkElj 3.5-10). That the Antichrist in the *Apocalypse of Elijah* can raise no one from the dead (ApkElj 3.11-13) is Jewish and Jewish-Christian polemic. In Acts as well the gift of raising the dead is reserved only for (the Jewish-Christian) Peter: see the Tabitha miracle, Acts 9:36ff.; and on the other hand, Acts 20:9ff., where a raising of the dead is intentionally not reported for Paul.

47 Kreyenbühl 1900, 214.

48 Ben-Chorin 1986, 35.

49 But see EpAp 31.

50 Cf. Dessau 1919

51 Translator's note: these attempts to replicate Detering's translation; cf. however, the translation by O.S. Wintermute, in Charlesworth 1983, I, 746, and the textual variations discussed there.

52 Preuschen 1901, 192ff.

53 Ibid., 194.

54 From the Greek *enkrateia* = "chastity" or "sexual continence."

55 NHC II,6

56 ATh 7

57 Clem Recog 2.12.4

58 Beyschlag 1974, 66, n. 135.

59 Dietzfelbinger 1991, 165.

60 Because Helena (= Athena) is ransomed by her "redeemer" Simon, faith in redemption becomes the faith of Helena, the figure of Helena becomes the symbol for faith itself; for the Simonians, faith is Helena. A reflection of this is to be found in Eph 6:14, where, in the same was as Athena, faith is conceived as an armored virgin.

61 Quispel 1995, 66.

62 Cf. Hippolytus, Haer 6.19.1; Clem Recog, 2.12.4.

CHAPTER 4: WHAT REMAINS?

1 Politeia 7. 514A ff.

2 Nietzsche, *Morgenröte*, Aphorism 84 (ET J.M.Kennedy): "What can be expected from the effects of a religion which, during the centuries when it was being firmly established, enacted that huge philological farce concerning the Old Testament ? I refer to that attempt to tear the Old Testament from the hands of the Jews under the pretext that it contained only Christian doctrines and belonged to the Christians as the true people of Israel, while the Jews had merely arrogated it to themselves without authority. This was followed by a mania of would-be interpretation and falsification, which could not under any circumstances have been allied with a good conscience.. ... They were engaged in a struggle, and thought of their foes rather than of honesty."

3 Cf. Johnson 1887, 213.

4 Schweitzer 1984, 553.

5 Uhland, Skeat 1864, 424

6 Rückert, Beyer, S. Vol. 4, 441: "Neuer Glaube".
7 Ratzinger 2004, 31
8 Ratzinger 2004, 31
9 Bergh van Eysinga 1947-52.
10 Nietzsche 1977, 1966, III, 646, 648.
11 Frater Smid 1958, 68.

Made in the USA
Middletown, DE
01 April 2024

52383731R00172